GREAT DECISIONS 2016

W9-BSC-371

About the cover

A Houthi militant walks by rubble from a part of the Qahira fort following air strikes in Yemen's south-western city of Taiz on May 12, 2015.

Photo Credit: Reuters

FOREIGN POLICY ASSOCIATION
1918

GREAT DECISIONS IS A TRADEMARK OF THE FOREIGN POLICY ASSOCIATION.

© COPYRIGHT 2016 BY FOREIGN POLICY ASSOCIATION, INC., 470 PARK AVENUE SOUTH, NEW YORK, NEW YORK 10016.

PRINTED IN THE UNITED STATES OF AMERICA BY DART-MOUTH PRINTING COMPANY, HANOVER, NH.

LIBRARY OF CONGRESS CONTROL NUMBER: 2015915676

ISBN: 978-0-87124-250-1

WITHDRAWN

Researched as of November 27, 2015.

The authors are responsible for factual accuracy and for the views expressed.

FPA itself takes no position on issues of U.S. foreign policy.

"Nessun dorma"

Like all great exploration discoveries also the Zohr discovery is full of surprises, the unexpected, intuitions, mistakes, skill, enthusiasm, and ups and downs in which the human element is as crucial as the technology. It's a story worth telling from the beginning because we already know what Eni has found in the Egyptian offshore and the geopolitical impact on the area, but still very little about how we arrived at this mega-discovery. A three-year journey – together with an extraordinary team of [...]

This beautiful story continues on **eniday.com/en**

Democracy is not inherited but taught and learned anew by every generation observed Alexis de Tocqueville. As yet another change of leadership is looming in Washington, what better time to reflect upon democratic renewal?

The emphasis America's founders placed on an educated citizenry is instructive. For James Madison, "The diffusion of knowledge is the only guardian of true liberty." And Thomas Jefferson admonished, "If a nation expects to be ignorant and free, in a state of civilization, it expects what never was and never will be."

It is distressing that, today, only two out of five Americans can identify the three branches of the federal government. Or that one out of two Americans is under the impression that the President can unilaterally suspend the Constitution. Disappointing too that only 54% of the voting age population participated in the 2012 presidential election. We can and should do better.

In foreign policy, even more than in domestic policy, much depends on what kind of leaders the American public votes into office. The character and vision of such leaders are key to sustaining our democracy, which should not be taken for granted. Indeed, John Adams wrote in 1814: "Remember, democracy never lasts long. It soon wastes, exhausts, and murders itself. There never was a democracy yet that did not commit suicide."

The Foreign Policy Association is deeply committed to public education in international affairs. The importance of our mission was recently demonstrated by the findings of a distinguished group of political scientists who asked a national sample of Americans what policy the U.S. should pursue in Ukraine. As part of the survey, they asked respondents to locate Ukraine on a map to see if this geographic knowledge (or lack thereof) affected the respondents' foreign policy views. They found that only one out of six Americans could find Ukraine on a world map, and that this lack of knowledge was related to policy choices: the farther the respondents' guesses were from Ukraine's actual location, the more likely they were to support U.S. military intervention.

Civics and geography may sound old-fashioned, but they never have been more relevant. At the Foreign Policy Association we are keen on expanding opportunities for social studies teachers. Our Great Decisions Teacher Training Institute brings together high school teachers from across the country for an intensive orientation program to familiarize them with cutting-edge classroom resources.

Let me widen the aperture of these remarks and posit that if we have a robust democracy and an informed public, we will optimize the probability that our foreign policy reflects American values and interests. Whether Americans will choose to have their country continue to play a leadership role in the world, however, is an open question. A recent Pew poll found that an unprecedented number of Americans believe that "the U.S. should mind its own business internationally and let other countries get along the best they can on their own."

Rejecting isolationism, in his last public address, FDR exhorted an audience of 1,600 members of the Foreign Policy Association thus: "The power which this Nation has attained — the political, the economic, the military, and above all the moral power — has brought to us the responsibility, and with it the opportunity, for leadership in the community of Nations. In our own best interest, and in the name of peace and humanity, this Nation cannot, must not, and will not shirk that responsibility."

Today, the U.S. enjoys preponderant military and economic power in the world. This primacy must be underpinned by a willingness to assume a leadership role in world affairs. Whatever level of involvement around the globe, Americans' understanding of international developments will be increasingly important. Former Secretary of State Henry Kissinger observes: "The U.S. must decide for itself the role it will play in the 21st century....At question is not the strength of American arms but rather American resolve in understanding and mastering a new world."

America's role in the world benefits from an unparalleled network of alliance treaties. Having recently visited the Demilitarized Zone between North and South Korea, a desolate no-man's land littered with 2 million landmines, I saw first-hand the crucial role of the U.S.-South Korea alliance in stabilizing the Korean peninsula. South Korea finds itself in an increasingly tense region — with China asserting "indisputable sovereignty" over 90% of the South China Sea, a channel for some $5 trillion in annual trade, and with North Korea threatening to test nuclear weapons. The tensions in northeast Asia are illustrative of growing international risks and the need for U.S. leadership to foster stability and economic growth across the region.

For the first time since the end of the cold war, geopolitical developments are causing fissures in what was widely believed to be a convergent global economy. Rising nationalism and growing regional conflicts are threatening to result in "deglobalization." In the annual Foreign Policy Association Andrew Carnegie Lecture on Conflict Prevention in honor of David Hamburg, former UN Secretary-General Kofi Annan spoke of "the new world disorder."

When Russia's foreign minister, Sergei Lavrov, addressed the Foreign Policy Association, he lamented his country's limited economic ties with the U.S. He also warned that Russia's relationship with the U.S. had reached an inflection point and was in danger of regressing. Economic interdependence is not empty rhetoric. Countries with strong economic ties have a vested interest in the prevailing order. As China narrows the economic gap with the U.S., the overriding question will be whether cooperation or conflict will characterize this relationship.

The world is changing. We cannot ignore the rise of new powers and the effects they will have on world order. The challenge for both the Foreign Policy Association and the International Relations Council of Kansas City is to help our fellow citizens understand and anticipate these developments.

* Excerpted from remarks delivered by President Lateef on November 5, 2015, when he received the International Statesman Award at the Sixtieth Anniversary Dinner of the International Relations Council of Kansas City.

Noel V. Lateef
President and CEO
Foreign Policy Association

Shifting alliances in the Middle East

by Curtis R. Ryan

The panel of Gulf Cooperation Council (GCC) attendees during the 24th session of the joint GCC-European Union ministerial council meeting on May 24, 2015, in the Qatari capital Doha. (KARIM JAAFAR/AFP/GETTY IMAGES)

The 2015 announcement of a major deal between Iran and six world powers, including the U.S., was but the latest in a list of major jolts to the Middle East regional system. In the last several years alone, the region has been rocked by the pro-democracy uprisings of the Arab Spring, followed by the dark turn toward civil wars, insurgencies and increasing terrorism in Syria, Libya and Yemen, as well as authoritarian backlashes from Egypt to Bahrain. Even before these tumultuous events, the single most destabilizing event for the entire region had occurred in 2003, with the U.S. invasion of Iraq. These developments have repeatedly shaken the system of regional alliances and alignments—including in inter-Arab relations—as states have tried to adjust to drastic changes in regional politics and security.

For all the changes and challenges to the regional system, however, some key aspects of regional politics continue to operate along familiar lines. If 2011 was the year of regime

change, the years since have seen the return of essentially reactionary regime security politics, against both internal and external challenges. Regime security dynamics, in other words, are all too familiar and pervasive. This does not mean that regional politics have not changed. Rather, it means that regimes are still playing with the old playbook, even as societies have changed dramatically and both democratic and militant movements alike challenge states. No matter what the next regional jolt will be, the focus of regimes on their own survival will remain the highest priority and will underlie their responses.

CURTIS R. RYAN *is a professor of political science at Appalachian State University in North Carolina.*

This article draws on two essays by the author for the Project on Middle East Political Science (POMEPS): "Inter-Arab Politics and International Relations in the Middle East," in Explaining the Arab Uprisings, *October 27, 2014, and "Regime Security and Shifting Alliances in the Middle East," in* International Relations Theory and a Changing Middle East, *September 17, 2015.*

1

Regime security and alliances

Regime security is a key driver of alliance politics in the Middle East. Even as regional alliances, alignments and coalitions change, these overall regime security dynamics continue to underpin international relations. Arab regimes remain frequently trapped in internal and external security dilemmas, largely of their own making, obsessed with ensuring the security of their ruling elites against both internal and external challenges. In the traditional (external) security dilemma, states unwittingly undermine their own security even as they bolster their military preparedness and defenses, by triggering alarm in their neighbors. In the internal security version, however, security measures create fortress regimes, ever more distant from their own societies, resistant to change and yet vulnerable to discontent from an alienated public. In short, the rise of the security state decreases the legitimacy and ironically the security of the regime, as it is increasingly estranged from its own society. Both types of security dilemmas refer to the dangers of trying to ensure security while actually creating a vicious cycle of insecurity.

Alliances in the Middle East then serve not just as bilateral defense pacts, but also as looser transnational support coalitions of ruling elites, as regimes help prop each other up against perceived security threats. These can be both material and ideational. Professor Laurie Brand has written on the former, in the form of a political economy of alliance-making and budget security, showing that regimes use alliances to secure their main state budget needs. Aid and economic security are therefore also part of regime security, leading aid-dependent states such as Jordan, Morocco and Sudan, not only to give diplomatic or verbal support for Gulf countries' security, but also to send military planes to take part in war efforts. For these states, regime security concerns were not rooted in fear of Houthi rebels in Yemen or even of Iranian regional ambitions, but rather in maintaining the good graces (and relatedly, the security and well-being) of rich aid donors such as the Gulf states. In that sense, when the Jordanian foreign minister referred to Gulf state security as a direct interest of Jordan, he was not merely being figurative. In terms of aid, investment, trade, labor remittances and oil, the security of the Gulf states does indeed correlate directly to regime security in Jordan, Egypt and other resource-poor states.

Professors Gregory Gause and Lawrence Rubin, however, have made clear that ideational threats can be every bit as dire in the eyes of regimes as those of a material nature. While material economic needs matter very much within alliance politics, so too do ideas, identities and ideologies. Regimes sometimes feel especially vulnerable to these latter nonmaterial challenges to their legitimacy. The importance of ideational as well as material political struggles in the international relations of the region can be seen especially in what some have called a "New Middle East Cold War" or a "New Arab Cold War."

A key fault line in Arab politics is a regime's perception of its own security and stability. When faced with a significant challenge, regimes respond by rearranging domestic support coalitions, increasing the active role of the internal security apparatus, and—in foreign policy—shifting alliances and alignments to better ensure regime survival. Regimes are continually tempted to provide quick fixes to security concerns via foreign policy and alliance choices, since adjusting external relations seems less risky to them than genuine internal restructuring and reform. In other words, the foreign policy focus of regime security politics also has domestic consequences, often bolstering existing authoritarian systems and thwarting hope for greater domestic change.

If anything, events since the start of the regional Arab Spring have only underscored the relevance of a regime security approach to understanding international relations and alliance politics in the Middle East. ∎

The changing balance of power

During the first three years of the Arab Spring, it was striking how different Middle Eastern regional politics were from earlier eras—not just in the collapse of heretofore long-lived autocracies, but also in terms of inter-Arab relations within the regional system itself. In earlier periods, Arab politics had seen struggles for dominance, often taking an ideological guise, between three main protagonists: Egypt, Iraq and Syria. In the early years of the Arab Spring, however, the names of these capitals—Cairo, Baghdad and Damascus—no longer implied centers of regional power, but rather of chaos, insurgency, civil war or revolution. The countries and capitals of the old Arab cold war were now no longer protagonists in regional leadership struggles, but instead had become arenas for struggle themselves.

By the time of the 2011 uprisings, this power vacuum in inter-Arab relations led to an unusual constellation of rising powers. Saudi Arabia, long used to playing a behind-the-scenes role in regional struggles, now openly asserted

Before you read, download the companion **Glossary** that includes definitions and a guide to acronyms and abbreviations used in the article. Go to **www.great decisions.org** and select a topic in the Resources section on the right-hand side of the page.

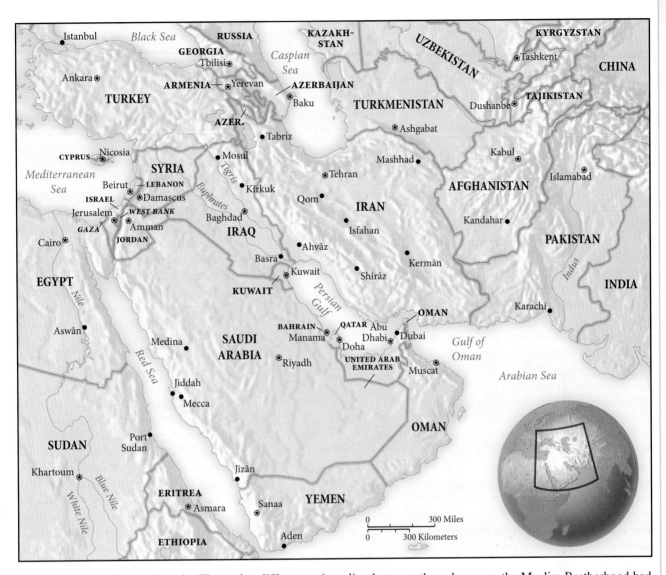

itself, with decidedly mixed results. The tiny emirate of Qatar became, temporarily, a major source of power and influence. It too attempted to play an assertive foreign policy role, stretching from Libya to Syria. Saudi Arabia, Qatar and other Arab Gulf monarchies in the Gulf Cooperation Council (GCC) intervened across the region, with money and arms, affecting domestic politics far beyond the Gulf itself. Their roles were in some cases supportive of revolution (against Muammar Qaddafi in Libya and Hafez al-Assad in Syria) but also counter-revolutionary (especially in securing the power of their own monarchies in the Gulf region itself). The GCC even launched a military intervention to secure the survival of the monarchy in Bahrain. Similar counter-revolutionary efforts across the Gulf have not ceased since. Yet, there are

also differences in policy between the GCC states. Saudi Arabia and Qatar, for example, engaged in heated rivalry and proxy conflict themselves, with different ideological preferences regarding what types of groups to support. Specifically, Saudi Arabia was more likely to back Salafi Islamist movements, while Qatar supported Muslim Brotherhood organizations in Egypt, Syria, Gaza and elsewhere.

The rapid changes in the regional balance of power in the Arab Spring years led to fleeting moments in which particular powers appeared to be ascendant, only to decline, in relative terms, almost as quickly. In 2013, Qatar appeared to be playing a regional role far beyond its means, with Islamist movements rising across the region and the Muslim Brotherhood in particular benefiting from Qatari support. By 2014,

however, the Muslim Brotherhood had been overthrown by a military coup in Egypt, and was subsequently banned in the country, as well as in Saudi Arabia and the United Arab Emirates (UAE). With the rapid decline of the Muslim Brotherhood's fortunes, Qatar too seemed to have been relegated once again to its role as a lesser power in regional affairs. Yet the Saudis were in no position to declare victory: Iran remained a powerful regional rival, and one that Western powers were negotiating with as an accepted part of the regional status quo. Concurrently, many of the Salafi movements that had received Saudi backing now took on a stridently anti-Saudi tone. When Saudi Arabia, the UAE, Bahrain, Qatar, and even Jordan took part in airstrikes against the militant self-declared "Islamic State" (also known as ISIS, ISIL

Pan-Arabism and the Arab Cold War

Most states in the Middle East became independent only after World War II, with borders inherited from European colonial powers. In the years after independence, especially in the 1950s and 1960s, many in the region rejected country-level nationalism as an artificial and imperial construct, and turned instead to Pan-Arabism. Pan-Arabism was rooted in the belief that the Arabs were one people, divided by foreign borders into almost 20 states. Pan-Arab nationalists called for unity and even political unification of the Arab states and peoples.

When ideologically motivated military officers launched coups to topple European-backed monarchies across the region and rose to power in Egypt,

Saudi Arabian King Saud ibn Abd al-Aziz (1902–69) (C) surrounded on his left by Egyptian president Gamal Abdul Nasser (1918–70) and on his right by Syrian president Shukri al-Kuwatli (1891–1967), arrives in March 1956 at Kubbeh Palace in Cairo for a Syria, Saudi Arabia and Egypt meeting. (AFP/GETTY IMAGES)

Syria, Iraq, Libya and South Yemen, they often turned to Pan-Arabism as part of their plans for a new Arab regional politics. In doing so, they clashed with the more conservative regimes in the region, as the various dynastic monarchies banded together to stop what they viewed as on onslaught of revolutionary, military-backed republics. The political, ideological, and at times military struggle that followed became known as the Arab cold war. It included the struggle between essentially Pan-Arab, socialist and military regimes versus conservative hereditary monarchies in Arab politics, but it also included struggles between the Pan-Arabist regimes themselves—especially Egypt's Gamal Abdel Nasser and his Baathist rivals in Syria and Iraq—over leadership in the Arab world.

Today, many have argued that a new regional cold war has emerged. This time it still includes conservative dynastic monarchies united to thwart the latest challenge to the status quo, but it also embodies a difference from the earlier era—this time there is no coalition of Pan-Arab regimes. Instead, the new regional cold war is marked by a glaring sectarianism, in which Sunni Arab monarchies led by Saudi Arabia have sparred with Shi'a (and largely Persian) Iran and its allies such as the Assad regime in Syria and the Hizbullah movement in Lebanon. The most devastating aspect of the current version of the regional cold war has been the intervention of these alignments and alliances in civil wars in Syria and Yemen, making already difficult local conflicts far worse and more deadly for the local populations.

the former imperial power attempting once again to intrude upon Arab affairs.

In some respects, multiple regional powers had attempted to grab power, yet all found themselves overstretched in various ways, and all faced unintended and unanticipated consequences of their activist and interventionist foreign policies.

What is most striking about the regional balance of power in the Middle East today is this: there is no balance of power. Iran remains powerful but largely friendless, tied to its own interventions in favor of the regime in Syria and against the regime in Yemen. Israel is engaged in yet another war in Gaza—with a staggering death toll that nonetheless failed at dislodging Hamas—leaving the country more isolated in regional politics than ever.

Within inter-Arab politics itself, the GCC remains a key alliance, albeit marked by intense rivalries and divisions, which seems to be a coalition of Sunni Arab monarchies and autocracies reprising their roles from the earlier Arab cold war. Again, they serve as a defensive front against material and ideological threats. But this time, the new regional cold war is not really Arab, but mainly a Saudi-Iranian struggle that manifests itself in competitive interventions with a pronounced sectarian tone. While the local sectarian violence was very real, the broader Sunni-Shi'a aspect of the new regional cold war was more symptom than cause. In short, primordial hatreds were not driving the international relations of the region; rather, material and ideational power struggles were actively manipulating sectarian and ethnic tensions as part of a broader and intensely cynical struggle for regional hegemony. This led regional powers, or would-be regional powers, to engage in competitive interventions across borders. Saudi Arabia and Iran backed opposite sides in civil wars in Syria and Yemen, for example, generally with devastating results for the local populations.

Insecurity and alliances

Just a few years ago, in 2011, the Arab League met in the wake of the Arab Spring, with new semi-democratic re-

or Da'esh), this was a measure of the weakness and severe insecurity of these regimes.

Similarly, in 2011, in part because of the power vacuum, and in part because it seemed to represent a case of successful and somewhat democratic Islamism, Turkey had clearly been the ascendant regional power. The irony of the moment was that the most popular leader across the Arab world was not Arab, but a Turk—Prime Minister Recep

Tayyip Erdoğan. But here too, fortunes soon changed dramatically. Like Qatar, Turkey was affected by the overthrow of the Muslim Brotherhood in Egypt, marked by a personal vitriolic animosity between Egypt's General Abdel Fattah al-Sisi and Turkey's Erdoğan. By 2014, both had become presidents of their respective countries, and the animosity, if anything, increased. Turkey had in a mere three years gone from regional superstar to its earlier image, as gimes sitting uncomfortably alongside increasingly nervous dictatorships. For some of the latter, the greatest threat did not appear to be Israel, Iran or militant jihadist movements, but rather domestic democratic grassroots activism and demands for regime change. For some, an even greater threat came from "reformist" and potentially revolutionary Islamist movements such as the Muslim Brotherhood.

The rise of Islamists, al-Nahda in Tunisia and the Muslim Brotherhood in Egypt, led alliances such as the GCC to close ranks and even to invite non-Gulf states such as Morocco and Jordan to join the GCC. They may not have been fellow Gulf states, but they were fellow Arab and Sunni monarchies with extensive ties to Western powers. As the tide of the Arab spring rose and toppled regimes—all authoritarian republics—the monarchies coalesced together in pursuit of a collective regime security. Yet the Syrian war continued to divide the core of the alignment itself, as Saudi Arabia and Qatar were more often than not at odds with one another in their (failed) attempts to determine regime change elsewhere.

Non-Arab states such as Turkey played ever-larger roles in regional politics, as Turkey's Justice and Development party, in alliance with Qatar, backed Islamist movements across the region. When former President Morsi's Muslim Brotherhood regime rose to power in Egypt, many Arab regimes were deeply alarmed. Islamists had, after all, taken power following a popular revolution and a democratic election. Egypt's regime change led to a closer alliance between Egypt, Qatar and Turkey, but in the same vein, another regime change would then rearrange regional alliances once again. The 2013 coup of General al-Sisi in Egypt ousted the Islamist regime, restoring secular and essentially authoritarian rule, while preserving the power and privileges of the Egyptian armed forces. The shake-up in regional alliances and inter-Arab relations was immediate. Within 24 hours, Jordan's King Abdullah II visited Cairo to support the new regime. Qatar pulled its financial support, but was soon out-

People hold pictures of Mohamed Morsi during a protest May 24, 2015, in Istanbul, Turkey, against an Egyptian court's decision to seek the death sentence for the deposed Egyptian president. (EPA/DENIZ TOPRAK/NEWSCOM)

shone by the vast support showered on Egypt by Saudi Arabia and the UAE.

The Arab Spring had given new urgency to the politics of regime security. The toppling of four regimes—in Tunisia, Egypt, Libya, and Yemen—each in a completely different way, got the attention of the surviving regimes in the region. The post-Morsi regional system saw the strengthening of regimes committed to thwarting security threats and propping up themselves and their allies. Specifically, Egypt, Saudi Arabia, the UAE and Jordan emerged as key allies, similarly suspicious of—or even outright hostile to—the Muslim Brotherhood. It was the perception of an internal, and to some extent transnational, threat to their own legitimacy, security and stability that led each of these regimes to work closely together—far more closely than they had in responding to severe regional crises like the Syrian civil war, or the rise of extremists like al-Qaeda and the Islamic State.

In short, the various states and regimes in the region had different security priorities, and a truly effective coalition against ISIS remained elusive. As dangerous as ISIS was, for most regimes in the region it was one of several threats. For example, Turkey remained focused on the Kurdish Workers' Party (PKK), even as it declared that it was striking ISIS.

Even when the Arab regimes did agree to work together against militancy and extremism, they had different security threats in mind. For the UAE and Egypt, the core threat remained the Muslim Brotherhood and other similar Islamist movements. For Jordan, meanwhile, the Muslim Brotherhood seemed a loyal opposition compared to rising Salafi movements within the kingdom and the transnational jihadists of the Islamic State who had taken huge swaths of Syria and Iraq, frequently testing Jordan's borders. While Jordan supported its allies, especially Egypt and the GCC, its main security concern remained the Islamic State. For Saudi Arabia and Bahrain, the key threat was Iran and Iranian influence in Syria, Lebanon, Iraq and Yemen, and even within Saudi Arabia and Bahrain themselves.

Even before the Iranian nuclear deal—between Iran and six major world powers—the region was already beset by crises and rising violence, and inter-Arab and regional solidarity remained as elusive as ever. Yet, the 2015 summit of the Arab League promised more than the usual platitudes. This time, the Arab regimes insisted, the summit would be meaningful and finally lead to regional cooperation to restore a semblance of regional order. Outsiders hoped that this would lead to

Iranian Foreign Minister Mohammad Javad Zarif gestures to journalists from a balcony outside of the Iran nuclear talks, being held in Vienna, Austria, July 10, 2015. (CARLOS BARRIA/POOL/AP)

unified action against ISIS. At least rhetorically, the Arab states seemed united: calling for a joint Arab military force for "rapid reaction" against militancy and terrorism. The force was to consist potentially of as many as 40,000 troops, to be drawn heavily from Egyptian, Jordanian, Moroccan, and GCC ground, air and naval forces.

Despite the flurry of temporarily unified rhetoric, actions failed to match the aspirations of yet another summit, to no one's surprise. The Arab League force never really came to pass. Instead an Arab coalition was organized by Saudi Arabia, but directed at Yemen rather than against ISIS. For Saudi Arabia, the war in Yemen seemed to be part of the broader Saudi-Iranian proxy war. The sectarian narratives that accompanied that intervention only deepened the importance of identity politics within the domestic politics and international relations of the region.

Identity politics

As states and the regional order suffer from a stability, security and legitimacy crisis in the eyes of many in the Middle East, multiple levels of identity challenge each other for the loyalty and support of individuals across the region. Even Pan-Arabism remains a force—but to a lesser degree when compared with the movement in the 1950s and 1960s. Then, it was led by relatively new, ideologically charged military regimes that soon found themselves in conflict, not only with conservative monarchies, but also with each other. That era was known as the Arab cold war, pitting these radical republics and their ideals of Pan-Arab unity against the more conservative hereditary monarchies of the region.

Today, it remains a staple of analysis to declare Pan-Arabism dead. But beyond this now outdated statist version, there remain powerful lines of Pan-Arab identification at the societal level. The new media revolution has facilitated this still further, and people in the region do follow the news in other Arab countries from North Africa to West Asia. Citizens and societies are today more aware of the cross-border issues and identities of the Arab peoples, in a kind of societal Arab identity without the ideological jargon or baggage of the Arab cold war era.

It would be impossible, for example, to accurately explain the dramatic regime shifts within Egyptian politics without turning to regional transnational relations. The Muslim Brotherhood in Egypt benefited from Qatari and Turkish support, but the military regime that ousted the Brotherhood was supported by Saudi Arabia and the UAE. Domestic politics mattered profoundly in these changes, but so too did the efforts of regional powers.

At the start of the Arab Spring, hopes were high that a new societal Pan-Arabism would lead youth and pro-democracy movements, perhaps even new democratic regimes, to form transnational support coalitions. The efforts were there, but so was the determination of authoritarian states to exploit identity politics, fuel divisions and divide and rule populations. In short, it is transnational authoritarianism, not transnational democracy, that—at least for the time being—seems to have gained the upper hand in regional politics. ∎

The Sunni-Shi'a Divide

The Sunni-Shi'a split in Islam represents the major sectarian divide within the faith. It was originally rooted in a political, not theological, struggle over succession and governance. When the Prophet Muhammad died in 632, the majority faction—the Sunnis—believed his political successor, or Caliph, should be chosen by consensus from the community. Shi'as, in contrast, believed that Ali (the Prophet's son-in-law) was the only legitimate successor, and that Muhammad himself had made clear that Ali was to succeed him as ruler. The issue was not over succession to prophethood, however, as all Muslims see Muhammad as the last of the line of prophets. Sunnis in effect "won" that early round of debate, establishing the Caliphate as an institution through many Islamic empires to follow. In the many years since the first succession debate, Sunnis came to follow the Caliphate as the legitimate governing authority, while Shi'as rejected this, following an alternative line of Imams related to Muhammad.

There are differences within the sects as well. For example, there are four different schools of Islamic law of Sharia within Sunni Islam. Similarly, there are different schools within Shi'ism, disagreeing over how far the legitimate line of Imams is believed to have gone (to the fifth, seventh, or twelfth Imam). But for the most part, the main differences became issues of identity more than theology. The two sects agree on all the main principles and pillars of Islam. And also for the most part have lived peacefully for most of the last 1,400 years.

These are not primordial hatreds that have simmered for millennia. Rather, sectarianism and identity politics tend to increase when political order collapses and people fall back on what they perceive as their main communities—whether they be sectarian, ethnic, national, tribal, or some other form of identity. Today, in the wake of multiple shattering events in the Middle East regional system, sectarianism has arisen where these communities live side by side and where political order has essentially imploded, as in Iraq, Syria and Yemen, among others. The Sunni-Shi'a split and regional sectarianism has also been goaded and manipulated by regional powers such as Saudi Arabia—a majority Sunni state that adheres to an ultra-conservative version of Islam— and Iran—the world's largest Shi'a majority country.

Alliances and regional challenges

By 2015, the early hopes of the Arab Spring seemed dashed by counter-revolution, military coups, civil wars and rising regional terrorism. The 2015 Sharm el-Sheikh summit in Egypt looked like it would be dominated by discussions on the Islamic State, with the Arab regimes uniting against ISIS. Instead, Saudi Arabia took the initiative to form an Arab military coalition, but used it to intervene in the Yemeni civil war, not to stop ISIS. In 2011, the idea of Arab states routinely crossing borders to intervene militarily, meddling directly in the affairs of neighbors, would have seemed highly unlikely. But in 2015, a Saudi-led coalition of Arab states was bombarding another Arab country—Yemen—in the name of regime and regional security.

Saudi Arabia and its allies backed the regime of President Abed Rabbo Mansour Hadi, while Iran gave its support to rebel militias, known as the Houthis. The Yemen conflict amounted to multiple dueling regimes, backed by still other regimes, with Yemeni society paying a terrible price for regime and prospective-regime miscalculations and failures. Not even the Syrian civil war, al-Qaeda or the Islamic State had triggered similar attempts at regional realignment or Pan-Arab security cooperation. Rather, it took seemingly less immediate threats—democratic street activism, the Muslim Brotherhood, or Iranian backing of local Shi'a movements—to trigger existential regime security fears, with corresponding shifts in alliances and even direct military action.

The nuclear agreement between Iran and major world powers then shocked the regional system yet again. But despite misunderstandings to the contrary, the agreement did not amount to a U.S. realignment away from Egypt, Jordan or the GCC states toward Iran. To be sure, regional allies feared abandonment by their main great power patron.

Militants loyal to Yemen's President Abed Rabbo Mansour Hadi gather in Taiz, Yemen, March, 30, 2015. At least 45 people were killed in north Yemen after an airstrike hit a camp for internally displaced people, while a Saudi-led coalition continued to strike Houthi targets around the country for a fifth day. (ANEES MAHYOUB/UPI/NEWSCOM)

Abandonment, and its counterpart entrapment (that is, having an ally drag one into an unwanted conflict) are the two traditional concerns in yet another security dilemma—one between allies themselves. But the U.S. actually increased its support, especially militarily, to each of these regimes and even more so to its ally Israel. In material terms, the U.S. alliances were stronger, even as the regime-to-regime distrust between allies had increased; making these partnerships seem distant and uncertain.

The U.S.-Iran relationship has a lot in common with U.S. arms control deals with the Soviet Union during the cold war. They were agreements between adversaries, with ambitions to work together on some issues, but against one another on others. They were not the beginning of a new alliance or a massive regional realignment on the part of the U.S. The deal is likely, however, to lead to further changes within the region: including deepening the already-existing alliance of Saudi Arabia, UAE, Egypt,

Jordan and other GCC states—and perhaps leading to a rapprochement with Qatar.

Still, perception matters more than reality in politics. Thus, the perceived realignment seems to be the dominant narrative within regional politics, as the system adjusts to what is indeed a dramatic change. The U.S. invasion of Iraq, the Arab Spring, the Syrian civil war, the rise of the Islamic State and the Iranian nuclear deal—each of these has shaken the regional system. And in each case, regimes responded by putting regime security concerns first, rearranging regional alliances accordingly, and ultimately allowing their multi-layered security dilemmas to dampen the democratic hopes and aspirations of those who had led the 2011 demonstrations and uprisings. As much as regional politics has dramatically changed over these last four years, regime security dynamics and security dilemmas continue to drive regional alliances, with profound implications for both internal and external politics. ∎

discussion questions

1. How do you think the Iran nuclear deal will affect regional political dynamics? Will the economic empowerment of Shi'a majority Iran further deepen the regional sectarian divide?

2. What role do you think sectarianism is playing in conflict in the region? Do you think that the apparent Sunni-Shi'a divide is a cause or a symptom of the violence in the Middle East?

3. Do you agree with the author when he claims that there is a new Arab cold war? If not, how would you characterize the current region-wide crisis?

4. Which "jolt" do you think had the biggest impact on the region—the 2003 U.S. invasion of Iraq and its subsequent withdrawal in 2011, the Arab spring and the ensuing civil wars, the rise of ISIS or the Iran nuclear deal?

5. In light of the aftermath of the Arab Spring—with many countries reverting back to reactionary authoritarian regimes—do you support democracy promotion abroad? Although democracy has inherent benefits, democratic transition typically involves an unstable and violent period. How can one balance democratic aspirations with the necessity for stability and security?

6. How does the dependence of many Sunni majority countries—Jordan, Morocco, Sudan—on the Gulf states' oil wealth foster transnational support for the regimes' ruling elites across the region?

7. Why is the Muslim Brotherhood so feared by entrenched regimes? Does this fear largely explain General al-Sisi's coup against Morsi's government in Egypt? Why do some countries like Qatar and Turkey support them?

8. Do you think that the system of alliances in the Middle East has brought about more or less stability? Why?

Don't forget: Ballots start on page 99!

suggested readings

Bank, Andre and Valbjorn, Morten, "The New Arab Cold War: Rediscovering the Arab Dimension of Middle East Regional Politics." **Review of International Studies**. Vol. 38 no. 1., 2012. The authors examine in detail the dynamics of a new cold-war style politics in the region, with emphasis on how this affects inter-Arab relations in the Middle East.

Brand, Laurie A., **Jordan's Inter-Arab Relations: The Political Economy of Alliance Making**, New York: Columbia University Press, 1994. A key work in the literature on alliance politics in the Middle East, introducing the concept of "budget security" as a prime motivator in alliance formation.

Gause, F. Gregory III, "Beyond Sectarianism: The New Middle East Cold War." **Brookings Doha Center Analysis Paper no. 11**. Doha: Brookings Doha Center, 2014. A leading scholar of Gulf and Middle East politics debunks arguments about primordial sectarianism in the region, showing how political powers manipulate the concept in their own regional power struggles.

Hinnebusch, Raymond and Ehteshami, Anoushiravan, eds., **The Foreign Policies of Middle East States**. Boulder: Lynne Rienner Publishers, 2014. This volume brings together multiple authors to explain the dynamics of international relations in the Middle East and also the foreign policies of 11 states in the region.

Kerr, Malcolm, **The Arab Cold War: Gamal Abdel Nasser and His Rivals, 1958–1970**. Oxford: Oxford University Press, 1971. This remains the classic study of the earlier Arab cold war, in the era when Egypt's Nasser made his country a regional power, but also with polarizing effects on regional politics.

Lynch, Marc, **The Arab Uprising: The Unfinished Revolutions of the New Middle East**. New York: Public Affairs, (2012). A leading scholar of the Middle East provides a highly readable account of the youth movements and democracy activism—as well as the anti-democratic regime repression—that shook the entire Arab world in the Arab Spring.

Rubin, Lawrence, **Islam in the Balance: Ideational Threats in Arab Politics**, Palo Alto: Stanford University Press, 2014. Drawing on cases such as Iran and Sudan, the author introduces the concept of the "ideational security dilemma" to show the security implications when regimes feel threatened by ideas and ideologies of other states.

Ryan, Curtis R., **Inter-Arab Alliances: Regime Security and Jordanian Foreign Policy.** Gainesville: University Press of Florida. This book develops a regime security framework for understanding inter-Arab relations and regional politics in the Middle East, and then traces the alliance shifts of the Hashemite Kingdom of Jordan through regional politics over a 40-year period.

———,"The New Arab Cold War and the Struggle for Syria." **Middle East Report** Vol. 262, 2012. pp. 28–31. Available free online at: http://www.merip.org/mer/mer262/new-arab-cold-war-struggle-syria. This essay examines the similarities and differences in the new and old versions of the Arab cold war, and why this has made the Syrian civil war particularly intractable.

To access web links to these readings, as well as links to additional, shorter readings and suggested web sites,

GO TO www.greatdecisions.org

and click on the topic under Resources, on the right-hand side of the page

The rise of ISIS

by Gregory D. Johnsen

Smoke rises after the U.S.-led coalition airstrikes pound ISIS positions at Harceli and Delhi villages in Aleppo, Syria, on November 20, 2015. (IZZET MAZI/ANADOLU AGENCY/GETTY IMAGES)

In the summer of 2014, an Islamist group calling itself the Islamic State in Iraq and al-Sham, or ISIS, captured several key towns in northern Iraq. The Iraqi military—funded and trained by the U.S. for years—fled in the wake of this advance, abandoning their posts and weapons. By August, as ISIS continued to take territory, the U.S. launched a series of air strikes against the group. ISIS responded by systematically beheading several Western hostages it held over a period of weeks. In the nearly year-and-a-half since ISIS' rapid advance, the U.S. has continued to bomb the group even as it has pushed into Syria and declared itself a caliphate, reviving the Islamic institution that had been dormant for nearly a century.

ISIS has, at times in its past, been affiliated with al-Qaeda. But, since its inception, the group has had a different approach with different priorities. Where al-Qaeda focused on defeating the West and corrupt Arab regimes as way to establish a caliphate, ISIS has concentrated its energies on killing Shi'a Muslims, whom it considers heretics. Al-Qaeda preferred a bottom-up approach, attempting to build popular support before announcing its rule, while ISIS has gone the other direction, relying on a top-down approach—it announced the caliphate as a way of attracting followers.

GREGORY D. JOHNSEN *is the author of* The Last Refuge: Yemen, al-Qaeda, and America's War in Arabia. *He has been a Peace Corps volunteer in Jordan, a Fulbright Fellow in Yemen, and a Fulbright-Hays Fellow in Egypt. In 2014, he was the inaugural Michael Hastings National Security Fellow for BuzzFeed, where he won a Dirksen Award from the National Press Foundation for his story "60 Words and a War Without End." That story also won a Peabody Award as part of a collaboration with Radiolab.*

Many of these differences can be traced back to the distinct vision of each group's founder. Osama bin Laden wanted al-Qaeda to be a popular movement, with the group's infrastructure and directed attacks reflecting that core desire. Abu Musab al-Zarqawi, on the other hand, cared less about popularity. A petty criminal early in his life in Jordan, he found religion in prison and wanted to re-create the world of the Prophet Muhammad and his earliest successors in a contemporary setting. Zarqawi read the same texts and studied the same sayings as bin Laden and al-Qaeda. The only difference was that ISIS interpreted them far more rigidly than al-Qaeda, and was determined to implement each and every part of the texts they read, sacrificing nothing for political expediency. ∎

The origins of ISIS

This image from a video released May 4, 2006, by the U.S. Department of Defense, shows Abu Musab al-Zarqawi, the leader of al-Qaeda in Iraq. According to the U.S. military, the video was found by U.S. forces during raids on alleged safe houses in Iraq. (U.S. DEPARTMENT OF DEFENSE/GETTY IMAGES)

Like most contemporary jihadi groups, ISIS has its roots in Afghanistan. In the late 1980s, thousands of young Arab men—with the backing of countries like the U.S. and Saudi Arabia—flocked to Afghanistan to fight the Soviet Union. These men, who became known as "Afghan Arabs," did not play much of a role in defeating the Soviet Union, but they did foster a myth, and in time, that myth would change the world. One of these men was a petty criminal and street thug from the Jordanian industrial city of Zarqa named Ahmad Fadil al-Khalayleh. On the

! Before you read, download the companion **Glossary** that includes definitions and a guide to acronyms and abbreviations used in the article. Go to **www.great decisions.org** and select a topic in the Resources section on the right-hand side of the page.

battlefields of Afghanistan he went by the name al-Gharib, or the Stranger, but he is more commonly known as Abu Musab al-Zarqawi and it is his vision that ISIS is living out today.

Shortly after his return to Jordan from Afghanistan, Zarqawi formed the first of what would become several militant groups called *Jund al-Sham*, or the Army of al-Sham (an area that roughly corresponds to greater Syria). Zarqawi's initial group did not last long. He was arrested in 1992 and the group folded. In a Jordanian prison, Zarqawi came in contact with the Islamic scholar Abu Muhammad al-Maqdisi, who would do much to shape his views and theology. Over the next several years, Zarqawi developed a reputation as an enforcer in prison, once suspending a guard from a coat hook in a fit of anger, according to a

book by *Washington Post* reporter Joby Warrick. But he also became more religious under Maqdisi's guidance, praying and memorizing the Quran. He also started to attract other prisoners, and fellow inmates started referring to Zarqawi and his companions as the *takfiri*s, or those who excommunicate, for the way they almost reflexively excommunicated anyone who disagreed with them. Zarqawi had always been tough, but prison made him hard and gave him both time and a fixed audience with which to develop his leadership skills. When he was pardoned along with several other prisoners in 1999 as part of King Abdullah II's ascension to the Jordanian throne, he was ready for the next step. Zarqawi left the country a few months later, returning to Afghanistan where he quickly came into contact with a growing al-Qaeda franchise.

Initially, al-Qaeda was mistrustful of Zarqawi. He had a prickly personality that did not lend itself well to collaboration, and he seemed overly focused on fighting Shi'a instead of the corrupt Sunni regimes and the U.S., which were al-Qaeda's two primary targets. In his book, *The ISIS Apocalypse*, William McCants of the Brookings Institution writes that Sayf al-Adl, one of al-Qaeda's leaders, was so wary that he had Zarqawi followed. Eventually, al-Qaeda agreed to support a separate training camp for Zarqawi in Afghanistan that would recruit Palestinians and Jordanians. But it did not invite him to join the organization, and Zarqawi did not ask. Instead, as McCants writes, the two coordinated and cooperated with each other "in service of our common goals."

After the September 11, 2001, attacks and the collapse of the Taliban—a group of local fighters in Afghanistan who had provided sanctuary to bin Laden and al-Qaeda— Zarqawi fled to Iran, before eventually making his way to Iraq. In the lead-up to the 2003 invasion, the U.S. attempted to establish Zarqawi as the link between al-Qaeda and attacking Iraq. This, of course, turned out not to be true. There was no connection between Saddam Hussein and al-Qaeda—Zarqawi was not a part of al-Qaeda and he was not yet in Baghdad. But both of these things would soon be reversed.

By the time U.S. troops arrived in Baghdad, Zarqawi was waiting for them, having established another group, this time calling it *Tawhid wa'l-jihad*, or Monotheism and Jihad. On August 19, 2003, Zarqawi ordered the bombing of the United Nations (UN) headquarters in Baghdad, killing more than 20 people including the UN's special representative Sergio Vieira de Mello. Ten days later he ordered a dual car bombing outside the Imam Ali Mosque in Najaf, one of the holiest sites in Shi'a Islam. In less than two weeks, Zarqawi had all but driven the UN out of Iraq and sparked a civil war between the country's Shi'a and Sunni populations.

A few months later, in February 2004, Zarqawi officially applied to join al-Qaeda. In October, al-Qaeda accepted his request, absorbing Zarqawi's Monotheism and Jihad group and re-naming it al-Qaeda in Iraq. But almost immediately issues arose. Bin Laden and his deputy, the Egyptian Ayman al-Zawahiri, wanted Zarqawi to tone down the violence, particularly when it came to beheading videos. Fighting U.S. soldiers was one thing—killing Iraqi Shi'a was another. But the violence in Iraq continued to grow, largely due to Zarqawi and his group. In April 2006,, Zarqawi established a council with representatives from several jihadi groups for the purpose of establishing an "Islamic state," which Zarqawi said would be operational within three months. But the Jordanian did not live that long. On June 7, 2006, a pair of U.S. jets flattened the house where Zarqawi was holding a meeting, killing him and five others.

The Islamic State

Zarqawi's dream of an Islamic state, however, was still very much alive. Later that year on October 15, 2006, Zarqawi's group, which by now had switched names several times, announced the establishment of an Islamic state, proclaiming that a man by the name of Abu Omar al-Baghdadi was now the *Amir al-mu'minin*, or the Commander of the Faithful, a loaded Islamic term that had also been adopted by Mullah Omar, the now deceased supreme leader of the Taliban.

One of the reasons for the quick announcement was that Zarqawi's successor, Abu Ayyub al-Masri, was convinced that the *Mahdi*, or Messiah, was about to return and he wanted a state in place for the apocalyptic battle that some believe will happen at the end of time. In his rush to prepare for the impending apocalypse, Masri announced the state and its commander—Abu Omar al-Baghdadi—before he had either. There was no state, just al-Qaeda's old organization in Iraq, and no one by the name of Abu Omar al-Baghdadi.

Masri eventually settled on a former police officer by the name of Hamid al-Zawi as the head of state, introducing him as Abu Omar al-Baghdadi. As Mc-Cants writes: "The selection of Zawi for the post of commander of the faithful was more like a casting call than anything resembling an Islamic procedure for choosing an emir or leader."

Not surprisingly, given the rollout, the Islamic state's early years were marked by mistakes and missteps. Like Zarqawi's earliest acolytes, the group seemed eager to fight anyone who disagreed with its stance. Baghdadi's followers fought other Islamist groups as well as the U.S. army, which was beginning to see gains as part of its "surge" approach. Bin Laden and Zawahiri criticized the group from Pakistan and Afghanistan, while in Iraq many of the Sunni tribes became fed up with the group's brutality.

By late 2009, it looked as though the group had all but disappeared. Both al-

(Left) An injured man emerges from the UN compound in Baghdad following a bombing, August 19, 2003. A truck bomb explosion ripped through the hotel used by the UN as its headquarters, leaving at least 10 people dead, wrecking the building and rocking the surrounding neighborhood. (JUSTIN LANE/THE NEW YORK TIMES/REDUX) *(Right) Iraqi Shi'a crowds protesting outside the Shrine of Imam Ali in Najaf, August 30, 2003. A car bomb that detonated following Friday noon prayers killed over 82 people including Ayatollah Mohammad Baqer al-Hakim (on banner) and wounded 229 others.* (RABIH MOGHRABI/AFP/GETTY IMAGES)

An Iraqi soldier guards the site where allegedly top al-Qaeda leaders in Iraq, Abu Omar al-Baghdadi and Abu Ayyub al-Masri, were killed in a joint U.S.-Iraqi military raid in Al-Dhahiriya in Salaheddin province, north of Baghdad, April 20, 2010. (MAHMUD SALEH/AFP/ GETTY IMAGES)

Masri and Abu Omar al-Baghdadi were killed a few months later in a joint U.S.-Iraqi raid in April 2010. In May, what was left of the group announced its new commander: Abu Bakr al-Baghdadi. For nearly two years there were no public statements, as al-Baghdadi resurrected his group in the shadows. By the time he made his first public statement, Iraq would look much different.

The Arab Spring

A few months after Masri and Abu Omar al-Baghdadi's death, a young street vendor in Tunisia named Mohammad Bouazizi set himself on fire to protest the confiscation of his fruit cart by police. That act sparked a series of popular uprisings throughout the Arab world, eventually forcing Tunisian President Ben Ali into exile. Next door in Libya, Muammar Qaddafi was eventually killed, while Egyptian President Hosni Mubarak went to prison. In Yemen, Ali Abdullah Saleh, the country's long-serving president stepped down in exchange for immunity. But in Syria, President Bashar al-Assad refused to budge, sending troops to confront the protesters in clashes that would eventually lead to a brutal civil war that has yet to end.

Throughout much of 2011—while

Abu Bakr al-Baghdadi remained silent—many commentators suggested that the Arab Spring would be the end of al-Qaeda. But neither al-Qaeda nor the struggling Islamic state saw it that way. Many of the same issues that animated protesters in 2011 would help fuel recruiting for the Islamic state in 2012 and 2013. Al-Qaeda was formed in the 1988 and although it came out of Afghanistan, an environment that was at war, it was speaking to a region—the Middle East—that was largely at peace. Gory videos and indiscriminate violence did more to turn people off than it did to attract new recruits.

But after more than a decade of conflict, that calculation has changed. In fact, four years after the uprisings of 2011, little seems to have improved across the Arab world. There is still high unemployment and a great deal of hopelessness. If anything, it is even worse now, as the Arab Spring artificially raised people's expectations, implicitly promising that, if they could only get rid of their corrupt leaders, their daily lives would change for the better. But that has not happened, and the comedown has been difficult. As Professor Bernard Haykel of Princeton University notes, "The Islamic State offers a utopian alternative, and

its propaganda trumpets a social order that is just and moral and in which corruption is severely dealt with." This is the same hope that drew hundreds of thousands of protesters into the streets in 2011.

Now, ISIS is both operating out of a warzone in Syria and Iraq as well as speaking to people who have primarily known upheaval and violence, at least in the Middle East. What would not have worked to attract followers in 2002–2003 now has an audience that, thanks to years of instability, has been prepared for a more violent presentation.

Beliefs

ISIS, like al-Qaeda, is a "jihadi-salafi" group. As Haykel points out, this means that ISIS and "its members adhere to a strict literalist interpretation of the texts of the Quran and the sayings of the Prophet Muhammad." ISIS is a "jihadi" group because it believes in using violence to achieve its means. It is a "salafi" group because it believes the Muslim community has lost its way and grown weak and divided. The only way to correct this drift is a return to the "pious forefathers," hence the emphasis on a literal reading of the Quran and the sayings of the Prophet Muhammad. It should be noted that not all salafi groups believe in violence as a means to an end, only jihadi-salafi groups do. What differentiates al-Qaeda from ISIS is, as Cole Bunzel noted in an influential paper for the Brookings Institution, the latter's "hardline approach." Both read the same texts and use the same means of jihad to achieve their goals and yet they are two separate groups with two different styles.

ISIS, as mentioned previously, favors a top-down approach to state building: announcing the caliphate as a way of attracting followers. Al-Qaeda, on the other hand, prefers to work from the bottom up, attracting grass roots supporters as a precursor to announcing an emirate, or statelet. But there are other differences as well—some of these are political, driven by personality conflicts, others have to do with the rigidity of thought and interpretation. For example, on the issue of slavery, which is attested to in the Quran, ISIS takes a literal approach, actively enslaving Yazidi women, whom it considers to be polytheists. Al-Qaeda never abrogated the verses or sayings endorsing slavery, but neither did it actively enslave non-Muslim populations. Another way in which the two groups differ is in their interpretation and implementation of the Islamic concept of *al-wala' wa-l-bara*, or association and disassociation. This is the idea of associating with true Muslims and disassociating with everyone else. Both ISIS and al-Qaeda see this as a key concept, but they differ in their interpretation. Once again, ISIS takes a hardline view, disassociating from everyone who is not a "true" believer. This is one of the reasons, along with Zarqawi's continued influence on ISIS thinking, for the emphasis on attacking Shi'a Muslims. Al-Qaeda, meanwhile, practices a more situational approach to al-wala' wa-l-bara, disassociating from non-believing Muslims in ideal circumstances but otherwise trying to play down potential divisions within the Islamic community in order to focus on attacking the U.S. and what it sees as corrupt Arab governments. In this, as in so much else, al-Qaeda favored political expediency over a rigid reading of the texts. As Cole Bunzel notes, "if jihadism were to be placed on a political spectrum, al-Qaeda would be its left and the Islamic State its right." ∎

ISIS matures

Abu Bakr al-Baghdadi issued his first public statement as the head of the Islamic state in early May 2011. At the time, little was known about him. The Islamic state's consultative council had elected him to replace Abu Omar al-Baghdadi in May 2010, but since then Abu Bakr had refrained from public speeches. Only 38 years old when elected to head the Islamic state, Abu Bakr's real name was Ibrahim Awwad Ibrahim al-Badri.

Born on July 1, 1971, Abu Bakr al-Baghdadi claimed descent from the Prophet Muhammad. But, by the time he was born, his family was surviving on farming and military service. Two of Baghdadi's uncles served in the military, as did a pair of his brothers. This in itself was not unusual, as one of the only avenues for political and economic advancement in Iraq was joining the Baath party, headed by Saddam Hussein.

As a child, Baghdadi's friends remember him as "quiet" and "introverted," a pious boy who earned the nickname "the believer." Low high-school test scores prevented him from studying law. Instead, he eventually settled on a degree in Quranic studies, graduating from the University of Baghdad in 1996. Three years later, he finished a master's degree and decided to pursue doctoral studies. But in February 2004, less than a year after the U.S. invasion of Iraq, Baghdadi was arrested and placed in Camp Bucca near Umm Qasr in southern Iraq where he was held for ten months as a "civilian detainee." In

In this March 16, 2009, file photo, detainees pray at former U.S. military detention facility Camp Bucca, Iraq. (DUSAN VRANIC/AP PHOTO)

the same way Zarqawi's experience in prison had shaped him, Baghdadi's time in Camp Bucca set his future course. The prison was known in jihadi circles as "the academy" because, as McCants writes, "it brought together so many jihadists and former members of Saddam's military and security services." The jihadists and the military learned from each other and young men like Baghdadi—who had been picked up by accident or without reason—came into contact with hardened jihadists, who provided a narrative and an explanation for what had happened to them.

In 2006, shortly after being released from prison, Baghdadi joined al-Qaeda in Iraq. But he was also working on other projects. In 2007, Baghdadi successfully defended his dissertation, and began to move up the ranks of what was now being called, at least internally, the Islamic state. When Abu Omar al-Baghdadi and Abu Ayyub al-Masri were killed in April 2010, the Islamic state needed to find a new leader. The Islamic state's consultative council was made up of 11 members, but because they were being hunted by the U.S. military they could not meet in person. Instead they relied on a clandestine network of couriers to deliver messages to one another. One member of the council, a former colonel in the Iraqi army, used this to his advantage, writing to each of the members of the council to tell them that everyone else had already agreed to support Baghdadi as the new leader. When the votes were counted, Baghdadi had been elected by a 9–2 margin.

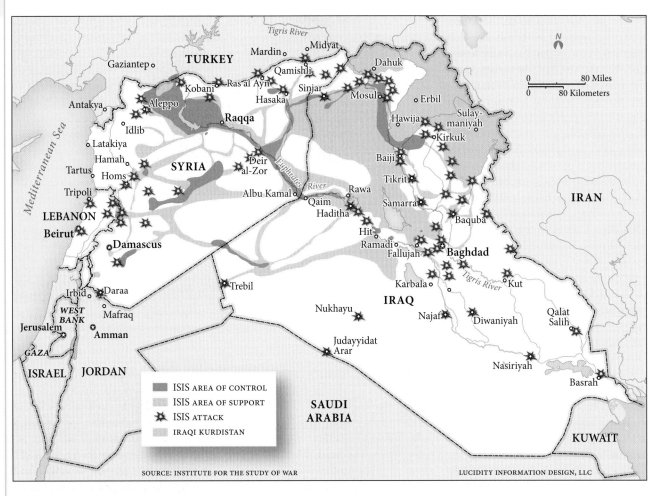

ISIS AREA OF CONTROL
ISIS AREA OF SUPPORT
✶ ISIS ATTACK
IRAQI KURDISTAN

SOURCE: INSTITUTE FOR THE STUDY OF WAR

LUCIDITY INFORMATION DESIGN, LLC

Baghdadi's first public statement, in May 2011, was a reaction to the death of Osama bin Laden. Although Baghdadi had been silent for a year since he took over, and it would be another year until he made his first speech, he was not inactive. At first, he set about consolidating control of the Islamic state and purging its ranks. By the end of 2011, as fighting in Syria between Assad's troops and protesters worsened, he sent a small contingent of fighters across the border. This group, which he called *Jabhat al-Nusra*, or the Nusra Front, was commanded by one of his deputies named Abu Muhammad al-Jawlani. But, much in the same way Baghdadi in Iraq had quietly defied al-Qaeda's orders from Pakistan and Afghanistan, Jawlani began ignoring his boss. Part of the conflict, as McCants and Bunzel suggest, was the revenue from oil that was being smuggled out of Syria. But there was also a strategic gulf between the two former allies. Jawlani, siding more with the local fighters in Syria, wanted to prioritize popular support in a

way that the Islamic state never had in Iraq. Baghdadi disagreed and throughout 2012 and early 2013, the two leaders conducted a slow-moving argument on the best way forward. Finally, in April 2013, fed up with Jawlani's reluctance to overtly recognize Baghdadi as his commander and the Nusra Front as part of the Islamic state, Baghdadi went public.

ISIS

On April 9, 2013, Baghdadi released an audio message announcing the formation of a new entity, which he called the Islamic State in Iraq and al-Sham. In his message Baghdadi explained that both Jawlani and the Nusra Front were part of the Islamic State, but that in the future only the name ISIS would be used. Jawlani wasted no time, releasing a statement of his own the next day, declaring the Nusra Front's independence from ISIS and pledging his loyalty to Ayman al-Zawahiri, bin Laden's successor as the head of al-Qaeda. The split that had been brewing between the two

for months was finally out in the open.

Baghdadi's next move was to send more ISIS fighters into Syria, this time to fight both Assad's government as well as their former allies in the Nusra Front. At the same time behind-the-scenes, Zawahiri was trying to broker an agreement between Baghdadi and Jawlani. Ultimately, the al-Qaeda leader sided with Jawlani, effectively making the Nusra Front al-Qaeda's franchise in Syria, and telling Baghdadi to stay in Iraq. That advice fell on deaf ears, and throughout the summer of 2013 Baghdadi continued to direct fighters to Syria, making good on his public claim of creating an Islamic State in Iraq and al-Sham.

The split between Baghdadi on one side, and Zawahiri and Jawlani on the other soon spilled over into scholarly circles as both sides attracted followers who argued for their respective leader. Finally, on February 2, 2014, al-Qaeda renounced any connection with ISIS, saying it could not be held responsible for any of ISIS' actions. The back-and-forth continued throughout 2014, as both ISIS and al-Qaeda sought to distance themselves from each other. At one point, an ISIS spokesman even argued that his organization had never been a part of al-Qaeda, although al-Qaeda quickly debunked that claim by releasing documents showing that ISIS had indeed sprung out of al-Qaeda in Iraq.

A few months later, on June 9, 2014, ISIS made a major push on the battlefield—taking Mosul in northern Iraq. Two days later and nearly 125 miles away it took Saddam Hussein's hometown of Tikrit. The rapid military advances seemed to surprise everyone, including U.S. military planners. ISIS continued its expansion, pushing toward the border with Syria, taking over large chunks of territory as the Iraqi army seemed to disintegrate in its path. ISIS even made a concentrated push for the small village of Dabiq, just north of Aleppo in Syria.

Dabiq was more of a theological target than a military one. According to an Islamic prophecy, the Day of Judgment is supposed to come after Muslims defeat a Western army at Dabiq. For ISIS, taking the town was a way to hurry on the apocalypse. In order to be properly prepared for the battle at the end of time, ISIS needed a caliphate in place to welcome the Mahdi that would supposedly arrive. And, on June 29, 2014, ISIS announced a caliphate that would be known as the Islamic State. This was the first time in nearly 100 years, since Ataturk abolished the Ottoman caliphate in 1924, that there had been this form of Islamic government. ISIS, of course, was not modeling itself after this more contemporary version, which it considered decadent and un-Islamic. In calling itself a caliphate, ISIS was harkening back to the beginning of Islam and the rule of Muhammad's first four successors, who are known collectively as the *rashidun,* or the rightly guided caliphs.

The Caliphate

On July 4, 2014, five days after the announcement of the caliphate, Abu Bakr al-Baghdadi gave a rare public sermon in Mosul, urging his followers to "walk

An image taken from a video released on July 5, 2014, shows ISIS leader Abu Bakr al-Baghdadi preaching during Friday prayer at a mosque in Mosul. (AL-FURQAN MEDIA/AN-ADOLU AGENCY/GETTY IMAGES)

in the way of jihad." By announcing the caliphate and having Baghdadi—the caliph—make a public appearance, ISIS was attempting to sideline al-Qaeda, taking the battle for the mantle of jihad out of the hands of scholars and placing it before the Muslim community worldwide. This drew an immediate reaction from al-Qaeda. Instead of simply denouncing the Islamic State's caliphate, Ayman al-Zawahiri suggested that there already was a caliphate and caliph: Mullah Omar in Afghanistan. That argument, however, broke down months later when it was revealed that Mullah Omar had died in 2013.

What these claims and counterclaims reveal is how vital an issue the caliphate is to groups like ISIS and al-Qaeda. Both want to bring it into being—they just differ on the means. When ISIS bypassed al-Qaeda and appeared to be gaining recruits at the expense of the latter, al-Qaeda reacted by trying to beat ISIS at its own game. This has had little success.

ISIS has an impressive online presence that allows it to reach recruits that al-Qaeda never did. Al-Qaeda relied on a personal link, someone to connect an individual in the West with a franchise in the Middle East or Southeast Asia. Initial steps could be taken online, but al-Qaeda preferred to deal

with recruits in person. ISIS has, once again, circumvented this step, essentially encouraging individuals in the West to "self-radicalize." It has been much more successful at this than al-Qaeda, both through the group's use of social media as well as videos and the English-language magazine, named after Dabiq. Additionally, when not primarily addressing a Western audience, ISIS has shown itself quite skilled in using poetry and jihadi anthems to attract recruits from around the Arab world. "Poetry," as Robyn Creswell and Bernard Haykel write in *The New Yorker,* "provides a window onto the movement talking to itself. It is in verse that militants most clearly articulate the fantasy life of jihad."

In the immediate aftermath of ISIS' declaration of a caliphate, its online fan base cheered and expanded. ISIS made the argument that, as much as it was possible, true believing Muslims should travel to the new caliphate to live under a government that implemented all of what it called God's law. This fits with ISIS' broader message of associating with true Muslims and disassociating from everyone else, and has been part of the group's driving ideology since Zarqawi. As the recruits, both male and female, traveled to Iraq and Syria to join ISIS—essentially validating the group's

Jordanian protesters carry an effigy of the Islamic State's leader Abu Bakr al-Baghdadi, during a march after Friday prayers in downtown Amman, February 6, 2015. Thousands of Jordanians gathered to show their loyalty to the King and to show solidarity with the family of the pilot, Muath al-Kasasbeh, killed by ISIS. (MUHAMMAD HAMED/REUTERS)

"announce-it-and-they-will-come" approach—it continued to push forward militarily.

In early July 2014, ISIS seized one of the largest oilfields in Syria near the town of Homs, and later that month it overran a Syrian military base in Raqqa. In August, ISIS fighters massacred thousands of Yazidi men, taking the women as slaves, in and around Sinjar in northern Iraq. With Kurdish forces in danger of being defeated and a humanitarian disaster in the making, the U.S. finally took direct military action. On August 8, President Barack Obama authorized air strikes against ISIS targets. Weeks later, the UK and France followed suit by launching their first air strikes against ISIS targets. Since then, the U.S. and its allies have continued to carry out air raids and, in some cases, special forces operations on the ground in Iraq and Syria.

On August 19, 2014, less than two weeks after the U.S. started bombing ISIS, the group released a video entitled "message to the American people" that showed a masked man beheading American journalist James Foley. Over the next few months, more gory videos would follow, including those of the beheadings of Steven Sotloff and Peter "Abdul Rahman" Kassig. A fourth American hostage, Kayla Mueller, was

also killed although the circumstances of her death remain unclear.

On January 3, 2015, ISIS burned to death a Jordanian pilot named Muath al-Kasasbeh whom it had captured after he bailed out of his plane in the midst of a bombing run two weeks earlier. The video was released a month later on February 3, during King Abdullah II's state visit to the U.S. Jordan was one of several countries—including Australia, Canada, France, the Netherlands and the UK—to fly air missions against ISIS. Despite the number of air strikes since the U.S. and its allies began bombing in 2014, ISIS seems largely unfazed. They continue to receive money from oil that they are able to smuggle out of Iraq and Syria as well as from seizures, and new recruits continue to flock to ISIS-controlled territory.

In early 2015, the group lost control of Tikrit. But weeks later, it managed to push into the historic city of Palmyra in central Syria, destroying several historic artifacts. IHS Jane's, a security and analysis firm, estimated that from June 2014 to June 2015, ISIS had carried out more than 3,000 attacks. The U.S. and coalition forces have carried out more than 6,000 airstrikes since bombing began.

In August 2015, the Pentagon's inspector general opened an investigation

to determine whether U.S. intelligence assessments of ISIS were being altered to portray a more positive outlook. A few weeks later, in late September, Russia began bombing what it said were ISIS targets in Syria, but many of the strikes seemed to be directed at other rebel groups fighting Assad's government.

In November, three teams carried out coordinated terrorist attacks throughout Paris, which left more than 129 people dead and at least 300 injured. The attacks were traced back to ISIS along with suspicions that the group was also behind the downing of a Russian passenger jet over Egypt weeks earlier. The Paris attacks have sparked calls for a greater international response to defeat ISIS.

ISIS branches

In addition to the caliphate in Iraq and Syria, ISIS has also announced other affiliate groups throughout the Middle East.

In Egypt, a group calling itself *Ansar Bayt al-Maqdis* pledged loyalty to Baghdadi in late 2014. In much the same way ISIS operates, the group adopted a new name tied to its geography, in this case the Sinai Province, and attempted to re-create the caliphate's top-down approach, announcing and then building. This has taken the form of several attacks against military installations, a few attempts to hold territory and the beheading of a Croatian engineer.

A similar dynamic has played out in Libya, with groups tied to ISIS announcing themselves as a "province," such as the Tripoli Province, and then carrying out attacks on behalf of ISIS. It has bombed luxury hotels and government buildings, taken control of cities and overrun prisons.

This pattern is also repeating itself in Yemen and, to a lesser extent, in Saudi Arabia. Once again, ISIS supporters announced a group tied to a particular territory, pledged allegiance to Baghdadi, and then started carrying out attacks. In Yemen, as in Iraq and elsewhere, many of these attacks have targeted Shi'a mosques in Sanaa, in an apparent attempt to recreate the

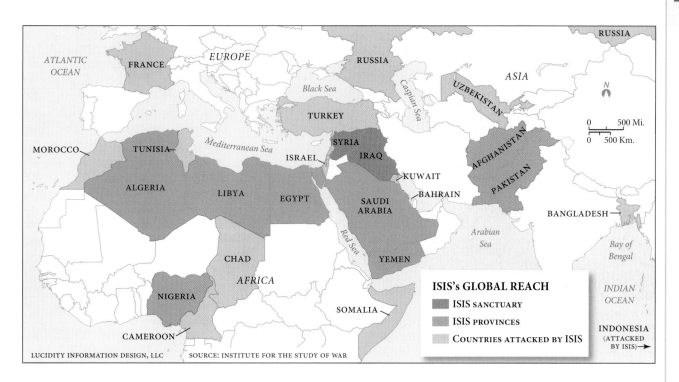

ISIS's GLOBAL REACH
- ISIS SANCTUARY
- ISIS PROVINCES
- COUNTRIES ATTACKED BY ISIS

LUCIDITY INFORMATION DESIGN, LLC   SOURCE: INSTITUTE FOR THE STUDY OF WAR

Sunni-Shi'a civil war that helped tear Iraq apart. Most recently, four suicide attackers targeted a hotel where United Arab Emirates troops were staying as part of the country's involvement in the Yemen civil war.

In early 2015, an ISIS-affiliated group announced the creation of a Saudi branch in the Najd Province. The group's first attack, bombing a Shi'a mosque, took place in May 2015. The group also bombed a Shi'a mosque in Kuwait.

Boko Haram in Nigeria has also pledged allegiance to ISIS, which Baghdadi accepted in March 2015. ISIS has also announced provinces in Algeria, Afghanistan, and Pakistan.

The goal appears to be to establish these provinces as outposts, and then build them to make the reality match the rhetoric. ISIS will likely continue to declare provinces in different countries throughout the Middle East, Africa and Asia, attempting to implement its vision for a caliphate that stretches from the Maghreb to Central Asia. ∎

Challenges ahead

The rise of ISIS has presented the U.S. and the international community with a number of security, humanitarian and political challenges. Chief among these has been the flood of refugees who have fled the war in Syria as well as ISIS' military advances in the region. Many of these refugees have fled to Turkey, which has relatively porous borders. Since the start of the conflict, Turkey has hosted nearly 2 million refugees and another 1.5 million have crossed into Jordan and Lebanon. Several hundred thousand of these have ended up in refugee camps. But for many, these bordering states are primarily transit countries for a dangerous journey to Europe—Turkey is particularly attractive because of its proximity to Europe. Significant portions of the refugee population either

escaped without proper documentation or crossed international borders illegally, which makes further travel increasingly difficult. As a result, in the first half of 2015, more than half a million refugees crossed the Mediterranean on their way to Europe, often paying smugglers to ferry them to Europe. The United Nations High Commissioner for Refugees (UNHCR) has established a Special Mediterranean Initiative to help European countries deal with the influx. But most appear overwhelmed by the number of refugees.

The problem is likely to get worse before it gets better. With winter approaching and dire warnings from the UNHCR, the EU still has not articulated a coordinated response. ISIS has responded to the refugee crisis by releasing several videos designed to en-

courage refugees to return to ISIS-controlled territory. There have also been reports, although largely unconfirmed, that ISIS has attempted to smuggle fighters into Europe along with the waves of refugees. Although not an impossible scenario, this is not a tactic ISIS has prioritized up to this point.

Kidnappings

ISIS has prioritized kidnappings, particularly in 2012 and 2013. Many captured, particularly Westerners, were freelance journalists or aid workers who had crossed into Syria. ISIS has offered to exchange many of these hostages for cash, which—despite the denials of some governments—appears to have been paid. In other cases, when countries such as the U.S. and UK refuse to pay ransom to the group, the hostages

(Left) Columns and the ancient Temple of Bel are seen in the historical city of Palmyra, Syria, June 11, 2009. The Syrian Observatory for Human Rights monitoring group and other activists said on August 30, 2015, that ISIS had destroyed part of the 2,000-year-old temple, one of Palmyra's most important monuments. (GUSTAU NACARINO/REUTERS) *(Right) More than 100 French police stormed an apartment in Saint-Denis, a Paris suburb, where several terrorists were hiding, including the Paris attacks mastermind, Abdelhamid Abaaoud. He and two other terrorists were killed in the raid, including one female who blew herself up.* (GROISARD/SG/JBV NEWS/POLARIS/NEWSCOM)

have been executed, often in particularly gruesome circumstances. In the U.S., ransom payments to terrorist groups have long been against federal law. But following sharp criticism of the current policy by the families of former hostages, the U.S. government announced in mid-2015 that it would no longer "seek to prosecute" individuals who attempted to negotiate ransom payments.

The kidnappings have presented a real problem for the U.S. and other governments. If countries pay ransoms or facilitate the paying of such, they, at least indirectly are supporting a terrorist group and encouraging future kidnappings. If they do not, those held captive are often killed. Western governments are still faced with the dilemma of either providing, or turning a blind eye to, money given to terrorist groups or being forced to watch its citizens executed.

Humanitarian challenges

Another concern for Western governments has been the human rights violations of minority groups in territory controlled by ISIS. The most obvious case has been that of young women and girls, particularly Christians or Yazidis, who are systematically raped by ISIS fighters. In a disturbing article for the *New York Times*, Rukmini Callimachi detailed what she called a "theology of rape." While rape has often been a byproduct of military conquest and occupation, ISIS has institutionalized

it, using the barter of young women as a reward for fighters. As Callimachi documents, ISIS has issued several "how-to" documents and even "celebrates each sexual assault as spiritually beneficial, even virtuous."

Destruction of cultural heritage

ISIS has also seemed determined to destroy any historical artifact it deems idolatrous. As in much of the group's theology, this necessitates a narrow and rigid reading of Quranic injunctions. Like the Taliban, who destroyed a pair of Buddha statues in Afghanistan in 2001, ISIS has appeared resolute to "cleanse" the territory under its control—including sites considered archeological marvels or world historic sites. Most recently, in early October 2015, ISIS destroyed the iconic nearly 2,000-year-old Arch of Triumph in Palmyra, Syria. UNESCO, the UN heritage agency, and others have described ISIS' destructive actions as "war crimes." But, as with the other challenges, Western governments have been unable to do much to reduce the threat to historic sites under ISIS' control.

Domestic attacks

Another primary concern is the potential for ISIS-linked attacks in the West, which has grown following the attacks in Paris. According to a *New York Times* database, ISIS has either inspired or directed attacks in 11 Western countries, includ-

ing the U.S., the UK, Canada, Australia, France and Germany. Unlike al-Qaeda, which prefers to maintain a degree of control over potential attacks, ISIS is eager for its supporters to self-radicalize. This is a relatively new phenomenon, and ISIS has utilized both traditional offerings such as magazines and videos as well as social media to reach supporters in Western countries.

ISIS is implementing a two-pronged approach. First, it is asking supporters in the West to travel to ISIS-controlled territory to live under the caliphate. But, if this proves impossible, ISIS has suggested that they take matters into their own hands, by carrying out attacks in their home countries on behalf of ISIS. This two-track approach also illustrates ISIS' priorities. Attracting members to live under the caliphate is the group's primary goal; attacks in the West are a secondary one.

ISIS also appears to be attempting to drive a wedge between host governments and refugees who are fleeing ISIS in Iraq and Syria by planning and launching attacks in the West. What remains unclear, however, is how monolithic of a group ISIS is, and how much command-and-control the group has over various plots in different countries.

This does not mean that ISIS will not carry out attacks in the West—it will. It means that a failure by ISIS to carry out attacks in the West will not erode the group's raison d'être. ∎

Policy options

The response to ISIS by the U.S. and the international community has been tepid. In 2011 and 2012, when it looked like al-Qaeda was on the run following the death of Osama bin Laden, ISIS took advantage of the West's inattention, reorganizing and growing under the leadership of Abu Bakr al-Baghdadi. Several factors contributed to ISIS gaining a foothold in Iraq and Syria, but two stand out. The first was the weakness of the Iraqi military—which the U.S. funded and equipped for years—in the face of ISIS assaults. The second contributing factor was U.S. reluctance to return to Iraq. In 2013 and much of 2014, as ISIS was making gains and taking territory, the U.S. watched and waited. As McCants notes, "some of the usual methods for dealing with jihadist statelets might have worked early on in Syria and Iraq. But ISIS is now too entrenched for quick solutions."

The U.S., for obvious reasons, is unwilling to commit ground troops to Iraq. President Obama reiterated this position in the wake of the Paris attacks in November. Instead it has opted for air strikes and training rebel groups, which it hopes will be able "to degrade and ultimately defeat ISIS." But both of these approaches have serious drawbacks. Air strikes can weaken ISIS targets but, on their own, they cannot defeat ISIS. The same is true for U.S.-trained rebel groups. They may be able to erode some of ISIS' hold on territory, but ultimately they will be unable to decisively roll ISIS back. Indeed, in late September 2015, press reports revealed that one group of U.S.-trained rebels had handed over ammunition and supplies to the Nusra Front apparently in exchange for safe passage. Around the same time Gen. Lloyd Austin, the head of the U.S. Central Command, which is responsible for military operations in the Middle East, testified to Congress that there were only four or five U.S.-trained rebels currently fighting in

Syria. Both of these revelations suggest serious problems with using proxies in the fight against ISIS. The U.S. might be able to train and equip them, but it cannot control them. Once these groups enter the battlefield, they will pursue their own objectives.

The U.S. has also backed Kurdish fighters who, in November 2015, pushed on the Iraqi town of Sinjar in an attempt to split ISIS' territory in two by taking the city and cutting off the supply line that ran through it. The U.S., however, is constrained here as well in that it does not want the Kurds to become so strong that they can form an independent state. Current U.S. policy seeks to ensure the territorial integrity of Iraq—even as the Kurds have set up a de facto state—which makes supporting the Kurds against ISIS a delicate balancing act.

The U.S. is also struggling to limit ISIS' finances, partly by working with Turkey and others to prevent oil smuggling. So far, this initiative's impact has been limited. Likewise, attempts to prevent foreign fighters from traveling to Iraq and Syria to join ISIS have not had a measurable impact on the group's strength. There is no silver

bullet to the problem that ISIS presents. The group did not arise overnight and it will not be defeated overnight. The U.S. and its coalition partners have been bombing for over a year and ISIS now controls more territory than it did when the bombing campaign began. The civil war in Syria is still going strong with no signs of abating, and ISIS affiliates throughout the globe appear to be multiplying.

Part of this is a political and sectarian issue. Abu Musab al-Zarqawi, although he did not live to see it, did an excellent job of sparking a Shi'a-Sunni civil war in Iraq that is now being exported to other countries like Yemen. Iraq's government is Shi'a and until it reaches some sort of a political agreement with Sunnis, the sectarian divide will continue to give ISIS the political oxygen it needs to survive.

In the face of all of these obstacles, the U.S. has decided on air strikes and support for various groups on the ground. It is, at best, a holding strategy, designed to prevent ISIS from further growing. But even this modest goal may be too much for the current policy. Still, there appear to be few other appealing options on the table. ∎

discussion questions

1. What steps can the U.S. and other Western countries take in order to stem the flow of recruits travelling overseas to join ISIS? Additionally, what should be done with former ISIS fighters once they return to their home countries?

2. Why are other Islamic insurgent groups like Boko Haram in Nigeria and Ansar Bayt al-Maqdis in Egypt pledging their allegiance to ISIS? Is that a demonstration of the caliphate's ideological attraction or the other groups' weakness? What can the U.S. do to prevent the spread of the ISIS brand across Africa, the Middle East and Asia?

3. How would you evaluate the success of the U.S. strategy against ISIS? When aiming at "degrading and ultimately defeating ISIS," are airstrikes and supplying weapons to local actors sufficient? Is the deployment of U.S. ground troops necessary to defeat the group?

4. Do you think the 2003 U.S. invasion of Iraq with the overthrow of Saddam and the subsequent 2011 withdrawal contributed to the situation in Iraq today? Would ISIS have conquered so much territory if Saddam was still in power? What if the U.S. still maintained a strong military presence in the country?

5. Which represents a bigger threat to the U.S.—al-Qaeda or ISIS? Although attacks against the West are not ISIS' primary objective, should the U.S. focus most of its attention and resources on it or worry about other terrorist groups?

6. Should the U.S. prosecute families who paid ransoms to ISIS in order to free hostages or should it abandon its current policy altogether? Would a policy change create a financial incentive for the group to kidnap even more?

Don't forget: Ballots start on page 99!

suggested readings

Bunzel, Cole. "From Paper State to Caliphate: The Ideology of the Islamic State." Washington, DC: **Brookings Institution**, March 2015. 45pp. Available free online: <http://www.brookings.edu/~/media/research/files/papers/2015/03/ideology-of-islamic-state-bunzel/the-ideology-of-the-islamic-state.pdf>. Gives a comprehensive overview of the intellectual history of the Islamic State's rise to power.

Callimachi, Rukmini. "ISIS enshrines a Theology of Rape." New York: **New York Times**, August 13, 2015. Available free online: <http://www.nytimes.com/2015/08/14/world/middleeast/isis-enshrines-a-theology-of-rape.html>. Presents a disturbing look into the world that ISIS rules, and how it has institutionalized rape as a method of control.

Haykel, Bernard. "ISIS: A Primer." Princeton: **Princeton Alumni Weekly**, June 3, 2015. Available free online: <https://paw.princeton.edu/issues/2015/06/03/pages/0027/index.xml>.A good introduction to the basic facts about ISIS: who they are and where they came from.

McCants, William. "The Believer." Washington, DC: **Brookings Institution**, 2015. Available free online: <http://www.brookings.edu/research/essays/2015/thebeliever>. Provides the best biography of Abu Bakr al-Baghdadi, current head of ISIS.

McCants, William. **The ISIS Apocalypse: The History, Strategy and Doomsday Vision of the Islamic State.** New York: St. Martin's Press, 2015. 256pp. Provides a brisk read outlining the roots and formation of the Islamic State. Of special interest are the translations of several of the key texts ISIS uses to form its ideological foundations.

Warrick, Joby. **Black Flags: The Rise of ISIS**. New York: Doubleday, September 29, 2015. 368pp. A good narrative overview of the life of Abu Musab al-Zarqawi, the spiritual founder of ISIS.

Wright, Lawrence. "Five Hostages." New York: **New Yorker**, July 6, 2015. Available free online: <http://www.newyorker.com/magazine/2015/07/06/five-hostages>. A compelling and heartbreaking piece of narrative reporting that looks at the families who negotiated with ISIS in an effort to get their children back, while also shining a light on U.S. policy toward hostages abroad.

Wood, Graeme. "What ISIS Really Wants." Washington, DC: **The Atlantic**, March, 2015. Available free online: <http://www.theatlantic.com/magazine/archive/2015/03/what-isis-really-wants/384980/>. Looks at whether ISIS is really as "Islamic" as it claims, how the group thinks and what texts guide its decision-making.

To access web links to these readings, as well as links to additional, shorter readings and suggested web sites,

GO TO www.greatdecisions.org

and click on the topic under Resources, on the right-hand side of the page

The future of Kurdistan

by Jenna Krajeski

Kurdish Peshmerga fighters fly a Kurdish flag in the city of Sinjar, Iraq, November 13, 2015. Deafening bursts of celebratory gunfire erupted after Yazidi fighters helped the Kurds gain control of the city, which has been under the brutal domination of the Islamic State for more than 15 months. (BRYAN DENTON/THE NEW YORK TIMES/REDUX)

In late July 2014, Massoud Barzani, the president of the autonomous Kurdish region in northern Iraq known as Iraqi Kurdistan, traveled west from the capital Erbil to the banks of the Tigris River, where he planned to deliver a speech. His audience were *Peshmerga*, the Kurdish fighters whose name loosely translates to "those who face death." At the time, the Peshmerga were embroiled in a brutal fight on the front lines with militants of the self-declared Islamic State (ISIS), suffering heavy casualties. Barzani, however, arrived ready to declare victory.

For a few months, ISIS had been reshaping Iraq, converting territories according to their definition of a new Islamic caliphate. Just across the Tigris river from where Barzani spoke, militants had established a stronghold where they planned to impose a new system of government and law based on their radical interpretation of the Quran, expelling, killing or enslaving any Iraqis who disagreed with their vision. Kurds had not fought a war since they sided with the U.S. during the 2003 invasion, and many of the Peshmerga were either new recruits or retired. These average Kurds suddenly found themselves as Iraq's best defense against attacks in the region.

But for Iraqi Kurds—who had long felt ignored in the broader discussion about the future of Iraq—the clash with ISIS was an opportunity. While the central government stumbled and the Iraqi army fled, Kurds proved their strength, both on the battlefield and in the political arena.

JENNA KRAJESKI *is a journalist covering the Middle East. Her work has appeared online and in print at* The New Yorker, The Nation *and* The Virginia Quarterly Review, *among many other magazines and newspapers. For four years she was based in Istanbul where, with the support of the Pulitzer Center on Crisis Reporting, she focused on the Kurdish minorities in Iraq, Turkey and Syria. She is a 2016 Knight-Wallace journalism fellow at the University of Michigan in Ann Arbor.*

Unlike in Baghdad, Kurds rallied around their leaders and the Peshmerga rushed to the fight. The Kurdistan Regional Government (KRG) welcomed thousands of Iraqis displaced by the conflict—Christians, Sunnis and Yazidis among them—into the remarkably stable north, adding to the significant number of Syrian refugees already living in KRG-controlled areas.

While the rest of Iraq buckled under the weight of the violence, Kurdistan rose to prominence. Politicians and reporters around the world celebrated its secular government, loyal fighters, reliable security, as well as its pro-Western attitude. So, by July 2014, when Barzani stood by the Tigris, he was inflated with confidence. "Our day is near," Barzani told the Peshmerga. In an interview with the BBC, he was less grandiose but no less clear. The fight with ISIS was proof that Kurds were capable of running their own nation; compared to the rest of Iraq, they were practically a different world. Kurdistan, he was sure, would soon be independent. "We will hold a referendum in Kurdistan," he told reporters. "We will respect and be bound by the decision of our people and hope that others will do likewise."

Barzani's determination, however, was not merely a response to ISIS; it came after generations of rebellions, betrayals, dubious negotiations and narrow escapes. To much of the world, the KRG's insistence on independence seemed to come on suddenly—a logical reaction, perhaps, to sectarianism, ISIS and a failed government in Baghdad—but for Kurds the wait has seemed interminable and the sacrifices vast in the pursuit of an independent Kurdistan. Barzani, it was clear, felt that Kurds had waited long enough. A few months later, however, it would become apparent to everyone that he had spoken too soon. ∎

Before you read, download the companion **Glossary** that includes definitions and a guide to acronyms and abbreviations used in the article. Go to **www.great decisions.org** and select a topic in the Resources section on the right-hand side of the page.

The dream for independence

The end of World War I signaled the collapse of the Ottoman Empire, and the Allied powers struggled to figure out how to divide up the Sultan's territories. Under the Treaty of Sèvres, Kurds were promised their own country, one that even included oil-rich Mosul, but Turkish authorities had their own ideas about sovereignty. Due to Turkish pressure, in 1923 the Treaty of Sèvres was replaced by the Treaty of Lausanne, which drew borders around modern Turkey and divided the Kurds across Turkey, Iran, Iraq and Syria, as well as a small corner of Armenia.

In 1923, when Iraqi Kurds experienced what they consider their first major betrayal by outside powers, they were led by Mahmoud Barzinji, a tribal sheikh determined to lead Kurds to independence from British-occupied Iraq. A photograph of the sheikh shows him in a rebel uniform almost identical to those worn by Kurdish rebels decades later, a knife and gun sticking out from under his thick traditional belt. Like future generations of Kurdish fighters, Barzinji is depicted in the mountains, leaning against a boulder

Sheikh Mahmoud Barzinji (BRIDGEMAN IMAGES)

as if to prove how at home he is in the remote and tough setting.

The failure of the Treaty of Sèvres became a rallying cry for Kurdish rebel leaders, both then and now. It was the first time Kurds truly had been taken into account by occupying powers—indeed, the first time they had been mentioned in a formal international document—and the closest they had come to the reality of an independent, and lasting, Kurdistan. Even a century later, Kurds feel the sting of this early loss. It is said that Barzinji wore a copy of the defunct treaty around his arm as part of his guerilla uniform.

Massoud Barzani was born into this tradition of determined leaders and thwarted rebellions, the son of Mullah Mustafa Barzani, Barzinji's successor. Mullah Mustafa led the first Kurdish rebellion against the British colonial government in 1930, and would continue to fight the central authorities until his death in exile in 1979, giving him the reputation as the 20th century's most active rebel leader.

In Iraqi Kurdistan, Mullah Mustafa has achieved an almost mythical status. Portraits of the rebel wearing a traditional Kurdish turban hang alongside those of Massoud in KRG government buildings and many private homes. His name is synonymous with the Kurdistan Democratic Party (KDP), which he founded in August 1946, as well as Kurdish self-governance in general. In 2014, as the war with ISIS intensified, Kurds in all sectors would credit Mullah Mustafa with the rights defended by the Peshmerga. "If it weren't for this man," an Erbil hospital supervisor told the author, gesturing toward Mullah Mustafa's picture hanging on the wall above his head, "we would all be speaking Arabic, not Kurdish."

Since the formation of Iraq in the aftermath of World War I, Kurds have rebelled against the central authority, from the occupying British through the brutal rule of Saddam Hussein. In retaliation, Kurds have been murdered and imprisoned, their villages razed, their culture suppressed, and their political leaders forced into the middle of political maneuverings of surrounding governments, usually with disastrous results. They have been massacred with chemical weapons that still manifest themselves in physical and psychological illnesses today. In the 1990s, after decades of internal fighting, Iraqi Kurds turned against one another in a civil war that lasted years and divided the region.

There have also been victories. In 1991, the U.S., UK and France began an effort to protect Kurds and Shi'a from Saddam Hussein by establishing no-fly zones in the country's Kurdish north and Shi'a-dominated south, which continued until the U.S.-led coalition invaded in 2003. This allowed the KRG to begin exploiting its oil reserves—an estimated 4 billion untapped barrels kept out of reach under Saddam, who used Iraq's oil wealth to suppress dissent — and developing its urban centers. Universities, hospitals, government buildings, parks and shopping malls have given the cities shape. Aside from the

government buildings, Erbil is notably free of blast walls, and people operate under the assumption that the Peshmerga and security services, called *Asayish*, are keeping them safe.

The landlocked KRG has also formed alliances with neighbors like Turkey—a political and economic calculation that now serves as a lifeline—and the U.S. Kurds proudly note that during the ten years of the Iraq War, not a single U.S. soldier was killed in Iraqi Kurdistan and say that, given the opportunity, the Peshmerga would gladly serve again alongside Americans. Although the U.S. has a history of abandoning the Kurds in favor of Baghdad or Turkey (which has historically oppressed its own Kurdish minority), most Kurds still refer to the 2003 invasion as a "liberation" and revere George W. Bush for ridding them of Saddam. U.S. support for independence, they thought, would surely follow, but so far it has not.

A post-2003 survey, conducted by the KRG, indicated that a mere 2% of Kurds wanted to remain part of Iraq, and the appearance of ISIS only increased Kurdish nationalist fervor. Moderates who reasoned that the KRG was not po-

Mullah Mustafa Barzani, 1963 (BRIDGEMAN IMAGES)

litically or economically ready to become its own country—claiming that within weeks of independence, Kurds would face potentially violent pushbacks from neighbors while watching their poorly built institutions unravel—were largely sidelined from the political debate. Both Kurdish patriotism and wartime fear spurred on that 98% of Kurds who thought they had waited long enough. ∎

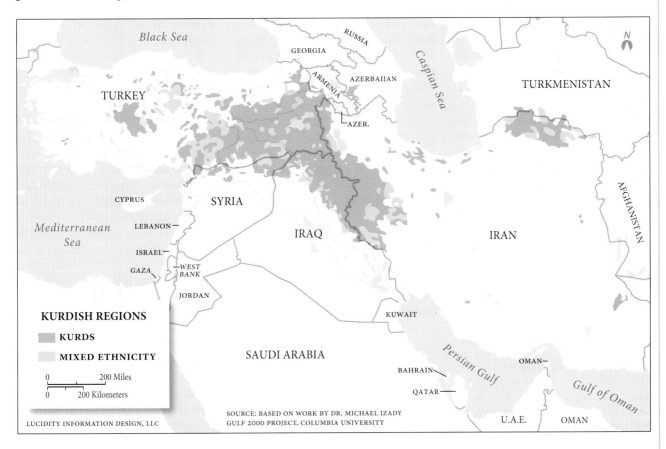

KURDISH REGIONS

KURDS

MIXED ETHNICITY

0   200 Miles

0   200 Kilometers

LUCIDITY INFORMATION DESIGN, LLC

SOURCE: BASED ON WORK BY DR. MICHAEL IZADY
GULF 2000 PROJECT, COLUMBIA UNIVERSITY

Civil war

In 1975 Jalal Talabani established the Patriotic Union of Kurdistan (PUK) as Iraqi Kurdistan's main opposition to the KDP—a status it would retain until 2009 when a PUK leader founded the *Gorran*, or "change," political party. The PUK presented itself as a more modern and secular political party, eager to leave the past behind and challenge the Barzanis' monopoly on power. For many Kurds, this was an appealing option, even though much of what they clung to were superficial and geographical differences. While Barzani wore the same traditional Kurdish outfit his father had worn in the mountains and throughout his political life, Talabani dressed in a suit. Talabani had authority in the east, near the Iranian border, where Kurdish society tends to be more open than in Erbil, and is rumored to prefer whiskey to tea.

Decades later, the two parties' core alliances—the KDP with Turkey and the PUK with Iran—would come to define them. But for many years after the split, Kurdish politics were characterized by a struggle for power over Kurdistan. Iraqi Kurdistan needed more than one political party if they wanted to be a full-fledged democracy, but those two threatened to tear the would-be nation apart.

Distrust between the two parties manifested in violence early on. In 1978, just three years after Talabani broke away from Barzani, KDP authorities captured two PUK commanders as they were crossing into Turkey, and sentenced them to death. Many PUK leaders tried to diffuse the situation by calling it an accident. But the deaths of the commanders were a spark that would lead to years of violence.

In the mid 1990s, after decades of escalating distrust between the two parties and the steady division of land and power, the Kurdish civil war began. In a city called Qala Diza, a tribal leader claimed that a relatively small plot of land belonging to his family had been unjustly taken by Baathists years earlier. By then, the land was being controlled by a KDP landlord but used by PUK shopkeepers, and the tribal leader, whose son was a

member of the Asayish, wanted the deed back. When representatives from both sides met to negotiate, violence broke out. The dispute over a small piece of land turned into a battle over Kurdish territory and the division of authority between the KDP and the PUK. Members of the parties—from civilian locals, to Peshmerga, to Barzani and Talabani themselves—took part in the war, and those who had once promised to lead Iraqi Kurdistan to independence seemed instead determined to divide the region.

The Kurdish civil war lasted from May 1994 until November 1997, resulting in the deaths of thousands of fighters and civilians on both sides. It split the country into two distinct parts, with the KDP ruling the northwest including the lucrative sole border crossing with Turkey and the PUK controlling the areas near Iran and, notably, oil-rich Kirkuk. Both had their own prime minister, Peshmerga, and checkpoints. Kurdistan's jails began to fill with members of the opposite parties, and prisoner accounts echo the torture under the Saddam regime. The Trauma Rehabilitation and Training Center in Sulaymaniyah treats Iraqis for PTSD and depression, and many of them trace their trauma back to the civil war. "We call it killing brothers," Dr. Ahmed Amin, the center's director, said. "Friends fighting each other. Families fighting each other. We always want to erase this from our minds."

By 2014, 17 years after the war, Amin still struggled to navigate a polarized KRG. If he appeared on a PUK television show advertising the clinic, he would make sure to appear on a KDP show the same night. When the Gorran Party was

SOURCE: INSTITUTE FOR THE STUDY OF WAR

founded in 2009, the clinic changed its logo, a candle floating in the sky—symbolizing hope, Amin said—determining that it was too close in appearance to the Gorran symbol, a white candle in front of a deep blue background. Still today, Kurds wince at the memories of the war. And the divisions created by the civil war in Kurdish politics, society and military greatly influence the Kurdish relationship with Baghdad and neighboring countries; the fight against ISIS; the alliance with the U.S.; and, most importantly, its own desire for independence.

Outside of Iraqi Kurdistan, the response to the civil war was ambivalence, and it took years for other forces to intervene. Some nations found the infighting helpful toward consolidating their own power and weakening the Kurdish opposition. Turkey, for instance, had been at war with its own Kurdish minority, who had organized under the guerilla army known as the Kurdistan Workers' Party (PKK), for over two decades. The Turkish government was adamantly opposed to the creation of a Kurdish state, particularly one that bordered the Kurdish areas of Turkey, convinced that an Iraqi Kurdistan fueled by oil would strengthen its armed forces with the goal of expanding their territory into Turkey. The civil war came at a critical moment in the quest for statehood, only three years after the no-fly zone presented the Kurdish north with the opportunity to thrive, protected from Saddam Hussein. The fighting greatly weakened the infrastructure and unity in the region, providing evidence, it seemed, that the possibility of a Kurdish nation along the Turkish border was remote.

Baghdad likewise welcomed the fighting between the PUK and the KDP. Saddam had kept his armed forces out of Kurdistan since the 1991 no-fly zone, and thought the Kurds had grown too strong. While Barzani and Talabani fought each other, they couldn't put their efforts into seceding from Iraq, taking over Kirkuk or exploiting their oil.

Washington, meanwhile, began to wonder if helping the Kurds had been a miscalculation, particularly when Talabani, in an attempt to balance his resources without access to Turkey, allied with Iran. In 1995, after Talabani had, with Iran's help, taken over Erbil, Barzani was desperate to reverse the course of the war and take back the capital city. To get what he wanted, he did the unthinkable—he took a course of action that is still hotly contested and often outright denied by KDP officials. Five years after the PUK won nearly half the Kurdish votes with an anti-Baghdad message, Barzani went to the Iraqi capital to ask Saddam for help.

The appeal was the nadir of the civil war and, arguably, Barzani's time in office. His visit to the Iraqi dictator was felt like an earthquake throughout all of Kurdistan. In his book *Invisible Nation*, journalist Quil Lawrence captures the gravity of Barzani's deal with Saddam. "In a region fabled for broken deals and rented loyalties," Lawrence writes, "Barzani's invitation to Saddam Hussein may go down as the most shocking bargain since God wagered with Satan that the devil couldn't break Job."

Iraqi tanks rolled into Erbil, scattering the PUK troops, and since then Erbil, the center of Kurdish government and economy, remains in KDP control. The act also helped to put an end to the war. Seeing Iraqi forces in Kurdistan, the U.S. called Barzani and Talabani to Washington, where they negotiated a peace deal. Both men returned home with a strict outward vision for unity, but the damage was done.

Today, Iraqi Kurdistan remains deeply divided along party lines. Not even the establishment of the Gorran party and the subsequent weakening of the PUK has lessened the partisanship. Even after 2003, when the U.S. removed Saddam and the elated Kurds were given the opportunity to participate fully in the new Iraqi government, Barzani and Talabani's rivalry shared the spotlight. The two leaders engaged in a tug of war over representation that reportedly even extended to disputes over the amount of space each party had in the newly established Green Zone in Baghdad.

When ISIS rose to prominence, Kurds recognized the need for unity and patriotism raged throughout the cities. The Ministry of Peshmerga was established to unify the forces aligned to the

In August 2014, PUK Peshmerga forces eat in the shadow of a an image of Jalal Talibani, founder and secretary general of the Patriotic Union of Kurdistan (PUK). Around 300 PUK Kurdish Peshmerga forces operate out of this base, one kilometer outside of Bashika, which is ISIS-controlled. (ANDREA BRUCE/NOOR/REDUX)

KDP or PUK, with the minister coming from Gorran. The call to arms was also a call for independence, and Kurdish Peshmerga entered disputed territories, like Kirkuk, which were under threat from ISIS. But the legacy of Kurdish divisions is difficult to overcome. Quietly, even the most patriotic politicians fretted over the loyalties among the Peshmerga; by early 2015, only a small percentage had been successfully united under the new ministry.

As refugees and internally displaced persons flooded Iraqi Kurdistan, the strains of the war increased and the optimism that Kurds had felt at the beginning—which prompted Barzani to declare his intentions to break away—began to dissipate. Internal ruptures slowed the response to the crisis and made out-

side governments, notably the U.S., more reluctant to send in the military aid that the KRG desperately needed in its fight against ISIS. Complaints of corruption in government and business, previously eclipsed by economic development, rose to the surface. As Kurds contemplated the possibility of an independent nation, they also confronted their own political challenges.

"This is a moment of truth for us," said a high-ranking opposition politician. "I know a Kurdish independent state would mean the Iranians, the Arabs, the Turks might be opposed to us, but I believe we can overcome that. The big question for us is domestic Kurdish politics. Can we really overcome that and can we be serious about Kurdish independence?" ■

Beyond Iraqi Kurdistan

In November 2015, following months of tension, ISIS-linked attacks, and renewed fighting between the PKK and the Turkish Army, Turkish citizens went to the polls to elect their parliament. For most voters it was a moment of unfortunate déjà vu. Only months earlier—in a resounding challenge to the decade-long majority rule of the Justice and Development Party (AKP)—Turkey

had voted into parliament the Peoples' Democratic Party (HDP), a left-wing opposition party with a pro-Kurdish ideology and disputed links to the PKK.

Kurds and Turks across the country—for whom the success of the HDP represented a focus on minority rights, as well as the vulnerability of the AKP—celebrated. For the first time in modern Turkish history, the country's Kurdish

A left-wing protester against Turkey's operations against Kurdish militants runs to avoid a police water canon, after he threw a petrol bomb at it during clashes in Istanbul, August 16, 2015. (CAGDAS ERDOĞAN/AP PHOTO)

minority, who make up around 20% of the population, would send parliamentarians from their own party to Ankara. The AKP would be forced to form a coalition government and President Recep Tayyip Erdoğan, who formerly served as prime minister for over a decade, would have to abandon proposed changes to the Turkish constitution granting him greater powers.

By voting for the HDP, Turkish citizens were illustrating an important shift in the country. No longer was the so-called "Kurdish issue" viewed solely as a problem of separatism and national security. Rather, Turkish citizens were sympathetic to the Kurdish movement and ready for politicians who promised greater rights for minorities and left-wing policies. Not even a ceasefire between the PKK and the Turkish Army, orchestrated largely by Erdoğan in 2012, could persuade voters to support the status quo.

The election was also more evidence of the Turkish public's increasing fear of Erdoğan's authoritarianism and dissatisfaction with his party. After the election, the dominance of the AKP, once considered all but guaranteed in the face of a weak and fractured opposition, appeared vulnerable. Turkey, a country whose intense nationalism has been both a force and a liability, seemed on the brink of real political change. In

Diyarbakir, a Kurdish-majority city in southeastern Turkey and the de facto capital of a would-be greater Kurdistan, Kurds filled the streets in celebration after the election's results. But the optimism was cut short by a surge in violence that, for many Turks and Kurds, seemed like a return to the past.

Tensions between Kurds and the AKP had begun to flare in late 2014, when Turkish forces blocked the passage of soldiers into Kobanî, a Syrian Kurdish city on the border with Turkey that had been under siege by ISIS militants for months. Eventually, because of domestic and international pressure, Turkey relented and allowed Iraqi Kurdish Peshmerga to enter Kobanî and help break the siege, but the damage was done by then. A distrust that many hoped had been quelled by the ceasefire was reignited. "The government does not care about the peace process," a Kurdish activist told the author. He had just returned to Diyarbakir, which had been locked in during protests over Kobanî, some of which had turned violent. Police swarmed the streets. "Turkey's policies on Rojava"—the Kurdish name for the Kurdish-majority areas of northern Syria—"and specifically Kobanî brought the peace process to a standstill."

November's snap elections, as well

as the renewed fighting with the PKK, are directly linked to the activities of Kurds of Rojava. Almost since the beginning of the war in Syria, the Turkish government has worried about PKK-linked Kurdish fighters and sympathizers establishing a stronghold in northern Syria along their border. Although trade relations had paved the way for diplomatic compromise between the AKP and the KRG in Iraq, Erdoğan and the AKP were unwilling to accept an autonomous Kurdish region that linked Iraqi Kurdistan to territories in Syria. Southeastern Turkey, they worried, could be next. "When you look at it from Ankara's perspective, they insist that Assad should be targeted because for them, that matters," Henri Barkey, a Kurdistan specialist and professor at Lehigh University, told the author. "Equally important [for Ankara] is that Syrian Kurds should not get an autonomous region… it's better for Kobanî to fall to ISIS than that Syrian Kurds should succeed in Syria. You can have one Kurdish autonomous region on your border"—Iraqi Kurdistan—"but two is a disaster."

Since 2012, Syrian Kurds had been governing and protecting the three cantons that comprise Syrian Kurdistan—Afrin, Kobanî and Jazira—as an autonomous entity. The Democratic Union Party (PYD), established in 2003 with ideological links to the PKK, had majority control while the borders and towns were being guarded with great success by the People's Protection Units (YPG). The YPG is widely considered the Syrian arm of the PKK (officially, they acknowledge an ideological connection and loyalty to the PKK founder Abdullah Öcalan, but deny direct ties) and for Turkish authorities their success within Syrian Kurdistan was anathema to Ankara's vision of a post-Assad Syria.

In the eyes of the Turkish government, Kobanî was a threat to national sovereignty and regional power. But the city quickly became a symbol of solidarity, not only between Kurds across borders but also between Kurds and Turks who oppose Erdoğan and support a peaceful and pluralistic Turkey. "Kobanî has turned into a metaphor of resistance against oppressive power," Abbas Vali, a Kurdish political theorist told me just after the siege was broken. "Clearly Mr. Erdoğan does not see the strategic importance of the metaphor of resistance, of people fighting for their life and land and honor."

The siege of Kobanî shifted public support from the AKP toward the Kurdish movement, both in Turkey and abroad. The YPG, like the Iraqi Kurdish Peshmerga, showed themselves to be worthy fighters against ISIS, with the U.S. implicitly confirming their importance by assisting them with air strikes. But soon the violence spilled across the border, changing the political climate in Turkey once again.

In July 2015, a month following the first election, a suicide bomber attacked a meeting at a community center in Suruç, a Kurdish-majority city within Turkey just across the border from Syria, killing over 30, most of whom were pro-Kurdish activists involved in a project to rebuild Kobanî. ISIS claimed responsibility for the attack, but a few days later PKK supporters killed two Turkish police officers in the southeast in retaliation, they said, for the Turkish government's cooperation with ISIS (the PKK officially denies responsibility for the two deaths). Turkey, meanwhile, responded by renewing strikes against PKK bases in northern Iraq and quickly the nation returned to a preceasefire, pre-election state of war. In August, citing the breakdown of negotiations among parties, Erdoğan announced snap elections in November. The country's very stability, he implied, was at stake.

In October, twin suicide bombs exploded at a Kurdish political rally in Ankara, underlining the new reality. ISIS had crossed the border and seemed to pose a real threat, while the Kurdish-Turkish conflict appeared to be back in full force. The ceasefire was dead, and along with it the promises of June's elections. When Turkish citizens returned to the polls in November, they did so in a climate of violence and instability. This time, Kurds lost.

For close to a century, since outside powers divided Ottoman territories into the modern Middle East, Kurdish minorities have been viewed as threats to fragile national sovereignty. In Turkey, Syria, Iraq and Iran—where most of the world's some 35 million Kurds live—central governments have oppressed their Kurdish populations, often brutally, in an effort to quell separatist rebellions and challenges to their power.

The Turkish state entered into a decades-long battle with the PKK, which was founded in 1979 and began using violent tactics in 1984. For Kurds in Turkey, the 1990s are remembered as a decade of terror. During those years, Turkish authorities razed hundreds of Kurdish villages; Kurds were killed or disappeared while thousands were tortured in one of the country's notorious prisons. Any expression of Kurdish culture was illegal, including speaking the Kurdish language, and police and army were stationed in the Kurdish southeast to keep tight control over the population. The PKK, meanwhile, responded with violence that, until Öcalan explicitly banned the tactics, targeted non-combatants as well as Turkish soldiers. As a result, Turkey, the EU and the U.S. consider the PKK a terrorist organization.

In the 1990s, a resolution to the Turkish-Kurdish war seemed remote, if not impossible, to the people living in the violence. No elected politician had approached the issue with genuine resolve

and fear, rather than hope, ruled Turkish politics. And yet by 2012, Erdoğan and Kurdish leaders including an imprisoned Abdullah Öcalan had entered into negotiations significant enough to convince the PKK to disarm and Turkish citizens to vote for Kurdish politicians.

The violence of the past few months, however, has bred fears among Turks and Kurds that the country could return to the chaos and paranoia of the past. It's a notion that has never been far from the minds of Kurdish politicians, many of whom have spent time in prison for their political activities. In 2013, Diyarbakir was celebrating at the beginning of the ceasefire. Throngs of people filled the city's main festival grounds, waiting for the official announcement; its promise was of a better future for Kurds living in Turkey and for the country itself.

But within this euphoria was caution. Sitting in his office the day after the celebration, dressed not in the bright colors of the Kurdish flag but in his usual black, then-mayor of Diyarbakir Osman Baydemir responded to Erdoğan's promises with reservation. "If this fails we will never be able to create an atmosphere of hope and peace," he said. "Every failure of this trust will bring a bigger and more violent process." He ended with a warning. "I believe this is the last chance," he said. "And it shouldn't be wasted." ■

U.S. and Iraqi Kurdish relations

In 2003, shortly after the invasion of Baghdad, U.S.-led coalition troops starred in one of the most lasting images of the Iraq War. In the middle of Baghdad's Firdos Square, and in front of a crowd of Iraqi spectators and foreign journalists, they tore down a massive bronze statue of Saddam Hussein, erected just the year before to celebrate the dictator's 65th birthday. The episode was seen to showcase the coalition's decisive victory over the Iraqi dictator, and it was referenced countless times in the years after eager journalists first broadcasted it across the world. But as the war dragged on, splintering Iraq internally and setting the stage for today's conflicts, the image of Saddam's likeness plummeting to the ground morphed into a different metaphor. "I had little awareness of the media dynamics that turned the episode into a festive symbol of what appeared to be the war's finale," journalist Peter Maass writes in The New Yorker. "In reality, the war was just getting under way."

For Iraqi Kurds, though, that moment signaled a different future—one in which their divergence from Iraq would be significant enough to earn Iraqi Kurdistan the nickname "The Other Iraq."

While most of the country dissolved into war, Kurds flourished. Since 2003, Kurds have lived in a different reality, if not a different country. Around the same time U.S. soldiers tore down Saddam's bronze likeness in Firdos Square, Kurds tore down their own statue of the dictator. But they did it by themselves and no one seemed to notice.

Iraqi Kurds played a vital role in the 2003 invasion, helping to provide passage and then fighting alongside the U.S. special forces in the Kurdish north. Kurds were convinced that Ansar al-Islam cells in Iraqi Kurdistan included members with links to Al-Qaeda—some of which, according to questionable Kurdish intelligence, had direct links to the perpetrators of the 9/11 attacks. From the north, the U.S. could also keep watch on the rest of the country and Iran, and the KRG was happy to help. Peshmerga and special forces proved an effective team, and those early battles made Kurds optimistic that the U.S. would consider them formidable allies in both the fight against terrorism and the war against Saddam.

Perhaps more than any other group in Iraq, Kurds welcomed the possibility of an end to Saddam's rule. They had been brutalized under the dictator, and had long looked to outside powers, particularly the U.S., to recognize their important role in the region and help them survive Saddam's brutal repression. America, though, has wavered in its relationship with Iraqi Kurds. The U.S. has consistently supported a unified Iraq, but America's interventions in modern Iraq have often revealed and intensified the country's deep divisions.

At times, Americans have been glad to stress their ties to the Kurds. In the lead-up to 2003, U.S. politicians, in their goal of intervention in Iraq, often alluded to Kurdish suffering. Since the end of the war, and even during the worst periods of fighting, Saddam's treatment of the Kurds and their post-2003 success have remained battle cries among some American officials. *New York Times* columnist Thomas Friedman, echoing politicians like John McCain, has more than once called Iraqi Kurdistan an "island of decency" in the region. But beneath the rhetoric of partnership there is doubt about America's commitment to the Kurdish future, fueled by a long history of American deceptions and miscalculations in the region.

In 1975, the U.S. formed a political alliance with the Shah of Iran against Baghdad. Iraqi Kurds, as among Iraq's strongest internal opposition to Baghdad, were encouraged by the U.S. to rise up against Saddam. Mullah Mustafa Barzani himself, bolstered by what he saw as the dual backing of the U.S. and Iran, led the Kurds in their rebellion against Baghdad. Soon after, though, Iran renewed its negotiations with Iraq, leaving the rebellious Kurds vulnerable on a shifting battlefield. U.S. officials were aware of the new dealings, but withheld the information from Barzani, and the effect was cataclysmic. Saddam attacked the Kurds and the Shah cut off aid, leaving Kurds without allies and scattering them across borders. To this day, Henry Kissinger, who, as secretary of state under Richard Nixon, led the talks with Iran, remains a despised figure in Iraqi Kurdistan.

When Saddam's air force dropped chemical weapons on cities in Iraqi Kurdistan during his al-Anfal campaign against them 12 years later, Kurds again felt betrayed by the U.S. The campaign, part of a response to the Kurdish rebellions and support of Iran over Baghdad, lasted three years and impressed upon Kurds the extent of their vulnerability under a regime intent on their suppression; many governments, including Britain's, now consider it a genocide. Experiences from those years still inform the vision for a Kurdish future, which relies on political and economic independence as well as a strong military and powerful allies. The U.S., Kurds hope, would be one of those allies.

Omar Ali Rashid was 14 on March 16, 1988, the day that Saddam's air force used chemical weapons on Halabja, the city in eastern Iraqi Kurdistan where Rashid lived with his family. At first, the bombs were met with confusion. "The first gas smelled like apples," he recalled, decades later in the lobby of the city's memorial to the attack, where papers sentencing Saddam to death are also on display. "People inhaled it because the smell was good. But it killed them."

Rashid was the only member of his immediate family to survive the attack, and he has never fully recovered. Like many, Rashid still feels the physical and psychological impact of that day. He has trouble breathing, he says, but he is less bothered by that than by his inability to connect with his wife, who he married in 2003, or feel close to the children they have had together. "I cry every day," Rashid said. "I want to live with my dead family."

At the time, the attacks did not appear to turn many heads in Washington, and Rashid, like other fellow survivors, felt abandoned by world powers. Americans, he thought, only cared about Kurds when they could help serve U.S. interests in the region. But, to him, the existence of Kurds in Iraq was about human rights, not U.S. interests.

It would take years before the U.S. would truly react to Saddam's atrocities in the north, and before they did they would again abandon the Kurds. In 1991, U.S. troops expelled Saddam's troops from Kuwait during Operation Desert Storm. But instead of continuing on to Baghdad to topple the dictator—which many Iraqis hoped would happen, in spite of constant assurance to the contrary—President George H. W. Bush gave a speech in which he seemed to encourage Iraqis, particularly the beleaguered Kurds and Shi'a, to stage a coup. With the U.S. withdrawing from the region, Bush asked Iraqis to "take matters into their own hands and force Saddam Hussein to step aside."

Millions of Iraqis, mainly Kurds and Shi'a, took Bush's encouragement to heart. Their uprising led them to confront the extent of Saddam's crimes, as well as their own capacity for revenge, an episode detailed in *Invisible Nation*. During a fight in Sulaymaniyah, close to the border with Iran, Kurdish Peshmerga broke into Saddam's Central Security Headquarters, where they found a hive of rooms smeared with blood. The corpses of executed women and children were evidence of years of torture.

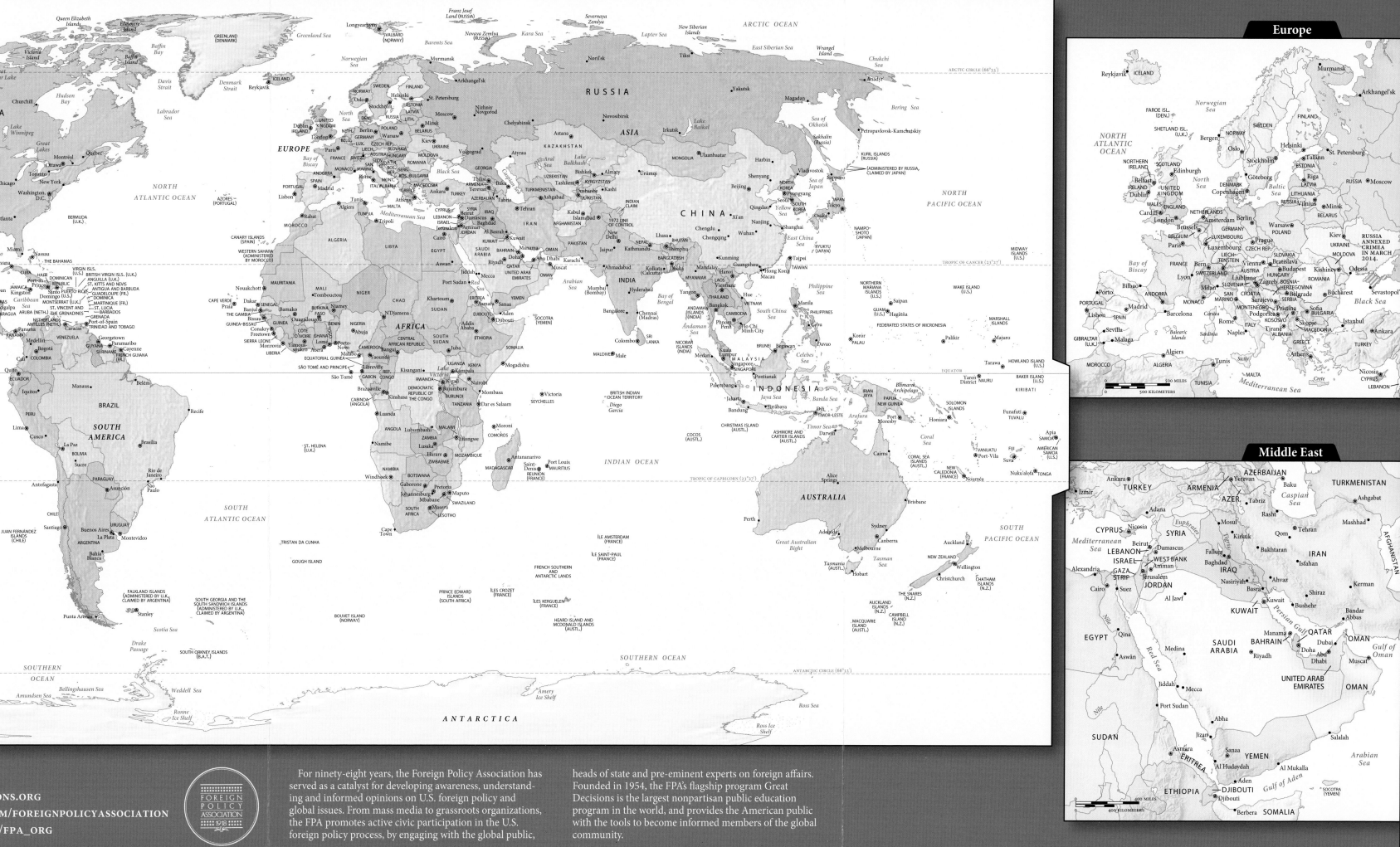

For ninety-eight years, the Foreign Policy Association has served as a catalyst for developing awareness, understanding and informed opinions on U.S. foreign policy and global issues. From mass media to grassroots organizations, the FPA promotes active civic participation in the U.S. foreign policy process, by engaging with the global public, heads of state and pre-eminent experts on foreign affairs. Founded in 1954, the FPA's flagship program Great Decisions is the largest nonpartisan public education program in the world, and provides the American public with the tools to become informed members of the global community.

The brutal scene threw Kurdish rebels into a fit of anger, and some attacked Iraqi police and officials—anyone they thought had ties to Saddam's Baathist regime. Americans, reacting to the mess of the uprising and seeing a connection between the Shi'a rebels and the Iranian regime, refused to aid the rebels, and Saddam swiftly quashed any hope of a coup. Millions of Kurds fled to Iran or Turkey, fearing another al-Anfal.

Kurds would never forget the moments they felt that the U.S. turned its back on them. During the fight against ISIS, Kurdish leaders have complained about the lack of financial and military support from Washington, not to mention the continued insistence on a unified Iraq. Weapons intended for Peshmerga, for instance, have to be routed through Baghdad and the U.S. does not support the independent Kurdish exploration and sale of the region's oil. Today, this presents both a tactical challenge—Erbil and Baghdad have been locked in an active feud over oil and disputed territories for three years—and a demoralizing message. Kurds are reminded of the aftermath of the Iraq War, when Americans armed the Iraqi Army and not the Peshmerga. Even after all these years of Kurdish autonomy and what the Kurds see as the proven strength of their Peshmerga relative to the Iraqi army in the war against ISIS, Americans still prioritize Baghdad. It was a hard truth. Most Kurdish officials, however begrudgingly, will acknowledge the importance of the KRG's relationship with Baghdad.

Still, the U.S. has been a catalyst for positive change in Iraqi Kurdistan. In 1991, following the failed uprising and recognizing the capabilities of Saddam to brutalize the Shi'a and Kurds, international powers including the U.S. decided to enforce a no-fly zone over the Kurdish north and the Shi'a south. Operation Provide Comfort, as the U.S. called it, led to the retreat of Saddam from the north, and Kurds began to transform their region. In the ensuing years, Kurds would elect their own parliament, begin exploring their own oil and build the institutions that they hoped would lead them to an independent Kurdistan.

U.S. Defense Secretary Ash Carter gestures to the guest book he just signed as he stands with Kurdish regional government President Massoud Barzani in Erbil, Iraq, July 24, 2015. (CAROLYN KASTER/POOL/AP PHOTO)

The most striking changes came after 2003. Without the yoke of Saddam threatening their very existence, Kurds began developing at breakneck speed. Five star hotels sprung up in Erbil, built to accommodate employees of foreign oil companies who had been courted by the newly appointed Minister of Natural Resources Ashti Hawrami. Even ExxonMobil, defying President Obama, bought stakes in the Kurdish countryside. The region was stable and secure, and sitting on top of known stores of untapped oil.

Still, Kurds remained skeptical of the U.S.'s role in the new Kurdistan. Their development and stability was held out to the U.S. as proof that they could, or even deserved to be independent. And yet, America remained firmly attached to the idea of a unified Iraq. Leaders, Barzani in particular, began to talk about independence without the approval of the U.S.; they had Turkey's partnership now, maybe that was enough. The U.S. lauded the Kurds and yet seemed unwilling to truly invest in their future.

Some saw U.S. favoritism of Kurds in Iraq as counterproductive and the potential chilling of the relationship as possibly a good thing. America praised the development of the region without pressuring Barzani and Talabani to confront their limitations as a would-be independent nation. "We have been coddling the Kurds since 2003," said Denise Natali, a Kurdistan expert and

fellow at the National Defense University. "It doesn't encourage them to make comprehensive changes." Non-Kurdish Iraqis, meanwhile, have the impression that the U.S. cares only about the secular, overtly Western-friendly Kurds, which exacerbates the kind of divisive crisis unfolding in Iraq today. "We created a situation that in the eyes of Iraqis was very, very imbalanced," Natali said. "This is not helping Iraq and this is not helping the Kurds."

"The relationship between Kurdistan and America is very good," a PUK official told me in 2014. "But there are two sides. If we go back to 1975… Americans were one of the most powerful factors in the collapse of the revolution. Then after 1991, Americans created the no-fly zone. And we appreciate that Americans came to liberate us [in 2003]." When it comes to America's steadfast support of a unified Iraq, the official laughed sardonically. To him, it was a reminder of how little the U.S. appreciated how much Baghdad had oppressed Kurds, and the dramatic strides that Kurds have taken to try to ensure that never happens again. Kurds, he thought, were a force for good in the region, and it was time the U.S. supported them fully "We have to consider that [Kurdistan's relationship with the U.S.] is a matter of the future of the nation and the pride and dignity of the nation," he said. "But I hope America will reconsider." ∎

discussion questions

1. Is U.S. favoritism of Iraqi Kurds anathema to its vision of a unified Iraq? Should Washington cool relations with Iraqi Kurdistan?

2. Should Washington reconsider its stance on Iraqi Kurdish independence? How would an unendorsed bid for Kurdish national sovereignty impact the regional balance of power?

3. Is there any reason to expect a lessening of Iraqi Kurdish partisanship? How do memories of the civil war manifest in contemporary inter-party relations? Are there any viable areas of accord between groups?

4. In 2013, the mayor of Diyarbakir called the AKP-PKK ceasefire "the last chance" to "create an atmosphere of hope and peace." Do you think this statement is accurate? Does the renewed violence that created momentum for the November 2015 snap elections portend a prolonged return to the pre-2013 situation?

5. Is continued U.S. characterization of the PKK as a terrorist group justified in the current context? Should the U.S. change its position on the issue?

6. How can the U.S. balance Turkish and Kurdish alliances in the fight against ISIS? Is Turkey a reliable partner? Does Ankara's Kurdish agenda hinder the success of the anti-ISIS coalition?

7. Think of other ethno-territorial conflicts: What insights do they offer into how to approach the Kurdish question?

Don't forget: Ballots start on page 99!

suggested readings

Filkins, Dexter, "ISIS Vs. The Kurds." **New Yorker**, September 29, 2014. Iraq expert reports on the possibility of Iraqi Kurdish statehood in the immediate aftermath of the war with ISIS. Rare access to Massoud Barzani, the president of the KRG, is the centerpiece of the work.

Krajeski, Jenna, "What the Kurds Want". **Virginia Quarterly Review**, Fall 2015. Available free online: < http://www.vqronline.org/reporting-articles/2015/09/what-kurds-want>. An exploration of a would-be leftist revolution in Kurdish-controlled northern Syria.

Lawrence, Quil, **Invisible Nation: How the Kurds' Quest for Statehood is Shaping Iraq and the Middle East**. New York: Walker Books, 2008. 357pp. This exhaustively researched book of narrative reporting explores the possibility of Iraqi Kurdish independence, as well as its impact on the region.

Marcus, Aliza, **Blood and Belief: The PKK and the Kurdish Fight for Independence**. New York: NYU Press, 2009. 363pp. Six years after its initial publication, this book remains the foremost insight into the PKK and the Kurdish struggle within Turkey and beyond. By based on interviews with former guerillas, the book provides a nuanced view of the polarizing and, in the West, greatly misunderstood war.

Meiselas, Susan, **Kurdistan: In the Shadow of History**. Chicago: University of Chicago Press, 2008. 472pp. Susan Meisalas spent decades in Iraqi Kurdistan, beginning in 1991, creating this rich visual history of Iraqi Kurds. Her photographs and descriptions help to illustrate the complicated and often tragic history of Kurds in Iraq.

Viviano, Franko, "Kurds in Control." **National Geographic**, January 2006. Available free online: < http://ngm.nationalgeographic.com/features/world/asia/iraq/iraqi-kurds-text>. The article challenges some of the mainstream narratives about Iraqi Kurdistan in the aftermath of the U.S.-led invasion of Iraq.

To access web links to these readings, as well as links to additional, shorter readings and suggested web sites,

GO TO www.greatdecisions.org

and click on the topic under Resources, on the right-hand side of the page

International migration

by Joseph Chamie

Refugees say goodbye to their translator at Ilaca train station on September 17, 2015, in Ilaca, Croatia. Crowds of migrants and refugees have scuffled with Croatian police in at least two places along the border with Serbia as they seek to enter the European Union. (CROPIX/ BARCROFT MEDIA/LANDOV)

International migration is an increasingly global issue with the world now experiencing the greatest mobility of people in human history. Millions of men, women and children are migrating—many without authorization— largely to the wealthier and more secure nations in both the North and South. The international migration flows are raising developmental opportunities and humanitarian challenges for communities, nations and international organizations, as well as for the migrants themselves. Governments of origin, transit and destination countries, international agencies and nongovernmental organizations are struggling on how best to manage the opportunities and challenges posed by the growing numbers of international migrants.

International migration is not a new global phenomenon, as it has been a continuous and prominent feature of hu- man existence for ages. Human migration has ranged from journeys of a few miles to epic travels across continents and oceans. In many instances, migrants sought freedom, oppor- tunity, fortune or power. Drought, plagues, famine, poverty and natural disasters have also triggered large international migration flows.

JOSEPH CHAMIE *is an independent consulting demogra- pher. He is the former research director of the Center for Mi- gration Studies in New York and editor of the* International Migration Review. *Also, he is a former director of the United Nations Population Division, having worked at the UN on population issues for more than 25 years. He has written numerous population studies for the UN—as well as under his own name—on population growth, fertility, estimates and projections, international migration and population and development policies.*

Migrant rights protesters in Mexico's southern state of Oaxaca faced off with riot police on April 15, 2015, on their annual march to demand greater human rights protections for the scores of Central American citizens who travel overland through Mexico en route to the U.S. (JORGE LUIS PLATA/REUTERS)

Slavery, invasions, conflict, human trafficking and persecution created forced international migration. The formations of empires, colonies and the modern nation states also permitted huge numbers of people to migrate to distant lands across the world's major continents. International migration has also supported the growth of the world economy and contributed to the evolution of societies, enriching many cultures and civilizations.

Over the past half-century, however, noteworthy changes have occurred in the magnitude, sources, causes and consequences of international migration, which in turn have transformed the phenomenon into a major issue of global concern. The number of international migrants, for example, has more than tripled from 76 million in 1960 to more than 232 million today. The remittances that migrants send home to assist their families in developing countries, estimated at an annual level of approximately $404 billion, far exceed overseas development assistance and are a key source of foreign exchange for many countries. In some countries major sectors of the economy and many public services are dependent on the contributions of migrant workers.

Refugee populations have also grown substantially during recent years and are now estimated to be at an all time high of 19.5 million, up from 16.7 million in 2013. Illegal immigration has also evolved into a serious worldwide challenge with millions of men, women and children risking their lives in order to reach and settle in another country, especially in the more developed regions.

The right to migrate was established internationally in 1948 with the adoption of the Universal Declaration of Human Rights. Article 13 of the Declaration states: "Everyone has the right to leave any country, including his own, and to return to his country." However, while everyone has the right to leave their country, they do not have the right to enter another country. This apparent paradox is the Catch-22 that the growing numbers of unauthorized migrants and destination nations are confronting.

In addition to voluntary forms of international migration, the international community also adopted the 1951 Convention Relating to the Status of Refu-

gees and the 1967 Protocol Relating to the Status of Refugees. These two key documents spell out who qualifies as a refugee, their rights and the legal obligations of nations. They also define a refugee's obligations to the host countries and indicate certain groups of people, such as war criminals, who do not qualify for refugee status. Initially, the 1951 Convention was generally limited to protecting European refugees following World War II, but the 1967 Protocol expanded the Convention's scope as the problem of displacement spread to all regions of the world.

In the aftermath of the tragic events of September 11th in the U.S. as well as terrorist bombings in India, Kenya, Tunisia, the UK and elsewhere, international migration has also become a matter of national security. Many countries have tightened their borders, stiffened their immigration entry requirements and monitored certain immigrant groups and individuals considered possible national security threats.

At the same time, many governments, especially in more developed regions, are continuing their policies of increased immigration, especially of highly skilled migrants. In contrast, however, majorities of the general public in many affluent countries in the West and in developing regions would like to see greater restriction of immigration and tighter control of borders.. This "migration gap" between public opinion and government policies in many receiving countries is contributing to political unrest and growing anti-immigrant sentiment.

Even though international migration has risen to the top of political agendas in many receiving countries, especially throughout Europe, the international community has shied away from effectively addressing it. Recognizing today's political realities and the continuing divergent perspectives between labor importing and exporting nations, it is unlikely that a worldwide international migration summit will be held any time soon. Informal dialogues among governments and nonbinding voluntary forums are likely to continue for the foreseeable future. ■

Before you read, download the companion **Glossary** that includes definitions and a guide to acronyms and abbreviations used in the article, as well as additional background material. Go to **www.great decisions.org** and select the topic in the Resources section on the right-hand side of the page.

Levels and trends

People have migrated from place to place from time immemorial. In addition to the pursuit of freedom, opportunities, challenges and adventure, the migrations of people were brought about by economic necessity, environmental change, persecution, slavery and conflict.

In the earliest stages, perhaps some 200,000 years ago, the mobility of humans was limited largely due to primitive levels of social organization and limited transportation and communication technologies. Approximately 60,000 years ago, human populations expanded not only along the coastal and inland areas of tropical Africa, but also to the coasts of Europe, South Asia and Oceania. This migration continued so that roughly 30,000 years ago most of Eurasia and significant portions of the western hemisphere, primarily North America, were settled by human populations.

Two thousand years ago virtually all areas of the world had been affected by human migration, with the result being that virtually no region at that time could be considered "empty." Consequently, most of the large-scale migration that followed consisted of settlers, refugees, slaves, traders or invaders moving into largely established human communities.

One of the most dramatic and sudden movements of any people was the expansion of the Arab Islamic Empire in the 7th century. Several years after the death of the prophet Muhammad in 632, the Muslims moved up from Arabia into Syria and Mesopotamia and subsequently into Persia and beyond. The Muslim empire also expanded westward capturing most of North Africa. In the beginning of the 8th century, the Muslims conquered Spain and moved into Gaul, where their advance was halted near Poitiers in 732.

In the 13th century the Mongol Empire emerged with migratory conquests and invasions across Central and Western Asia and into Europe. In addition to the killings and destruction of many societies, the Mongol migratory incursions induced massive population displacement and loss on a scale never seen before.

Large migration flows among continents began in the 16th century with a period of rapid European population growth and spatial expansion. The conquest, exploitation and settlement of the Americas and Oceania by European powers led to huge human migration streams between the continents and rapid population growth in Europe's New World. By 1750, it is estimated that less than 3% of the world's population of nearly 800 million lived in the western hemisphere. Two hundred and fifty years later, the world's population had grown to more than six billion and the proportion residing in the western hemisphere increased nearly sixfold to 14%.

Perhaps the predominant and certainly the most tragic international migration flows in the 18th and 19th centuries were the forced migration of slaves from mainly western Africa to the Americas. It is estimated that at least 12 million people were moved as slaves to North and South America between 1500 and 1850. In addition, between 1830 and 1930, 12 million people, mainly Chinese and Indians, were brought to the Americas as indentured workers.

The slave ships traveling from Africa to the Americas had extremely difficult and unhygienic conditions. Many of the ships transported hundreds of slaves, who were chained to their wooden plank beds. Dehydration, dysentery, scurvy and poor nutrition resulted in high mortality rates. While more than one in seven captive African slaves perished at sea, death rates were considerably higher in Africa during the process of capturing and transporting indigenous peoples to the ships.

Europe's geographic expansion also involved large numbers of voluntary immigration to other continents. Key European powers, in particular Britain, France, the Netherlands and Spain, facilitated the migration of workers, orphans, dissident soldiers and convicts to their respective colonies. By the close of the 19th century, European migration came to an end with the rise of anti-colonial sentiment and related political movements.

Migration of Europeans to the Americas and the forced importation of Africans as slaves brought on centuries of conflict between Native Americans and those of European origins. In addition to warfare, European migration spread epidemic diseases to populations that had little resistance. Between 1500 and 1650 the population of the Americas declined significantly, with estimates varying broadly from 50% to 90%.

With the establishment of Australia as a British penal colony, about 131,000 convicts mainly from Europe had arrived there by the middle of the 19th century. Furthermore, during the period from 1820 to 1932, expanding economic opportunities attracted 52 million people from Europe to the Americas, with 32 million landing in the U.S., and 3.5 million in Australia and New Zealand.

Following the First World War and then the Great Depression, international migration bottomed out. This was short lived, however, as migration rebounded markedly during and after the Second World War with millions dislocated and resettled abroad.

Decolonization also led to large international migration flows. The 1947 British India partition, for example, involved massive population transfers of an estimated seven to eight million Hindus and Muslims between India and Pakistan. Also the partition of British Palestine and the subsequent creation of Israel led to the movement of millions of Jews and Palestinians.

Recent past

During the second half of the 20th century the number of international migrants grew rapidly. By 1960, the number of international migrants as defined by the UN was 76 million worldwide. Forty years later, the number of persons residing outside their country of birth more than doubled to 175 million people. The numbers of international migrants have continued to increase, reaching 232 million in 2013, and are likely to be close to a quarter of a billion people today.

While the numbers of migrants have grown rapidly over the past five decades, the world's population has also increased markedly, doubling from three to six billion between 1960 and 2000. Consequently, the proportion of the world's population who are international migrants—about 3.2% in 2013—has varied in relative terms, but within a narrow range of between 2.2% and 3.2% (Table 1).

If the current proportion of international migrants were to remain constant at 3.2%, the numbers of migrants worldwide would necessarily increase in size as the world's population grows. In this case, the projected number of international migrants would reach 314 mil-

lion by mid-century and 362 million by the end of the century (Table 1). If the proportion of migrants globally were to increase slightly to 3.6% and remain at that level, the number of international migrants worldwide by the century's close would be in excess of 400 million.

The majority of the 232 million international migrants, approximately 60%, reside in the more developed regions. Nearly one third of the total—72 million migrants—lived in Europe, close to one fourth resided in Northern America and 3% lived in Oceania. Also about one third of all migrants resided in Asia, with Africa at 8% and Latin America and the Caribbean at 4%.

The numbers and proportions of international migrants vary greatly across major regions and countries. In devel-

Table 1: World Population, International Migrants and Percent: 1960–2100

YEAR	WORLD POPULATION (MILLIONS)	INT'L MIGRANTS (MILLIONS)	PERCENT
1960	3,018	76	2.5%
1970	3,682	82	2.2%
1980	4,440	100	2.2%
1990	5,310	154	2.9%
2000	6,127	175	2.8%
2010	6,930	221	3.2%
2013	7,182	232	3.2%
2025	8,142	263	3.2%
2050	9,725	314	3.2%
2075	10,702	346	3.2%
2100	11,213	362	3.2%

Source: UN, International Migration Report 2013; after 2013 UN population projections (medium variant) and percent migrants held constant at 3.2%.

oped regions, for example, international migrants constituted 11% of the total population in 2013 compared to 2% in developing regions (Table 2).

Also the countries with the largest numbers of international migration are largely found in developed regions (Table 2). The U.S. has the largest number of migrants, about 46 million or one fifth of the world's total, followed by Russia (11 million) and Germany (9.8 million). Among the remaining seven top ten receiving countries, all are located in developed regions except for Saudi Arabia (9.1 million) and the United Arab Emirates (7.8 million).

In contrast to the absolute levels, the highest proportions of international migrants among countries are mostly in developing regions, especially in the Persian Gulf (Table 2). The economies of oil-exporting countries are heavily dependent on the labor of the vast numbers of migrant workers who are primarily from Asia. The largest proportions of migrants globally are found in the UAE at a remarkable level of 84%, followed by Qatar and Kuwait at 74% and 60%, respectively. High proportions of migrants are also observed in Bahrain (55%) and Saudi Arabia (31%).

Developed regions have been net receivers of international migrants, while

Table 2: Countries with Largest Number and Largest Percent of International Migrants: 2013

	TOTAL (THOUSANDS)	PERCENT OF TOTAL MIGRANTS	PERCENT OF COUNTRY POPULATION	PERCENT FEMALES
World	231,522	100%	3%	48%
Developed Regions	135,583	59%	11%	52%
Developing Regions	95,939	41%	2%	43%
Largest Number				
United States	45,785	20%	14%	51%
Russian Federation	11,048	5%	8%	51%
Germany	9,845	4%	12%	52%
Saudi Arabia	9,060	4%	31%	29%
United Arab Emirates	7,827	3%	84%	25%
United Kingdom	7,824	3%	12%	52%
France	7,439	3%	12%	52%
Canada	7,284	3%	21%	52%
Australia	6,469	3%	28%	50%
Spain	6,467	3%	14%	51%
Largest Percent				
United Arab Emirates	7,827	3%	84%	25%
Qatar	1,601	1%	74%	21%
Kuwait	2,028	1%	60%	30%
Bahrain	729	0%	55%	28%
Singapore	2,323	1%	43%	56%
Jordan	2,926	1%	40%	49%
Saudi Arabia	9,060	4%	31%	29%
Oman	1,112	0%	31%	19%
Switzerland	2,335	1%	29%	51%
Australia	6,469	3%	28%	50%

Source: United Nations, International Migration Report 2013.

Africa, Asia and Latin America and the Caribbean served as net senders. Also, while on average annual net migration to Europe, North America and Oceania between 2000 and 2015 was 2.8 million persons per year, the scale of net migration has recently increased.

During the last decade, the number of international migrants increased in about 75% of all countries. The largest gain occurred in the U.S., with more than 1 million additional immigrants annually. Spain and the UAE follow with about half a million annually.

Countries experiencing the lowest levels of net migration—or the largest net emigration—were mostly developing ones. Bangladesh had the largest net outflow of migrants during the last decade, at more than one-half million per year. Other large net exporters of migrants during this period were Mexico and India at slightly under one-half million annually, followed by China (418,000), Pakistan (360,000) and the Philippines (236,000).

In 2013, about 74% of all international migrants were of working age, 20 to 64 years old, with the majority living in developed regions. About 15% were less than 20 years old, with notable differences between developing and developed regions, 23% in the former and less than 10% in the latter.

Of the international migrants worldwide, 11%, or about 25 million, were aged 65 years or over. The large majority of the elderly, approximately 70%, resided in developed regions. This distribution is chiefly because many developed countries have long histories of immigration and because of the greater propensity of international migrants living in the developing regions to return to their home countries.

In 2013, women comprised 48% of all international migrants worldwide (*Table 2*). Again, notable differences exist across regions. While women constituted 52% of migrants in the developed regions, they accounted for 43% in developing regions. Also, some of the lowest proportions of women migrants were found in the Persian Gulf: 19% in Oman, 21% in Qatar and 25% in the UAE. ∎

Major issues

Demographic consequences

While of little demographic significance at the world level, international migration can be an important component of demographic change for a given population, affecting its size as well as altering its age structure and composition. Moreover, migration's demographic impact is not only due to the number of migrants, but also to the subsequent descendants of migrants. Several examples help to illustrate the significant demographic impact that migration can have on population change (*see Box 1 on next page*).

Migration's demographic impact may be better appreciated by comparing it to population change due to natural increase (births minus deaths) in the European Union (EU). Taking the 28 EU member countries as a whole, population change in 2014 due to net migration (immigrants minus emigrants) was nearly six times as great as the EU's natural increase: 952,000 versus 161,000.

However, considerable variation in the demographic effects of international migration exists among EU countries. In some, such as Germany and Italy, net migration was fully responsible for population growth because natural increase was negative. In other countries, such as Greece and Portugal, natural increase and net migration were both negative, each thereby contributing to population decline. In France, natural increase substantially exceeded net migration (265,000 compared to 32,000) and in the UK, both were at similar levels (206,000 and 210,000).

An examination of the trends in the components of population change for the EU over the past half-century provides additional insights into the important demographic role played by international migration. From 1960 to the early 1990s natural increase exceeded net migration and largely followed the total rate of population change, which was declining due to falling birth rates. Since then, net migration has remained

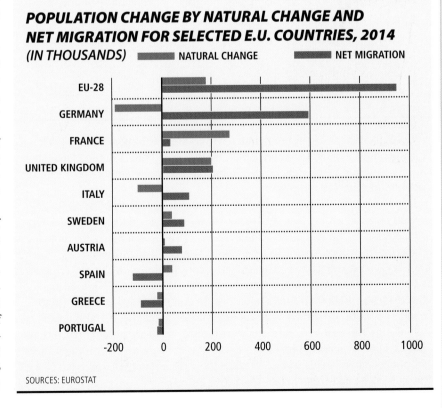

POPULATION CHANGE BY NATURAL CHANGE AND NET MIGRATION FOR SELECTED E.U. COUNTRIES, 2014
(IN THOUSANDS) ▬ NATURAL CHANGE ▬ NET MIGRATION

SOURCES: EUROSTAT

Box 1: Immigration to the United States

From its very founding in 1776, immigration has greatly affected the growth, structure and composition of the U.S. population. Indeed, it is the dominant force fueling America's demographic growth. This is largely because immigrants not only add their own numbers to the nation's overall population, but also contribute a disproportionate number of births whose effects are compounded over time.

If international migration had ceased after the signing of the Declaration of Independence in 1776, when the colonies numbered several million, today's U.S. population would be no more than 143 million, far short of its current size of approximately 322 million. Immigration's contribution accounts for more than half of America's past population growth.

U.S. POPULATION WITH AND WITHOUT MIGRATION, 1770 – 2100 (IN MILLIONS)

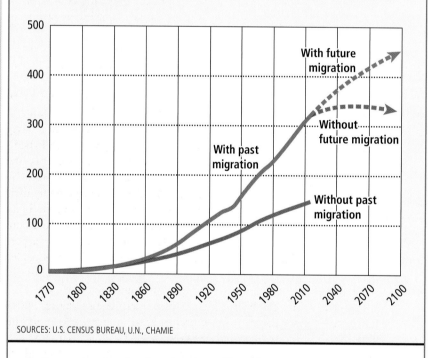

SOURCES: U.S. CENSUS BUREAU, U.N., CHAMIE

In the coming decades, immigration will continue to have a dominant demographic impact on the U.S. population. By the year 2060, assuming an annual net migration of approximately 1 million, the U.S. population is projected to reach more than 400 million.

However, if future immigration were to cease, the U.S. population in 2060 would be considerably less, at around 340 million. Again, this illustrates that the addition of immigrants and their descendants is the major driver behind the projected growth of America's population (about 80% in this instance).

For each fiscal year the U.S. president, in consultation with Congress, sets an admissions ceiling for refugees as well as regional allocations. The total ceiling for 2015 was 70,000 refugee admissions. In contrast, the number of persons obtaining lawful permanent status is much larger, averaging 1.1 million annually during the past ten years. About two-thirds of the total legal permanent flow is family-sponsored immigrants. The largest major admission category is the immediate relatives of U.S. citizens (46%), consisting of spouses (27%), parents (12%) and children (8%).

greater than natural increase and in recent years has accounted for nearly all of the growth of the EU population.

The potential impact of international migration on the future size of a population may also be appreciated by considering the percent change with and without migration across countries with very different demographic conditions (*see chart on next page*). For some countries, especially the traditional immigration countries such as Australia, Canada, New Zealand and the U.S., international migration accounts for a sizeable amount of future population growth over the next five decades. And in the case of Canada, the future size of its population would decline in the absence of international migration .

In other countries, such as Italy, Japan, Germany, Hungary, Spain and Russia, international migration reduces the expected declines in their future populations due to their negative rates of natural increase. And for traditional emigration countries such as Bangladesh, Kyrgyzstan, Mexico and the Philippines, their future populations would be decidedly larger in the future without their outflow of emigrants.

In addition to its impact on the future size of populations, international migration can also have important consequences on a country's age structure. Notably, immigration can add working-age people, and thereby stabilize or increase the size of the labor force as well as contribute to slowing population aging. However, by and large immigration is not a solution to a graying population insofar as the immigrants themselves also age and eventually retire.

A population's composition can also be affected by international migration. Many of those migrating today are ethnically, religiously and culturally different from the populations of the receiving countries, boosting anxiety about integration and cultural integrity and fears about ethnic conflict.

In countries such as Japan and South Korea, ethnic homogeneity is widely viewed as a positive characteristic. While foreign workers would add to the shrinking Japanese and Korean la-

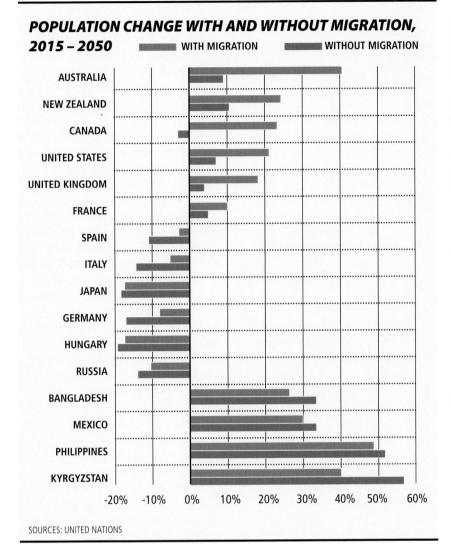

POPULATION CHANGE WITH AND WITHOUT MIGRATION, 2015 – 2050

WITH MIGRATION | WITHOUT MIGRATION

AUSTRALIA
NEW ZEALAND
CANADA
UNITED STATES
UNITED KINGDOM
FRANCE
SPAIN
ITALY
JAPAN
GERMANY
HUNGARY
RUSSIA
BANGLADESH
MEXICO
PHILIPPINES
KYRGYZSTAN

-20% -10% 0% 10% 20% 30% 40% 50% 60%

SOURCES: UNITED NATIONS

Development

During the past several decades there has been a growing consensus that international migration is an integral feature of global development in both sending and receiving nations. While not always beneficial, especially for indigenous populations, it is widely acknowledged that international migration is a key aspect of globalization and can play a positive role in socioeconomic development. If managed in ways that facilitate safe and empowering mobility, while ensuring that migrants' human rights are respected and protected, international migration can be advantageous to the economies and welfare of the populations in both the host and home countries, as well as to the migrants themselves.

International migration can complement the developmental efforts of countries by being more fully integrated into national strategies. In particular, to ensure that migration is voluntary, governments need to prioritize poverty reduction and good governance. In addition, sending countries may leverage the benefits of migration for development by recognizing the skills acquired by their citizens while abroad and capitalizing on the potential contributions of diaspora groups. Promoting the transnational portability of acquired benefits also enables migrants to participate more easily in circular and return migration.

With modern transportation, telecommunication networks and the persistence of large demographic differences and economic and social inequalities across regions, people are increasingly migrating to other countries to improve their personal well-being as well as that of their family members. However, the outflow of highly skilled men and women from the less developed countries, particularly in Africa, is also likely to further challenge and undercut developmental efforts in many of these countries. Among other things, brain drain prevents the origin countries from benefiting from the investments they have made in the education and training of their citizens.

Nevertheless, many developing countries have found it attractive and

bor forces, which would help to pay for the pensions and healthcare of the elderly, introducing large numbers of immigrants from other cultures is seen as increasing the chances of social unrest as is frequently reported in ethnically diverse nations throughout Africa, Asia, Europe and elsewhere.

In contrast to the recent past, the composition of recent immigrants in many instances differs markedly from that of the receiving country. In Europe, for example, many of the immigrants after World War II came from the relatively poorer countries such as Italy, Spain and Portugal. Many of today's immigrants to Europe are ethnically different from the native populations and many are also poorly educated and low skilled. These conditions are contributing to increased ethnic diver-

sity as well as tensions within several European countries, raising concerns about national identity, assimilation and public safety.

International migration is also continuing to mold the composition of the traditional immigration countries. In the U.S., the relatively recent large influx of immigrants has altered and diversified the country's ethnic composition and culture, making it less European and more Latin American, Asian and African. Throughout the 19th and most of the 20th centuries, the U.S. foreign-born population was predominately from European countries such as Germany, Ireland, Italy and the UK. Today the top five countries are Mexico, China, the Philippines, India and Vietnam, with Mexico accounting for nearly a third of the U.S. foreign-born population.

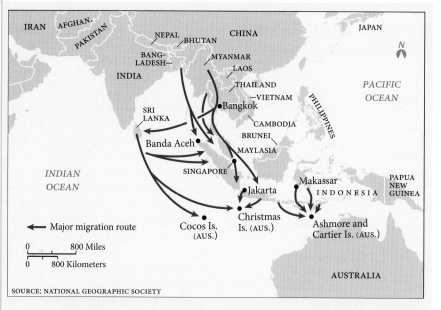

← Major migration route

0 — 800 Miles
0 — 800 Kilometers

SOURCE: NATIONAL GEOGRAPHIC SOCIETY

The Rohingya

A Muslim minority population numbering about one million, the Rohingya have long been denied residence in Myanmar's (Burma's) majority-Buddhist Rakhine state, located on the country's western coast. The government maintains that the Rohingya are illegal Bengali immigrants. It refuses them rights to citizenship and self-identification, and restricts mobility and access to basic services.

A spate of extreme violence erupted between the Buddhist and Rohingya populations in 2012–13, leaving 140,000 Rohingya stranded in refugee camps around the state capital, Sittwe. Camps in neighboring Bangladesh shelter over 30,000 Rohingya, but 200,000 more reside in the country illegally—meaning that they lack services, face deportation and are particularly susceptible to smuggling.

Since 2012, around 100,000 Rohingya have fled Myanmar by sea. Deteriorating conditions in camps, as well as escalating discriminatory policies, including a plan announced in the fall of 2014 to round up and deport Rohingya who cannot prove residence of over 60 years, resulted in a fresh wave of refugees.

The crisis came to a head in May 2015 when, after the discovery of mass migrant graves, the Thai government began cracking down on human smuggling. As Thailand pushed boats back from its shores, so did Malaysia and Indonesia, leaving nearly 8,000 migrants stranded at sea.

Under international pressure, an emergency meeting was called in late May to discuss a solution to the crisis. Malaysia, Thailand and Indonesia agreed to receive stranded migrants on the condition that they be relocated within the year. While the countries in question are bound by customary law not to turn away asylum-seekers, they—like the majority of governments in the Association of Southeast Asian Nations (ASEAN)—are not signatories to the 1951 UN Refugee Convention or its 1967 Protocol. A coordinated framework for long-term response remains elusive.

—*Lillian Marx*

During the past several decades, the amount of remittances being sent by migrants has grown rapidly. Whereas 20 years ago remittances amounted to less than $100 million, today they are estimated at over $500 billion per year, well in excess of official development assistance.

The largest estimated remittances in 2014 were to India ($70 billion), China ($64 billion), the Philippines ($28 billion), Mexico ($25 billion) and Nigeria ($21 billion). The largest sources of migrant remittance outflows in 2013 were from the U.S. ($54 billion), Russia ($37 billion), Saudi Arabia ($35 billion), Switzerland ($23 billion) and Germany ($20 billion).

Some of the most advanced programs promoting overseas employment are in the Philippines and Mexico. The Philippine Overseas Employment Administration, established more than 25 years ago, has become an integral part of the country's Department of Labor and Employment. Mexico also has agencies to aid citizens working abroad, such as the Program for Mexican Communities Living Abroad. In addition, the government started a program known as "3x1"—for every $1 sent from a Mexican emigrant club or association for a development project in Mexico, the government contributes $3.

For many countries, individual monetary remittances are a major factor in their economies. For example, migrant remittances represent a significant proportion of the gross domestic product (GDP) in Tajikistan (49%), Kyrgyzstan (32%), Nepal (29%) and Moldova (25%).

Refugees

People are sometimes forced to migrate to avoid persecution due to their ethnicity, religion, political opinion or membership in a particular social group. In the past, wars between countries yielded large streams of escaping men, women and children. More recently, ethnic and religious conflicts within countries have produced millions of refugees and asylum seekers.

According to the 1951 Refugee Convention, a refugee is someone who

profitable to facilitate the departure of workers and their families. By having their citizens work abroad, sending countries have the opportunity to gain valuable foreign exchange through remittances, reduce domestic unemployment and poverty levels, as well as diminish the risks of civil unrest. Remittances provide direct and immediate financial assistance to family members that increase educational and business opportunities.

Europe

In 2015, Europe experienced record inflows of migrants at its borders, with over 900,000 recorded in the first 11 months, as compared with 280,000 for the whole of 2014. The swell in irregular migration began in 2011 and 2012, following unrest in Tunisia and Libya. The latest increase is attributed to the ongoing conflicts in Syria and Afghanistan, and to human rights abuses in Eritrea. Syrians fleeing their country's four-and-a-half-year-old civil war made up nearly 40% of migrants entering the EU in the first nine months of 2015.

Europe has struggled to achieve a united response to the crisis. Under the current Dublin Regulation, ports of entry are solely responsible for processing asylum applications. This has placed a disproportionate burden on countries like Greece, Italy and Hungary, where migrants arrive via the Mediterranean or Western Balkans routes. Consequently, enforcement is haphazard, and migrants have functionally been given carte blanche to continue on to wealthier EU destination countries, primarily Germany and Sweden, which have higher rates of asylum acceptance.

In September 2015, Germany temporarily reinstated border controls after an influx of 40,000 migrants arrived over the course of one weekend; neighboring countries followed suit, resulting in the most restrictive environment for mobility in Europe since the abolishment of internal border controls in the Schengen Area 20 years ago.

European Commission President Jean-Claude Junker promoted a system of mandatory quotas for the distribution of migrants between EU countries. However, a vocal bloc of Eastern European states, including Hungary, the Czech Republic, Poland and Slovakia, stymied efforts in this area. At a meeting of EU members in September, for instance, Hungarian Prime Minister Viktor Orban illustrated the general attitude saying, "We do not like the consequences of having a large number of Muslim communities that we see in other countries.… I do not see any reason for anyone else to force us to create ways of living together in Hungary that we do not want to see." Hungary subsequently completed a 110-mile-long fence along its border with Serbia, and began criminalizing unauthorized migrants.

While the European crisis makes international headlines, regional neighbors continue to bear the brunt of migration flows. Syrian refugees, for example, number around 2 million in Turkey, 1 million in Lebanon and 630,000 in Jordan. Increased aid to regional asylum-takers is one of the deterrence solutions proposed by European policymakers. Other proposals include the creation of asylum centers in the Mideast and North Africa, crackdowns on smuggling and the creation of a "safe-countries list" to expedite application processing and deportations. The UN High Commissioner for Refugees has warned that the current European system of piecemeal national legislation could strand migrants in "legal limbo," effectively denying them the protections guaranteed under international law.

—Lillian Marx

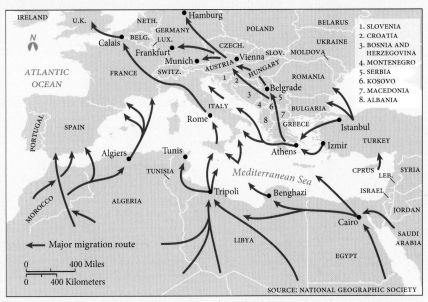

1. SLOVENIA
2. CROATIA
3. BOSNIA AND HERZEGOVINA
4. MONTENEGRO
5. SERBIA
6. KOSOVO
7. MACEDONIA
8. ALBANIA

← Major migration route

SOURCE: NATIONAL GEOGRAPHIC SOCIETY

"owing to a well-founded fear of being persecuted for reasons of race, religion, nationality, membership of a particular social group or political opinion, is outside the country of his nationality, and is unable to, or owing to such fear, is unwilling to avail himself of the protection of that country." The 1951 Convention prohibits the expulsion or forcible return of persons accorded refugee status. The 1967 Protocol extended the application of the 1951 Convention, removing temporal and geographic restrictions, which had been limited to persons fleeing events occurring before January 1, 1951, and within Europe.

Worldwide, the numbers of refugees have increased markedly in recent years. In 2014–15, we have seen a dramatic growth in mass displacement from civil turmoil, conflicts and wars, reaching levels unprecedented in the recent past. The latest estimate places the total global number of refugees at nearly 20 million at the end of 2014, with 14.4 million under the mandate of the UN High Commissioner for Refugees (UNHCR), and 5.1 million Palestinians registered with the UN Relief and Works Agency for Palestine Refugees (UNRWA).

The 14.4 million refugees under UNHCR's mandate in 2014, including persons in refugee-like situations, number some 2.7 million or 23% more than at the end of 2013. That level was the highest since 1995, when an estimated 14.9 million persons were considered to be refugees at the end of the year.

Migrants, who are to be repatriated from Myanmar to Bangladesh, cross the Myanmar-Bangladesh friendship bridge at the Taung Pyo near the Bangladesh border, Rakhine State, western Myanmar, June 8, 2015. (NYUNT WIN/EPA/LANDOV)

In 2014, an estimated 2.9 million people became refugees. UNHCR historical data over the past half century suggests that such a year-to-year gain in the number of refugees is almost unprecedented. Only in 1980 and 1990 were net additions of more than two million refugees recorded.

The unprecedented scale of displacement has put the global refugee system under visible strain, as humanitarian agencies and host communities struggle to provide for ever-rising needs. According to the UNHCR, "We are witnessing a paradigm change, an unchecked slide into an era in which the scale of global forced displacement as well as the response required is now clearly dwarfing anything seen before."

The world's refugees are concentrated in a few regions, with the Middle East and North Africa hosting 41%, followed by Asia and the Pacific at 20% and Sub-Saharan Africa at 19%. In addition to the Palestinian refugees, the major source countries of refugees at the end of 2014 were Syria (~4 million), followed by Afghanistan (2.5 million), Somalia (753,000), Sudan (627,000), South Sudan (615,000), the Democratic Republic of the Congo (488,000), the Central African Republic (410,000) and Eritrea (240,000).

In addition, a small number of de-veloping countries host the majority of refugees under the mandate of UNHCR. For the first time, Turkey became the largest refugee-hosting country, with an estimated 1.9 million refugees. The next highest countries hosting refugees were: Pakistan (1.51 million), Lebanon (1.15 million), Iran (982,000), Ethiopia (660,000) and Jordan (654,000).

The proliferations of war and internal struggles, and the resulting displacements, have been major contributors to increasing strains on asylum and protection systems. In addition, the failure of the international community to provide returns to normal life within reasonable time frames for many of the displaced has led to new refugees in overburdened host communities.

UNHCR reports that during 2014 about 127,000 refugees returned to their countries of origin. Approximately half of the returning refugees went to the Democratic Republic of the Congo (25,200), Mali (21,000) and Afghanistan (17,800). This number was the lowest level of refugee returns since 1983.

The continuing civil wars in Syria and Iraq, regional conflicts and crises in Afghanistan and the Middle East as well as in some African countries have triggered the recent dramatic increases in the flow of refugees and others fleeing to Europe. The scale and scope of those migration flows have produced a refugee crisis of historic proportions for the EU. The economic crisis in Greece has also led to weaknesses in border controls, especially in Greek islands near mainland Turkey. Consequently, in addition to the flows across the Mediterranean Sea, growing numbers of refugees have been crossing into Europe through the Balkans in recent months. Since the beginning of 2015, it is estimated that more than 900,000 migrants have arrived in the EU.

The number of refugees and migrants who crossed the Mediterranean sea to Europe during the first six months of 2015 to flee conflict or persecution hit the highest recorded level, approximately 137,000 compared to about 76,000 in the first six months of 2014. Greece, Italy, Malta and Spain recorded an 83% increase in refugees and migrants crossing the Mediterranean between January and June. One third of those who arrived by sea in Italy or Greece were from Syria. The second and third most common countries of origin arriving in Europe were Afghanistan and Eritrea.

Illegal immigration

While a precise global figure on the number of migrants unlawfully resident is difficult to establish, it is estimated to be at least 50 million. The number varies from time to time due to amnesty, regularization or normalization programs. For example, in 2005 Spain regularized 700,000 migrants, granting them legal status. Over the last several decades Belgium, Canada, France, Greece, Italy, Portugal, Spain and the U.S. have also implemented amnesties or regularizations aimed at reducing the number of migrants unlawfully resident.

Countries estimated to have the largest numbers of unauthorized migrants include the U.S. (12 million), India (at least 10 million), South Africa (10 million), Russia (4 million), the UK (nearly 1 million), Malaysia (800,000), Brazil (500,000) and South Korea (at least 300,000).

A major underlying reason for illegal migration—and why increasing numbers resort to human smuggling—is that the demand for migrants in immigrant receiving countries is far less than the supply of potential migrants wishing to go abroad. While every year countries are receiving millions of immigrants of their choosing, the pool of potential immigrants is many times larger.

In contrast to legal migration, broad agreement exists both among governments and the public concerning the undesirability of illegal migration, especially when it involves smuggling and human trafficking. In fact, governments—especially at intergovernmental gatherings such as the United Nations—uniformly stress their sovereign rights to determine who may enter and remain within their respective countries. In particular, they emphasize their rights to monitor borders, manage immigration and pass laws aimed at deterring illegal immigration.

However, and this seems to be the crux of the issue, perspectives differ greatly between sending and receiving countries as well as within countries on how best to deal with the millions of men, women and children that are unlawful residents *(see Box 2)*. At one extreme are those who wish to regularize the unauthorized migrants, granting amnesty or legalization. At the other extreme are those who wish to repatriate migrants, contending that deportation is the appropriate and needed solution to address illegal immigration.

The political will necessary to implement wide-scale deportation is typically lacking or weak at best. Politics, voting patterns, economic interests and labor needs, especially evident in Europe, Asia and the U.S. push political leaders to avoid taking a strong position on illegal immigration and the prickly issue of repatriation.

However, others contend that illegal migration has negative consequences, not least to the potential migrants who often risk their lives to make the journey to another country. Among their concerns are social cohesion, political stability, public safety and the rule of law. Illegal migration may also contribute to anti-immigration views in host communities, making integration more problematic for those who immigrated legally.

In addition, the costs of identifying, detaining, processing and deporting are not inconsequential. In the UK, for example, the enforced removal of an unlawfully resident migrant has been estimated at approximately £15,000 ($22,800). In the U.S. simply detaining an unauthorized migrant in a governmental facility has an average cost of about $160 per day.

Legal deportation proceedings, if they take place at all, frequently give rise to ethical and humanitarian concerns. Sending illegal migrants back to countries with civil turmoil or searing

Central America

In 2014, the surge of unaccompanied migrant children and families crossing the U.S.' southern border reached crisis levels. Nearly 70,000 unaccompanied children were apprehended at the border in 2014, a 77% increase year-on-year. In previous years, the vast majority of unaccompanied children entering the U.S. came from Mexico. Now, nearly 80% originate from Central America's Northern Triangle countries: Honduras, Guatemala and El Salvador.

Regional asylum requests for children and families increased more than sevenfold between 2008 and 2013. Migrants fled crumbling economies and some of the highest homicide rates in the world.

The U.S. turned to Mexico to help stem the overwhelming tide, encouraging the country to increase policing of its southern border. Deportations of unaccompanied minors in Mexico doubled in the first eight months of 2015, while the number apprehended at the U.S. border was cut by half.

Central American migrants entering Mexico face a bureaucracy that

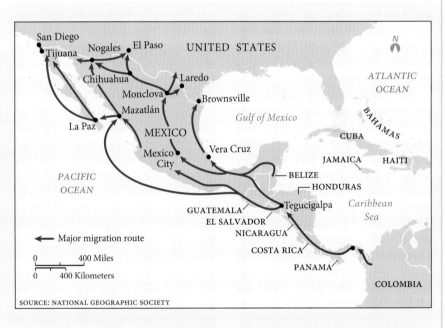

SOURCE: NATIONAL GEOGRAPHIC SOCIETY

is poorly equipped to handle asylum requests. Uncertain immigration status can leave migrants susceptible to abuse, exploitation and human trafficking. Heightened border controls in both the U.S. and Mexico have encouraged smuggling. The White House estimates that three quarters of unaccompanied child migrants in Central America now make their journeys with the help of *coyotes*. In December 2014, the Obama administration established the Central American Minors Program, meant to discourage young asylum-seekers from attempting such hazardous trips by allowing them to apply for refugee status from within their home countries. Almost a year later, bureaucratic obstacles have prevented any of the 5,400 applicants to the program from reaching the U.S.

—Lillian Marx

poverty, for example, may violate their human rights.

Objections to deportation also arise in the countries of origin. Some nations, such as China, Ethiopia, Eritrea, India, Iran, Jamaica, Laos and Vietnam, refuse to repatriate many of the illegal migrants coming from their countries. Also, some origin countries, such as Cambodia, El Salvador, Guatemala and Jamaica, are understandably not eager

to receive deported citizens convicted of violent crimes abroad or linked to organized crime.

In addition to the loss of valued remittances, returning unauthorized migrants are likely to contribute to unemployment rolls, additional costs and political unrest. Besides new and uncertain economic circumstances, deported migrants often face re-entry difficulties, including stigmatization and depression.

Legalization is often coupled with commitments for increased border, interior and work place enforcement, as well as public information campaigns aimed at discouraging future illegal migration. However, governments acknowledge that offering "last chance" legalization programs likely encourages others to attempt unlawful entry or overstay their legal visit in hopes of being eligible for the next amnesty. ∎

Policy options

Government policies play an important role in determining the flows, types, conditions and consequences of international migration. This critical role relates not only to the regular flows of immigrants, but also to the involuntary migration of refugees, asylum seekers and human trafficking victims as well as illegal immigration.

In recent years more countries have put in place policies that reflect openness to regular immigration. In 2013, 73% of countries reported policies to maintain the current level of immigration and 15% had policies to lower it. About 11% of countries had policies to raise the level of international migration, primarily to attract highly skilled and technical workers. However, relatively few governments have adopted policies to raise immigration for permanent settlement or for family reunification.

The majority of governments recognize that successful integration of immigrants is vital in order to maximize the benefits of international migration. Worldwide, 63% of governments had policies in place in 2013 to promote the integration of non-nationals, an increase from 44% in 1996. However, while nearly all governments in more developed regions (94%) had policies to promote integration of non-nationals, less than one half of governments in less developed regions (49%) had such policies, and less than one third in least developed countries (29%).

While the proportion of governments with policies to lower emigration has remained the same at about

25% during the past two decades, the proportion with policies to raise emigration has increased steadily. At the same time, more governments have adopted policies to encourage the return of their citizens, increasing from 43% in 1996 to 63% in 2011.

Also, approximately three quarters of governments consider irregular migration within their borders as a major concern. Some have responded to irregular migration by reforming their immigration laws, promoting the return of unauthorized regular migrants and implementing regularization programs.

An increasing number of countries consider fences, walls and barriers coupled with increased border surveillance, including the use of satellite imagery and drones to monitor borders, as effective preventive measures to discourage people from undertaking illegal migration and hazardous journeys. Such policies have become increasingly evident in Australia, Canada, Greece, Hungary, India, Israel, Italy, Malta, Russia, Saudi Arabia, Spain and the U.S. Also, a recent EU initiative to thwart illegal migration across the Mediterranean aims to identify, capture and destroy vessels before smugglers use them.

While governments appear to be continuing their policies of increased immigration, especially of highly skilled migrants, the overwhelming majorities of the public in most countries wish to see immigration reduced. This "migration gap" between public opinion and government policies is likely to lead to further social upheaval and political unrest concerning immigration.

Governments, business leaders and various ethnic, social and political organizations may view more immigrants as beneficial—a partial solution to addressing the consequences of declining and aging populations—and sometimes even politically and economically advantageous. In contrast, the general public appears less willing to accept the arrival of large numbers of immigrants, often perceiving it as threatening employment conditions and opportunities, depressing wages, raising the costs of local services and internal surveillance, and benefiting from social service entitlements. A survey of 24 nations taken in mid-2015, for example, found that nearly one half of people in the world's most advanced economies—including Belgium, France, the UK, Hungary, Israel, Italy and Russia—believe that there are too many immigrants in their country, immigration is causing their country to change in ways they do not like and has placed too much pressure on public services in their country.

Public opinion in many countries is particularly negative toward those unlawfully resident and working. Increased unemployment, poor enforcement of laws and regulations and a flourishing shadow economy that relies on unauthorized low-wage workers are also contributing to rising anti-immigrant attitudes. Surveys in many countries often show that the majority of the public wishes to reduce current immigration levels and prefers that unauthorized migrants return to their countries of origin.

In addition to national policies, regional agreements for managing international migration have been adopted by groups of countries. The EU has adopted various directives relating to international migration, including family reunification, asylum and temporary protection and the human rights of third country migrants. The regional conferences on migration for the Americas have also adopted guidelines and recommendations relating to managing migration flows and the human rights of migrants.

At the global level, the UN and other intergovernmental agencies have also adopted a significant number of noteworthy international conventions and protocols over the past half-century touching on a variety of issues relating to international migration. The issues addressed in the conventions and protocols include the rights of migrants, labor migration, refugees, human trafficking, smuggling, stateless persons, working conditions of migrants, domestic migrant workers, protection of migrants and their families, and equality of opportunity and treatment of workers. These instruments have contributed to the goal of establishing a comprehensive international legal and normative framework for managing the migration of people across international borders and protecting the rights of migrants.

Opportunities and challenges

International migration is one of the most important issues on today's global policy agenda. Migration has enormous demographic, economic, social, political and cultural consequences for sending and receiving countries as well as for many transit countries. The levels of international migration are expected to remain high during the 21st century. Over the next half-century approximately 100 million people are expected to immigrate primarily to the large cities of more developed nations. Consequently, international migration offers opportunities as well as challenges for governments, international organizations and the migrants themselves.

If international migration is managed properly, it is widely recognized that it can be beneficial for all concerned. More specifically, international migration offers large-scale opportunities for socio-economic development, transfer of technology and new ideas, rebalancing labor markets, remittance flows, societal enrichment and marked improvements in the well-being of millions of men, women and children.

In many countries, economic and demographic developments coupled with concerns over the future of labor supplies provide encouraging opportunities for managed labor migration. In order to formulate effective migration policies and programs, governments of sending and receiving countries will need to reconcile their respective interests and needs with the supply of millions of potential migrants seeking meaningful employment opportunities and improved living standards abroad.

At the same time it would be naïve to ignore the challenges posed by international migration. Given current global affairs, including widening conflicts and refugee flows, rapid population growth, brain-drain and frustration with attempts at multiculturalism, international migration may become even more divisive and problematic to manage in the coming years. In addition, those challenges are not likely to be confined to the developed countries; developing countries are finding themselves progressively more concerned with international migration issues, especially refugee flows.

Also, in the aftermath of the tragic events of September 11th, international migration has become an issue of national security. As a result, many countries have tightened their borders and stiffened their migration policies. Concurrently, economic and political crises in many less developed countries, together with rapid population growth and urbanization, have increased pressures and desires, especially among young men, to migrate to comparatively wealthier and safer nations.

The world's population—currently at 7.4 billion—is projected to add more than 2 billion additional people by the middle of the 21st century. Nearly all of this future population growth will take place in developing regions, mainly in Africa. Many developed countries, in

Migrants crowd the border crossing between Rigonce in Slovenia and Harmica in Croatia, September 19, 2015. After Hungary sealed its borders, migrants began taking an alternative route to Western Europe via Croatia, the EU's newest member. (IGOR KUPLJENIK/EPA/NEWSCOM)

contrast, will either experience little demographic growth or even population decline, as well as facing aging populations. Together, those demographic ingredients will create powerful push and pull forces for increased international migration, perhaps bringing about an additional 100 million migrants by mid-century.

For many high-income countries, international migration is expected to be the major driver of future population growth. Over the next five decades, migrants and their descendants are projected to account for approximately 80% of future population growth in those countries.

In addition, the international refugee system and host communities are under enormous pressures, with an unprecedented scale of forced human displacement. As is widely acknowledged, the levels of global forced displacement—estimated at more than 60 million—and the responses needed to address these crises are now dwarfing anything previously experienced.

Concerns have also been raised that a large number of people may become climate or environmental refugees as

Box 2: Pros and Cons for Amnesty or Legalization of Unlawful Migrants

PROS	CONS

PROS

1. Abuse: Granting legalization will reduce abuses against illegal aliens, who are often afraid to report crimes and mal-treatment against them for fear of being deported.

2. Compassion: As most illegal aliens are simply seeking work in order to better the lives of their families and to escape from poverty, compassion should be extended by permitting them to become legal residents.

3. Costs: In addition to the logistical problems, consider-able financial costs are incurred in sending illegal aliens back to their home countries.

4. Crime: Legalization of illegal aliens will reduce crime because they will be more willing to come forward to report crimes to the authorities.

5. Economics: In addition to paying taxes, many impor-tant sectors of the economy, especially agriculture, depend on the labor of illegal aliens, who often work on tasks that natives eschew.

6. Entitlement: As they have resided, worked and con-tributed to their new communities for years, illegal aliens should be entitled to remain in the country legally and to apply for citizenship.

7. Exploitation: As they fear being reported to the authori-ties and subsequently deported, illegal aliens are reluctant to complain about labor exploitation and sub-standard working conditions.

8. Fairness: It would be unfair to deport these people back to their home countries, which are often plagued by poverty, lack of opportunity, political instability and armed conflict.

9. Family: Many of the illegal aliens have family members, including children, who are citizens or legal residents in the country. Every effort should be made to keep families intact, which is in the best interests of the children and society at large.

10. Logistics: It is an enormously difficult undertaking for gov-ernment authorities to identify, locate and deport illegal aliens.

11. Rights: It would be a violation of basic human rights to expel people seeking to improve their lives simply because they lack the legal documents permitting them to remain in their new homes.

12. Security: It is in the national interests of the country to permit legalization and a path to citizenship for illegal aliens, as it strengthens and revitalizes the nation—and also increases its overall security.

CONS

1. Borders: Amnesty increases the pressures for further illegal immigration at the nation's borders.

2. Costs: It will be costly to taxpayers to grant amnesty to illegal aliens, especially with regard to providing education, health care, welfare and other social services.

3. Crime: Amnesty encourages trafficking and smuggling of illegal aliens who are willing to pay high prices to enter a country that periodically grants amnesty for illegal im-migration.

4. **Environment:** Granting amnesty increases the size of a nation's population, thereby negatively impacting its environment.

5. Fairness: Providing amnesty to illegal aliens penal-izes legal aliens who have properly followed the rules, and delays the immigration of others patiently waiting abroad.

6. Governance: Democratically elected governments ought to respect public opinion, which is opposed to granting am-nesty to illegal aliens.

7. Law: As it is clearly unlawful to enter, remain or work in a country without proper governmental authorization, granting amnesty undermines the rule of law among a na-tion's citizens.

8. Logistics: Granting amnesty is a costly bureaucratic nightmare and very difficult to implement without corrup-tion at nearly every stage of the process (e.g., fraud, intimi-dation, bribes, etc.).

9. Rewards: Granting amnesty to illegal aliens rewards unlawful behavior and encourages others, especially family and community members, to sneak into the country in hopes of a future amnesty, which often happens not too long after the initial amnesty is granted.

10. Security: As illegal aliens enter or reside unlawfully without proper initial security clearance and health screen-ing, granting amnesty threatens national security and public health.

11. Wages: Amnesty of illegal aliens depresses the wages of native and lawful workers by increasing the supply of workers, many of whom are willing to work for much less than the prevailing wages.

12. Trust: Granting amnesty to illegal aliens undermines the public trust, as past amnesties were to be "the last."

---

a result of natural or man-made disas-ters and climate change. In the coming decades, especially in the develop-ing regions, people will increasingly be forced to adapt to changing global environmental conditions with many deciding to migrate in order to survive. For example, a third of Bangladesh's

coastline may be flooded if the sea rises one meter during the next half century, leaving some 20 million persons dis-placed from their homes and farms.

Human trafficking and smuggling are also growing global concerns. Due to worldwide demands for cheap and compliant labor, sexual exploitation,

as well as the associated low risks and high profits, criminal groups are in-creasingly involved in human traffick-ing and smuggling in virtually every region of the world. As a result, grow-ing numbers of men, women and chil-dren are falling victim to deception and mistreatment, including debt bondage, torture, unlawful confinement, sexual abuse and violence against them.

Another major concern is illegal migration, which appears to be growing in scale and becoming more hazardous. For example, more than three times as many migrants entered the EU illegally in July than a year ago and the numbers of asylum seekers have soared in countries such as Germany, Greece and Italy. Also, during the first seven months of 2015 more than 2,000 people died and nearly 200,000 people were rescued attempting to cross the Mediterranean to enter the EU.

For many governments, illegal migration is viewed as threatening national sovereignty and security, undermining the rule of law and eroding public support of legal migration. In a number of destination countries, such as Denmark, Germany, Hungary and the UK, host communities have become increasingly concerned about the presence of unlawfully resident migrants, especially those coming from very different cultures and plagued by conflict, violence and extremism.

Properly managing international migration and deriving its benefits in the coming years will require considerable efforts by the governments of destination, transit and origin countries as well as improved cooperation and coordination at the regional and international levels. Laws, policies and programs will need to confront a broad array of challenges. Perhaps foremost among those challenges is ensuring the basic human rights of migrants and their families, and especially persons who have been victims of human trafficking. Closely related to this objective is protecting refugees and seeking durable solutions to their plight.

While the international community has not shied away from convening global conferences on a broad range of issues, it has not held such a conference on international migration. The primary explanation for this omission is that governments of the wealthier, more influential labor-importing countries and their allies have resisted. Those governments fear that if such a conference were convened, the more numerous

A father gives his son to a coast guard officer, second from left, as he disembarks from a vessel at the port of Mitylene after being picked up by the Greek coast guard near the northeast Greek island of Lesbos on June 17, 2015. (THANASSIS STAVRAKIS/AP PHOTO)

labor-exporting nations might adopt an international program of action setting legal norms and passing recommendations incompatible with their own national agendas and interests.

Another major challenge facing nations is establishing legal mechanisms and increased opportunities for international migration. Succesful addressing that challenge will involve taking into account the needs of the destination countries and the desires of potential migrants in origin countries. While the demands for labor in many destination countries are sizeable, they remain far below the enormous supplies of labor in less developed regions.

In the coming decades, the population increases in developing nations, especially among the least developed, are projected to greatly surpass those of the developed countries. For example, whereas the population of the 48 least developed countries, most of which are in Africa, will more than triple in size adding more than 2 billion people by the century's end, the population of the developed regions will increase by 2% or 26 million people. Clearly, international migration cannot be a realistic solution for the hundreds of millions of men, women and children facing dire living conditions.

For migrants unlawfully resident in countries, and those attempting to en-

ter or remain outside authorized legal channels, governments should properly review their circumstances and conditions and decide on the appropriate actions. If unauthorized migrants are found to have legitimate claims to remain in the country, authorities should ensure their basic rights and assist in their integration. In those instances when repatriation is found to be suitable, governments should return and reintegrate the unauthorized migrants back to their countries of origin. Also, governmental authorities need to identify and prosecute those responsible for human trafficking and smuggling.

With regard to the millions of authorized migrants and their families now residing and working in host countries, governments should facilitate their social, economic and political integration. Governments need to recognize the rights and contributions of migrants, promote labor force participation consistent with qualifications, encourage active civic participation, provide educational opportunities and effectively address discrimination and xenophobia. At the same time, the migrants themselves need to acknowledge their responsibilities and obligations as new societal members and endeavor to participate fully in their transition and integration into their host communities. ∎

discussion questions

1. Should national borders be open to free movements of international migration? Does the current global refugee crisis portend insularity of destination countries, or will it herald expanded international cooperation and supranational solutions?

2. Given national security concerns, how can governments address the potential migration of those wishing to carry out violence and terrorist acts?

3. How should governments deal with multiculturalism, especially when the cultural practices and behavior of migrants are at odds with host country norms and culture?

4. Currently, a small number of countries have a disproportionate refugee burden while others are far removed and have relatively few refugees. How should the burden of protecting and caring for refugees be equitably shared among countries?

5. How should the issues of illegal immigration and migrants who are unlawfully resident be addressed? What should be the consequences of illegal migration and what are likely to be the most effective policies and programs to combat smuggling?

6. Do remittances contribute to long-term GDP growth sufficiently to counterbalance the concurrent outflow of human capital—brain drain—in developing countries? If not, how could we fix this disparity?

7. Is international migration manageable per se, or are solutions to underlying issues—socioeconomics, climate change and conflict—a precondition for functioning response frameworks?

8. Should the definition of refugees be expanded to include those displaced by environmental disaster and climate change?

Don't forget: Ballots start on page 99!

suggested readings

Castles, Stephen, de Haas, Hein and Miller, Mark J., **The Age of Migration: International Population Movements in the Modern World**. New York: Palgrave Macmillan, 2013. 420 pp. This book investigates the scope of modern international migration, with accompanying regional case studies. It is supplemented by a website, <www.age-of-migration.com>.

Department of Economic and Social Affairs (DESA), **International Migration Report: 2013**. New York: United Nations, 2013. Available free online at: <http://www.un.org/en/development/desa/population/publications/migration/migration-report-2013.shtml>. This report examines levels and trends in international migration, as well as relevant existing legal frameworks.

World Population Prospects, The 2015 Revision: Key Findings and Advanced Tables. New York: United Nations, 2015. Available free online at: <http://esa.un.org/unpd/wpp/Publications/Files/Key_Findings_WPP_2015.pdf>. This 2015 revision presents the latest key findings on global demographic estimates and trends.

Koser, Khalid. **International Migration: A Very Short Introduction**. New York: Oxford University Press, 2007. 140 pp. Available free online at: <http://lms.hse.ru/content/lessons/35035/Koser%20International%20Migration.pdf>. Khalid sketches a succinct history of international migration and considers its relevance.

Koslowski, Rey, ed. **Global Mobility Regimes**. New York: Palgrave MacMillan, 2011. 298 pp. This book examines possibilities for international cooperation on the movement of persons, working from a concept of "global mobility" as differentiated from "international migration."

OECD, **International Migration Outlook 2015**. Paris: OECD Publishing, 2015. Available free online at: <http://www.oecd.org/els/international-migration-outlook-1999124x.htm>. The text examines migration trends and policies, primarily in OECD countries. It also looks at the impact of immigration on labor markets.

United Nations High Commissioner for Refugees, **Global Trends: Forced Displacement in 2014**. Geneva: UNHCR, 2015. Available free online at: <http://unhcr.org/556725e69.html#_ga=1.193262565.97356199.1436220213>. This report offers a comprehensive review of the refugee situation worldwide in 2014.

To access web links to these readings, as well as links to additional, shorter readings and suggested web sites,

GO TO www.greatdecisions.org

and click on the topic under Resources, on the right-hand side of the page

Korean choices

by Scott Snyder

Park Geun-hye salutes during her inauguration ceremony as the 11th South Korean president, at the National Assembly in Seoul, South Korea, February 25, 2013. (LEE JIN-MAN/AP PHOTO)

On a brisk day in February 2013, Park Geun-hye celebrated her inauguration as the 11th president of the Republic of Korea. What looked like the start of a new administration was for Park a homecoming as her election returned her to the Blue House, the Korean equivalent of the White House and her childhood home. But transformation of Korea in the period between the presidency of the dictator Park Chung-hee, who took power in 1961, and the administration of his democratically elected daughter would have been virtually unfathomable when Park Geun-hye was a youth.

When Park Chung-hee came to power, 15% of the Korean population lived in poverty, 8% of Koreans went to college, most Koreans were farmers and the GDP per capita was $1,458 a year. By the time Park Geun-hye became South Korea's popularly elected president over 50 years later, the country's income per capita had reached over $24,000, it was home to business conglomerates with global reach and over 90% of Koreans aged 18–22 enrolled in college.

Many older Koreans remember Park for her poise amidst tragedy, when she stood in for five years as de facto first lady following her mother's assassination by a North Korean

SCOTT SNYDER *is senior fellow for Korea studies and director of the program on U.S.-Korea policy at the Council on Foreign Relations, where he had served as an adjunct fellow from 2008 to 2011. Snyder's latest books include the co-authored volume* The Japan-South Korea Identity Clash: East Asian Security and the United States *(Columbia University Press, 2015) and* Middle-Power Korea: Contributions to the Global Agenda *(Council on Foreign Relations, June 2015) He currently writes for the blog, "Asia Unbound."*

A file photo dated 1974 showing Park Geun-hye (left) posing with her father, President Park Chung-hee, when she became acting first lady at 22 after her mother Yook Young-soo was shot to death by a North Korean agent in an attempted assassination of her husband in 1974. (YONHAP/EPA/CORBIS)

sympathizer in 1974. Five years later, she left the Blue House and experienced political exile following her father's assassination at the hands of his security chief. The personal experiences of that tragedy, the political betrayal it signified, and the test of personal loyalty forged by her isolation during almost two decades out of politics has left an indelible stamp on her own character and leadership.

In the decade and a half since she entered Korean politics on her own in 1998, Park Geun-hye has shown herself to be a savvy politician with a solid support base, excellent political intuition, a fiercely independent moral righteousness and a knack for pulling out electoral victories in the face of impending disaster. She has been dubbed the "Queen of Elections," repeatedly winning support for her party on election day against long odds. Her elec-

toral success has occurred even despite criticism of her leadership and failed choices for cabinet appointments. But in demonstrating these political qualities, more than anything Park Geun-hye has proven to be the daughter of her father, the authoritarian leader and architect of South Korea's successful rapid development in the 1960s and 1970s that earned the appellation "Miracle on the Han River."

Park's experiences following her return to politics in the late 1990s have reinforced lessons she learned while in exile in the 1970s and 1980s. In the 2004 parliamentary elections, with her party in the opposition and poised at the brink of collapse due to a bribery scandal, the party leadership turned to her as its interim leader during the election period, perhaps with the idea that she would also take responsibility for the party's losses. When they did better than expected, the "old boys" who had previously controlled the party were unable to dislodge her. During a political campaign in 2006,

Park suffered a gash on her face from an attacker at a rally in Seoul; in the aftermath of the attack her concern for her party's fortunes over her own welfare won high marks as evidence of her determination.

These experiences make her a sympathetic figure, especially among older Koreans, but they also make her a politician who is not to be underestimated. Park is the closest figure in contemporary Korean politics to political royalty. As an unmarried Korean woman, Park's reputation has been flawless because she has no competing allegiances that can plausibly trump her devotion to the country. She seemingly sacrificed her personal life, as well as strong social norms to marry and have children, for service to her country. Because of her special place in the mind of the Korean public, corruption scandals have surrounded her but have not personally ensnared her.

Park has taken advantage of her family credentials by forging a reputation for consistency based on principle,

! Before you read, download the companion **Glossary** that includes definitions and a guide to acronyms and abbreviations used in the article. Go to **www.great decisions.org** and select a topic in the Resources section on the right-hand side of the page.

LUCIDITY INFORMATION DESIGN, LLC

most notably in her defiance of her predecessor Lee Myung-bak's efforts to reverse a political decision to relocate the administrative national capital to Sejong City, about an hour outside of Seoul. Observers view Park's politics as informed by principle (when one agrees with her) and by stubbornness (when one disagrees).

Park's reputation and family history gained her a surprisingly high electoral turnout and support rate among Koreans 50 and older in the 2012 presidential election. But her victory masked an extreme generational polarization since the majority of Koreans under the age of 40 voted against her. Unlike most of her father's elections, which involved state manipulation, Park's slim majority was hard-won. Periodic accusations of electoral fraud involving alleged illegal electioneering on the part of the National Intelligence Service and the Korean military have surfaced, but none of these accusations has led to widespread questions about her legitimacy.

Mirroring her personal story, the first two years of Park Geun-hye's homecoming to the Blue House have been filled with unexpected challenges, tragedies and deviations from what she had originally planned. Many of her initial personnel choices to lead her administration were hung up in the National Assembly, in some cases as a result of gridlock between the ruling and opposition parties and in other cases because of ethical or financial management flaws that had not been properly vetted prior to candidate nominations. Campaign promises to expand welfare benefits for Korea's aging population and to provide subsidies to counter exploding childcare and education costs proved to be too expensive to keep.

Another pillar of her campaign was economic democratization, which came to the fore in response to growing income inequality and efforts to build a creative economy driven by innovation. However, Park's creative economy initiatives have been sidelined due to dependence on South Korea's largest conglomerates as the primary source of export growth and the only real source of strength in an otherwise slowing

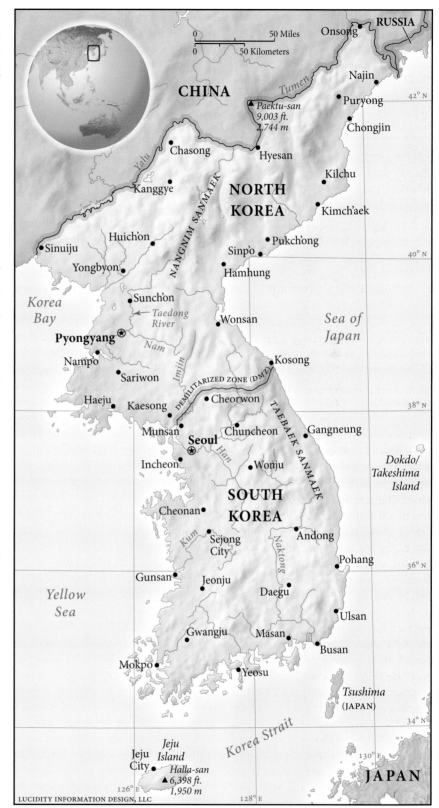

Korean economy. Looking abroad, rising regional rivalries in Northeast Asia have intensified, particularly between Japan and China. While Park's signature foreign policy initiatives seek to place a self-proclaimed middle-power Korea as a regional convener and even bridge, its diplomacy has been unable to address larger geopolitical tensions or overcome political stalemates with Japan or North Korea. As president, Park has experienced unexpected man-made and public health tragedies that have paralyzed the government, eviscerated domestic economic growth and challenged her leadership.

Through all of these trials, Park Geun-hye has worked hard to apply leadership models and traits that she learned from her father. But Korea's democratic and economic transformations have been so successful that the leadership characteristics that Park adopted from her father often seem outdated. Park Chung-hee successfully piloted South Korea's developmental take-off, but the task of political leadership in contemporary South Korea cries out not for a skilled pilot, but for an air traffic controller with the ability to provide a "control tower" capable of preventing mishaps instead of trying to pilot a single plane. ∎

Domestic tragedy

No one expected on the morning of April 16, 2014, that a routine trip by an overloaded ferry between Incheon and Jeju Island would result in national tragedy, dampen South Korea's economic growth or paralyze South Korean politics for months. But those were the consequences of the sinking of the *Sewol* ferry that resulted in 304 casualties, including 250 high school students and 11 teachers on a break from studying for Korea's all-important college entrance exams. The terrible tragedy, and the months-long search in treacherous waters for the bodies, severely damaged the Park administration's legacy. They raised searching questions about Korean disaster-response capacity and safety and regulatory standards, and provoked national self-reflection and re-criminations about the cultural values of a society that seemed to systematically prioritize efficiency or profit over human life.

The debate over causes and consequences of the ferry sinking was intense and broad, with fault to be found on every side. One person in focus was the young, inexperienced junior skipper who had been left in charge of the vessel as it made routine course corrections on a well-traveled waterway. The effects of these adjustments were too much for the overloaded ship and efforts to compensate made matters worse as the boat listed irretrievably and started to sink.

While the crisis was unfolding, the crew requested passengers to remain in assumedly secure areas rather than initiating early evacuation procedures that might have saved hundreds of lives. Lifeboats remained tethered to the ship for too long. Local coast guard teams arrived on the scene, but confusion, indecision and poor communication in the early moments of the crisis unnecessarily cost lives. The 69-year-old captain, who was absent from the bridge, was one of the earliest survivors to depart the sinking vessel, resulting in severe public criticism, including from Park herself, and court-imposed jail sentence of 36 years. A few heroes among the crew saved lives and went down with the ship, but those stories were rare compared to poignant videos and text messages sent by the students once they realized they were trapped in the ship and could not be saved.

Investigation showed that the *Sewol* should not have been authorized to sail that day; the routine safety and weight checks that should have been conducted to ensure that the vessel was seaworthy did not take place. Nor did regulators, including former government officials with close ties to the operators, prevent modifications to the ship so that it could carry more cargo, which endangered the stability of the craft. Compounding these failures was the shadowy story of the ownership structure of a company ultimately controlled by an elite cosmopolitan family with a history of eclectic business operations and cultural interests that also led a Korean religious cult.

The failures at the lowest levels of government to save more people gradually filtered up, especially as the central government took control of a months-long recovery operation to bring the bodies of the dead home for proper burial. This herculean effort involved deep-sea divers who spent weeks combing the inside of the wrecked ship amidst treacherous currents and low visibility. All but nine of the bodies were recovered.

Park made a series of public apologies in response to public outcry and sacked her prime minister and other cabinet officials. Park also made several administrative changes designed to improve South Korea's maritime regulatory and crisis management as well as its response capabilities. But her effort to fire the prime minister was unsuccessful. As her choice to take over the job could not win confirmation at the National Assembly, the former prime minister had to return to his position. Families of the bereaved high school students led political protests as the legislative opposition in the National Assembly feuded with the government over the composition and scope of an investigation into the tragedy. Yellow ribbons of protest and remembrance migrated through down-

South Korean President Park Geun-hye looks at the site of the sinking of the Incheon-Jeju Island ferry Sewol *from a Coast Guard ship on April 17, 2014.* (YNA/EPA/LANDOV)

(Left) Bereaved families of the victims of the April 16 sinking of the ferry Sewol *hold pictures of their loved ones as they sit behind yellow ribbons (with messages for the missing) on their way to the presidential office as policemen block their path in Seoul, South Korea, early on May 9, 2014.* (KIM CHUL-SOO/EPA/CORBIS) *(Right) A family member of passengers missing from the* Sewol *ferry kneels at a memorial in Paengmok Harbor in Jindo, South Korea, April 27, 2014.* (JEAN CHUNG/THE NEW YORK TIMES/REDUX)

town Seoul and became a seemingly permanent fixture at Gwanghwamun Plaza in the center of the capital. Over one year following the tragedy, a Chinese company was contracted to raise the boat in accordance with Park's pledge.

In the summer of 2015, the Park administration faced a public health crisis that also tested the South Korean government's coordination and response capabilities. This time, a South Korean man caught Middle East respiratory syndrome (MERS) while traveling to the region and brought it back to South Korea. While waiting for treatment at a hospital emergency room, he spread the disease to other patients, who in turn spread the disease further to additional hospital waiting rooms.

After an initial phase of public panic, which included the closure of many elementary schools, the South Korean public health system effectively implemented a public awareness campaign, quarantine and treatment system that brought the disease back under control within weeks. However, 166 people were diagnosed with MERS during that period, with 36 casualties. The outbreak dissuaded many tourists from visiting South Korea during the summer of 2015, thus dampening South Korean economic performance.

The *Sewol* ferry tragedy and the MERS crisis unfortunately distracted the Park administration at the cost of its capability to address many pressing domestic and international issues. Its response to both these complex crises engendered much public criticism, revealed South Korean governance failures and distracted the Park administration from achieving many of the political goals it had originally set for itself. ∎

Socio-economic challenges

Park Geun-hye pledged in her inauguration speech that she would work together with the Korean people to build "a new era of happiness and hope" and to create the "Second Miracle on the Han River." Although expressed in wildly overambitious terms, Park's pledges grapple with four interrelated social and economic challenges: demography, welfare, equity and happiness. A 2013 McKinsey Global Institute report on the Korean economy entitled "Beyond Korean Style: Shaping a New Growth Formula" has been remarkably influential in providing the Park administration with a template for pursuing these objectives.

Demographic challenge

The country's fertility rate has fallen to one of the lowest levels in the world at 1.2 births per woman, far below replacement rate of 2.1. The primary cause for the drop in fertility rates is the soaring cost of housing and educational expenses that has made the task of raising a child expensive. Moreover, the decision to have children in Korea comes at the expense of women's professional careers, given the high cost of childcare and cultural discouragement to return to the workplace. The government has offered modest education subsidies and has encouraged childbearing following decades of official support for birth control in the 1970s and 1980s, but with little effect.

This means that South Korea is losing some of its most talented workers while the costs of raising children have skyrocketed. South Korea's demographic challenge is slowly reverberating through the society in the form of increased competition in the educational sector for fewer students, lower numbers of available manpower for military service, and the need for more effective immigration and social integration policies for mixed-race families in a historically ethnically homogeneous society.

5

An elderly couple sit on a bench under cherry blossom trees near the national assembly in Seoul on April 8, 2015. (JUNG YEON-JE/AFP/GETTY IMAGES)

These pressures are even changing Korean conceptions of nationalism from an ethnically based concept to one resting on citizenship and participation in Korean society.

Welfare challenge

With a low birth rate comes an aging society. The size of South Korea's work force will peak in 2016–17 and the country is set to become one of the most rapidly graying societies over the next two decades, inverting the demographic pyramid. This challenge requires South Korea to spend more on welfare to support its aging population at the same time that expectations for elder care have shifted from the extended family to the government. Indeed, many of South Korea's elderly are living in poverty and desperately need an expanded social safety net, but the government budget and the pension system necessary to support an older population are small compared to other OECD members—a club of mostly rich countries. Park entered office vowing to expand South Korea's welfare system, but pulled back from her ambitious pledge when it became clear that there was no budget to implement most of her campaign promises in this area.

Equity challenge

A buzzword during Park's election campaign was "economic democratization." This term referred in general terms to the sensitive problems in the Korean economy that have resulted from globalization, increased efficiency and concentration of economic growth among large Korean conglomerates, all of which have left the rest of the economy behind. The small and medium enterprise sector and the service sectors have been unable to replace or provide the high quality jobs that the multinational conglomerates—*chaebol*—had provided during Korea's economic take-off, serving as the engine for growth.

Today, the chaebol provide exports and income from their global operations, but relatively few jobs, leaving the Korean government dependent on the chaebol for tax revenues while responsible for finding and creating new jobs in a stagnant economy. In addition, relations between employees and management have historically been fraught as Korean labor costs have skyrocketed compared to OECD counterparts, constituting a further drag on Korean economic growth.

Park's solution has been to promote innovation through a "creative economy," but to support these efforts the Park administration has had to turn to the chaebol for help as an incubator for localized innovation hubs. This uneasy coexistence means that the chaebol are able to scout or buy out the most productive Korean fledgling innovators before they can grow competitive within South Korea. Another large obstacle to innovation is the education system, which is built on fear of—and high costs associated with—failure, in contrast to the most vibrant innovation cultures, which count failure as an essential learning experience on the pathway to success.

Happiness challenge

Perhaps the most bold and simple of Park's inauguration pledges has been her promise to bring happiness to the people. But in a "pressure-cooker" society—so hypercompetitive that parents risk their family savings to secure their children's future by getting on an elite track for entry into one of the SKY universities (Seoul National, Korea, Yonsei)—happiness is elusive. The divorce rate is soaring and the suicide rate is the highest in the OECD. During South Korea's development take-off in the 1970s and 1980s, shared growth meant social mobility, but if the growth pie is stagnant or shrinking, the prospects for happiness appear slim. Recent polls show that South Koreans are increasingly unhappy. The structural conditions for rapid growth appear to be in Korea's rear view mirror rather than on the horizon. The happiness Park has promised will be hard-won without social restructuring that improves quality of life—especially work-life balance—and reduces competitiveness. But a "Second Miracle on the Han" does not seem to be within the grasp of the government. ■

Students line up outside the Veritas study center where lectures and classes run from morning till evening to help students prepare for the civil service or bar exams in Goshichon (literally "Exam Village"), Seoul, South Korea, March 26, 2013. (SIM CHI YIN/VII MENTOR PROGRAM)

Inter-Korean relations

Park Geun-hye's North Korea policy has been full of ambiguity and contradictions. It has been defined by pragmatism and an unusual willingness to learn from past South Korean experiences of both confrontation and cooperation with North Korea. The co-existence of these contradictions has rubbed off onto the ambivalent and wary inter-Korean relationship. The relationship has been further complicated by North Korea's hereditary leadership transition from Kim Jong Il to Kim Jong Un.

Park's views toward North Korea are marked by a striking personal complexity. Her father opened a dialogue with Kim Jong Un's grandfather despite deep mistrust. She lost her mother to a North Korean sympathizer in 1974. Yet she was the only conservative political leader in South Korea to visit Pyongyang at the invitation of Kim Jong Il in 2002. Many of Park's advisers are hardliners who would prefer to defeat rather than open up to North Korea, yet the banner for Park's policy approach to North Korea is known as Trustpolitik. However, a close reading of Park's Trustpolitik reveals that while she identifies lack of trust as the essential barrier

North Korean employees working at an apparel factory at the industrial complex in the North's border town of Kaesong, September 2013. (YONHAP/EPA/CORBIS)

to progress in inter-Korean relations, this is really a statement that North Korea must take actions to show that it is trustworthy in order to make real progress.

Despite Park's calls for dialogue based on trust, Kim Jong Un appears to have gone out of his way to project to the South untrustworthiness and contradiction. In the early months of Park's presidency, North Korea shut down the Kaesong Industrial Complex that had provided hundreds of millions of dollars in cash subsidies to the government as payment for over 50,000 North Korean laborers who work at the site for South Korean companies under South Korean supervision. The shutdown constituted an early test of Park's leadership. Negotiations to restart the complex dragged on for months, and Park did not blink in the face of North Korean demands. Finally, the North Koreans returned to Kaesong under putatively binational arrangements for administration of the complex, a remarkable concession on paper for the regime in Pyongyang.

This was followed by on-again, off-again calls for family reunions, including two rounds that took place over the Lunar New Year in 2014. North Korean authorities appeared dissatisfied with this experience as well, resisting South Korean calls to continue these meetings as a humanitarian gesture between the two sides.

Park Geun-hye subsequently laid out a more detailed vision for inter-Korean cooperation in a speech in Dresden that year where she introduced a three-phase formula for humanitarian, economic, and political exchange and integration. The North complained vociferously that the speech was given in the former East Germany, interpreting the venue as a veiled call for unification by absorption on the model of German reunification in 1990, and lobbing harsh and vulgar personal criticisms at Park herself. Subsequently, North Korea has insisted that the South Korean government quash human rights' NGO efforts to float large balloons into North Korea with propaganda designed to reach its people. Despite public noise, virtually nothing sustainable has materialized in the inter-Korean relationship.

There have been moments of hope—dashed by reality. A triumvirate of top advisers to Kim Jong Un requested to attend the closing ceremonies of the Asian Games held in Incheon to cheer a better than expected North Korean athletic performance, but did not bring any political message to Park that could be used to jump-start dialogue and cooperation. Park and Kim have both used New Year's statements to float vague public overtures, suggesting the ever-present possibility of another inter-Korean summit. But these overtures have come to naught, and in Park's case have been

Park Geun-hye (left), daughter of South Korea's former military ruler Park Chung-hee, poses with North Korean leader Kim Jong Il, May 13, 2002 in Pyongyang, North Korea. (GETTY IMAGES)

North Korean soldiers guarding the border at Panmunjom where all official contact between the militaries of North Korea, South Korea and the U.S. takes place. The border runs through the center of the blue buildings. (GARY KNIGHT/VII)

overshadowed by her expression that Korean unification will be a "bonanza," or unexpected windfall, if it can be achieved. This phrase seems to have been targeted more at South Korea's youth, who are increasingly pessimistic about Korean unification and likely associated costs, than toward Kim Jong Un. Park chairs the Presidential Committee for Unification Preparation that takes a comprehensive look at social, economic, political and security dimensions of unification. But the establish-

ment of that committee has neither facilitated inter-Korean dialogue nor had a discernible impact on the prospect that instability might lead to regime change or collapse in the North.

Surprisingly, the most significant moment of inter-Korean progress was forged in the face of a spiraling escalation of inter-Korean tensions. A landmine placed near a lookout post on the South Korean side of the DMZ maimed two South Koreans on August 4, 2015, precipitating a steady escalation of ten-

sions. South Korea turned on propaganda loudspeakers near the DMZ for the first time in 11 years, and North Korea responded with threats of further retaliation. But an exchange of fire near the DMZ on August 20 surprisingly led to a North Korean offer of high-level talks. The result of marathon negotiations between top-level officials was a modest six-point agreement that rolled back tensions and opened the way for a renewed round of family reunions held in October of 2015. But this progress remains fragile in the absence of broader inter-Korean cooperation measures and commitments to peaceful coexistence.

Fifteen years following a surprising June 2000 inter-Korean summit that opened up unprecedented possibilities for exchanges and cooperation, the prospects for further contact appear increasingly limited. The two Koreas are moving apart more than ever before, as a younger generation led by Kim Jong Un doubles down on a nuclear development policy that only deepens division and confrontation. Many younger South Koreans appear ready to move on from the decades-long inter-Korean legitimacy competition and obsession with unification—but irrelevance is the one thing North Korea under the Kim family dynasty will never willingly accept. ■

Korea's role in Northeast Asia

President Park's Trustpolitik, or trust-based relations with North Korea, has two foreign policy objectives. The Eurasia Initiative, linking the Korean peninsula by rail through Russia to Europe, and the Northeast Asia Peace and Cooperation Initiative (NAP-CI). Both were designed as an antidote to what she termed in her presidential campaign as the "Asian Paradox" of rising regional tensions that threaten to undermine Asia's growth and place in the heart of the global economy.

The Asian Paradox has proven a prescient depiction of a Northeast Asia beset by rising regional rivalries—Rus-

sian distraction resulting from its own aggression in the Ukraine, growing tensions in the South China Sea, and competing nationalisms in China, Japan and South Korea—but it has thus far not served as a platform for foreign policy achievements. Instead, at a time when South Korea's capacity to influence its own strategic environment as a middle power is arguably greater than it has ever been in its history, regional rivalry limits its ability to act, reminding Koreans that they live in a tough neighborhood, surrounded by larger and more powerful countries.

The vulnerability to rising tensions

with North Korea, incomplete reconciliation with Japan, and regional tensions are all factors that ironically underscore the logic and commitment of South Korea to the promotion of multilateral mechanisms for regional cooperation. But they also illustrate the difficulty of the challenge South Korea faces as it attempts to constructively influence its own strategic environment. Trustpolitik depends on North Korean reciprocation, and the Eurasia Initiative has been upended by Russian aggression, leaving only the NAPCI as a diplomatic opportunity for South Korea.

Park's initiative at first blush seems far-fetched. It envisions an Asian version of the Organization for Security and Cooperation in Europe, an institution that successfully bridged systemic and ideological divides and established a basis for cooperation on specific security and humanitarian issues in Europe at the height of the cold war. In Asia, functional cooperation has developed within the region despite political divisions, most notably as a result of trilateral cooperation projects among China, Japan, and South Korea on cross-border issues such as the environment. Despite an adverse political backdrop, it is very important that working-level projects have proceeded under the Trilateral Cooperation Secretariat (consisting of China, Japan, and South Korea and housed in Seoul). South Korea seeks to harness that cooperation to advance regional cohesion, but that aim means that it must provide the connective tissue by having good relationships with all of its neighbors.

Thus, the major stumbling block to Park's proposal of establishing a multilateral mechanism for peace and cooperation in Northeast Asia has been the diplomatic standoff between South Korea and Japan that stems from unresolved differences over historical issues from the period of Japanese colonization. Currently the most contentious and visible issue between the two is Korea's call for Japan to acknowledge state responsibility for Korean women forced or coerced into sexual slavery for Japanese troops before and during World War II; other issues still disputed are each country's public school textbooks, which contain government-approved narratives that reaffirm respective competing territorial claims on the small islets Dokdo/Takeshima (Liancourt Rocks).

South Korea has an interest in normalizing and managing differences in its relations with Japan while maintaining the strong Sino-South Korean relationship that has developed between Park Geun-hye and Xi Jinping. South Korea must therefore play a connecting role and provide conceptual leadership and salesmanship on the benefits of regional cooperation as a way of counteracting the rising tensions that will impose ever-greater constraints on South Korean foreign policy. In this way, South Korea can also maximize its diplomatic influence with Washington and Beijing, not by trying to medi-

ate between them, but instead by using its connecting capacity in the region as a source of leverage to encourage peaceful settlement of disputes.

The use of multilateral mechanisms to encourage cooperation and to support existing normative behavior is characteristic of the middle power diplomacy to which South Korea aspires. But Park's

initiative will not be successful unless South Korea is an effective connector, operating with support from its main ally, the U.S.. The U.S.-South Korean alliance is a factor that gives South Korea strategic weight to pursue effective regional diplomacy and demonstrates the capacity of U.S. alliances to promote and support regional stability. ∎

The future of North Korea

As the only three-generation socialist dynasty in the world, North Korea's leadership system is a political anachronism and throwback to 19th-century Asia. Yet its harsh mechanisms for political control, relative isolation and continued flow of economic benefits from neighbors such as China have kept the regime afloat despite momentous shocks and political changes. Ironically, the timing of Kim Jong Il's death in December of 2011 and subsequent successions in neighboring states makes the thirty-something Kim Jong Un the longest-serving political leader in Northeast Asia.

Despite its relative longevity, there are visible cracks in the system over which Kim Jong Un presides. The regime founder Kim Il Sung was able to

consolidate political control based on loyalty, and Kim Jong Il relied on two decades of patronage as his father's designated successor by assigning appointments to induce loyalty or through bribes. The main source of Kim Jong Un's authority is derived from the fear of getting on the wrong side of his absolute authority within the North Korean system. Kim's brutal execution of his uncle Jang Song Thaek and continuing demotions, rotations and even executions of senior defense officials suggests that disloyalty to Kim has extreme consequences and perceived slights can be fatal.

Ironically, Kim's impulsive behavior and willingness to execute his subordinates for disloyalty may ultimately generate the biggest risk to his

BY PARESH NATH, THE KHALEEJ TIMES, UAE, 4/28/2013

South Korean protesters with defaced portraits of North Korean leader Kim Jong Un shout slogans during an anti-North Korean rally in Seoul, South Korea, August 21, 2015. The sign at right reads: "Explode the statues of Kim Il Sung and Kim Jong Il !" (ULIEYOON/AP PHOTOJ)

rule over a system that has otherwise shown stability and adaptability amidst grave challenges. The Kim family has survived past coups and purges, as well as a great famine in the mid-1990s that removed the state's control over distribution of goods in favor of a barter economy through informal markets. Ultimately, marketization could be tolerated, but not at the expense of Kim family political control. The system exacted bribes and concessions from its people, but appears to have allowed little social mobility in the absence of patronage from top-ranked elites who preside over a rigid caste system that has strictly determined social rank and privileges within North Korea.

As Kim Jong Un consolidates his power internally, he has pursued two notable initiatives that appear to be contradictory but that define his leadership thus far. First, he has tied North Korea's nuclear capabilities to the legitimacy of the regime. His assumption of rule coincided with North Korea's designation as a nuclear state in the preamble of the constitution, and the nuclear program was touted as a primary accomplishment attributed to the rule of Kim Jong Il, implying that North Korea's nuclear accomplishments have become a pillar of regime legitimacy.

Second, Kim Jong Un has promoted economic improvements as a way to better the socio-economic situation. He stated in his first public speech that the North Korean people should no longer have to "tighten their belt" and has encouraged limited agricultural reform measures as well as devolution of economic decision-making to lower levels within the North Korean system. Reported crop yields improved sufficiently in the first three years of Kim's rule so that Pyongyang no longer relies on food contributions from the United Nations system to meet its annual cereal requirements, although the regime still secures limited bilateral food donations and makes commercial purchases on the international market to make up the gap between indigenous production and total cereal needs. North Korea's refusal of in-person UN FAO field assessments itself is evidence of improvement in domestic production; the rejection of UN FAO access would not occur if the leadership felt it was still dependent on international contributions to meet its food needs. The UN FAO claims that food rations in 2015 have declined 21% from a three-year average, but reports that official and black markets are now a significant source of food purchases.

The pursuit of these parallel objectives—nuclear and economic develop-

ment—was affirmed as North Korea's main "strategic line" by the Workers' Party of Korea on March 31, 2013. Although continued pursuit of a nuclear program has limited North Korea's attractiveness as a destination for foreign investment due to international norms, security concerns and UN sanctions resulting from North Korea's missile and nuclear tests, external estimates of the country's economic growth show marginal improvement, and anecdotal evidence from visitors to Pyongyang suggest that it is enjoying economic stability.

More problematic is Kim Jong Un's nuclear and missile development. Within a few years, it could lead to North Korea having a mid- to long-range nuclear strike capability, a sufficient number of bombs and a mobile launch capability that would make it able to survive a nuclear first strike. This circumstance poses risks related to North Korea's nuclear doctrine, particularly regarding the possibility that Pyongyang could threaten nuclear use for blackmail purposes or in desperation.

Finally, the North Korean human rights situation has been exposed over the past two decades as one of the worst in the world. A UN commission of inquiry on North Korean human rights has documented witness testimonies from escaped North Koreans that graphically outline crimes against humanity, use of food and withholding of food as a political weapon and severe punishments for expressions of disloyalty toward the regime.

The combination of North Korea's threat to South Korea, the expansion of its nuclear and missile capabilities so as to threaten the region, and the appalling stories of human rights conditions inside North Korea will continue to make North Korea a source of concern, especially to the extent that Kim Jong Un is perceived by the international community as prone to taking unnecessary risks or miscalculating. Given Kim's international isolation and absent a change in the regime's priorities, North Korea will continue to be a source of concern and a potential threat to international stability for the foreseeable future. ∎

U.S.-South Korean relations

South Korean views of the U.S. have been highly favorable in recent years, with the U.S.-South Korean alliance enjoying the support of over 90% of South Koreans polled. This is a remarkable turnaround from a relationship that appeared to be frayed and plagued by "anti-American" attitudes in South Korea as of the mid-2000s. At that time, contentious bilateral issues, namely debate over the Status of Forces Agreement (SOFA) with the U.S. and a decision to lift a ban on U.S. beef imports that ran alongside U.S.-Korea free trade agreement negotiations, caught national attention and induced massive protests in central Seoul. But more recently, South Korean appreciation for the relationship with the U.S. has grown. Over 60% of South Koreans now believe the U.S. to be the most important partner for South Korea's security. The numbers remain relatively unchanged when South Koreans are asked to predict the preferred future partner in an era of Sino-U.S. competition—about 59% choose the U.S. and 30% choose China.

South Koreans feel greatest affinity for Americans compared with its immediate neighbors—5.3 on a 10-point scale, compared to 4.5 with North Koreans, 4.6 with Chinese and 3.0 with Japanese. The U.S. is seen as a fair partner committed to a liberal world order with a market economy from which South Korea has benefited. In service of maintaining this world order, over 70% of South Koreans advocate U.S. leadership in world affairs, while support of Chinese leadership is at 50%. However, despite this sympathy for the U.S., 44.5% of South Koreans in a recent survey responded that U.S. and South Korea do not share the same national interests.

At the same time, China has become the most important trading partner for export-dependent South Korea. Its trade with China is twice that of trade with the U.S. and Japan, combined. Thus, it is not surprising that 55% of South Koreans view China as the most important country for their economy, compared to 34% who chose the U.S.

U.S. Secretary of State John Kerry, left, talks with South Korean President Park Geun-hye at the Presidential Blue House in Seoul, South Korea, May 18, 2015. (JEON HEON-KYUN/ POOL/AP PHOTO)

South Korea's other neighbor, Japan, evokes a more conflicted view from South Koreans. It has a security treaty with the U.S., South Korea's closest ally, but it is also a former aggressor, having annexed and later colonized the Korean peninsula from 1910 to 1945. Thus, the legacy of Japan's colonization of the peninsula is a perennial shadow that negatively affects the relationship. Despite having normalized relations in 1965, ties have been characterized by cycles of rapprochement and rupture due to differences over textbooks, history, and a longstanding territorial dispute over the island of Dokdo/Takeshima. Moreover, Koreans have viewed the return to office of Prime Minister Shinzo Abe with suspicion due to Abe's reputation as a historical revisionist.

A 2015 poll reported that approximately 72% of South Korean respondents view the Japan-South Korea relationship as competitive, 84% see the bilateral relation as having already worsened, and 62% project it to further worsen in the future. At the same time, South Koreans recognize the need for a stable relationship with Japan: in March 2015, 70% of South Koreans polled supported a Korea-Japan summit, recognizing the importance of improving ties with Japan. (This number represents consid-

erable improvement compared to the 49.5% of South Koreans who supported a summit in December 2013, following Abe's visit to the controversial Yasukuni Shrine.) The U.S. has encouraged the two leaders to reconcile. President Barack Obama was able to bring President Park and Prime Minister Abe together on the sidelines of the Nuclear Security Summit at The Hague in 2014.

One important factor in South Korean public opinion is the generational gap in perceptions of the region. Koreans in the "386 Generation," influenced by their experiences with democratization in the 1980s and contested civil society-government relationships, have the lowest level of support for the U.S. alliance and are more willing to see China favorably as a future partner. Among South Koreans in their 40s, 43% prefer the U.S. and 44% prefer China. However, 75% of 20-somethings who have grown up in a modernized, democratic South Korea view the U.S. as a preferable future partner. These preferences are similar to South Korea's "development generation" in their 60s and above, who view the U.S. as a security protector, based on collective memory of the American intervention to save South Korea from communist North Korea. ∎

discussion questions

1. Is immigration a viable solution to Korea's demographic challenge? Can official policy ameliorate traditional popular attitudes that pose barriers to social integration? Will basic conceptions of Korean national identity have to change?

2. Is *Trustpolitik* a viable framework for inter-Korean relations given an increasingly belligerent North Korea? Could it be applied to other situations around the world?

3. What obstacles stand between South Korea and the successful assertion of its middle power influence? Which issues obstruct stable Japanese-Korean relations, and what plausible actions can be taken to overcome them?

4. The Park administration's promotion of a "creative economy" has been stymied by dependence on *chaebols*. Does the administra-

tion have options for socio-economic restructuring that circumvent *chaebol* influence?

5. Is the U.S.-South Korea alliance a forward-looking partnership? How would the regional balance of power change if North Korea became significantly more or less threatening, and would the structure of the alliance necessarily be affected?

6. What are the prospects for unification of the Korean peninsula? How strong is South Korean popular support for unification and to what extent is this reflected in foreign policy priority setting? Is South Korea prepared for the possibility of sudden reunification, as in the case of West Germany?

7. Should the U.S. and other international players consider regime change in North Korea as a policy option? What might be the potential costs and benefits of this approach

Don't forget: Ballots start on page 99!

suggested readings

Connell, Sean P., "Creating Korea's Future Economy: Innovation, Growth, and Korea-U.S. Economic Relations."**Asia Pacific Issues**, Honolulu: East-West Center, January 2014. Available free online at: <http://www.eastwestcenter.org/sites/default/files/private/api111.pdf>. This analysis explains South Korea's "creative economy" agenda and outlines opportunities for Korea-U.S. economic cooperation.

Suh, Jae-Jung,"The Failure of the South Korean National Security State: The Sewol Tragedy in the Age of Neoliberalism." **The Asia-Pacific Journal**, October 6, 2014. Available free online at: <http://japanfocus.org/-Jae_Jung-Suh/4195/article.html>. This article argues that inadequate government oversight and regulation contributed to the Sewol ferry disaster.

Choi, Wonsik, et al., "Beyond Korean Style: Shaping a New Growth Formula." **McKinsey Global Institute**, April 2013. Available free online at: <http://www.mckinsey.com/insights/asia-pacific/beyond_korean_style>. This report identifies challenges facing Korea's economy and suggests potential responses. It places particular focus on the country's growing wealth gap.

Park, Geun-hye, **An Initiative for Peaceful Unification on the Korean Peninsula**, March 28, 2014. In her speech, President Park sets out her vision for reunification of the two Koreas.

———."A Plan for Peace in North Asia." **The Wall Street Journal**, November 12, 2012. Available free online at: <http://www.wsj.com/articles/SB10001424127887323894704578114310294100492>. This opinion piece by President Park locates reconciliation, cooperation and peace in Northeast Asia as government priorities, arguing that regional relations must be approached with a "correct understanding of history."

Snyder, Scott, ed., **Middle-Power Korea: Contributions to the Global Agenda**. New York: Council on Foreign Relations Press, 2015. 114 pp. Available free online at: <http://www.cfr.org/asia-and-pacific/middle-power-korea/p36623>. This report proposes strategies for maximizing Korea's influence on the global agenda.

Cha, Victor D.,"Powerplay: Origins of the U.S. Alliance System in Asia," Cambridge: **International Security**, Winter 2009/2010. This article explains the origins of East Asia's current system of security bilateralism, locating them in the U.S. cold war era foreign policy.

Armstrong, Charles K., **The Koreas**. New York: Routledge, 2007. 210 pp. This book explores modern North and South Korean identities as fluid and multifaceted. It further addresses the countries' differing approaches to globalization.

Wit, Joel S. and Sun Young Ahn, "North Korea's Nuclear Futures: Technology and Strategy." Washington DC: **U.S.-Korea Institute at SAIS,** Johns Hopkins University, 2015. Available free online at: <http://38north.org/wp-content/uploads/2015/02/NKNF-NK-Nuclear-Futures-Wit-0215.pdf>. This paper provides an overview of North Korea's nuclear and missile programs.

To access web links to these readings, as well as links to additional, shorter readings and suggested web sites,

GO TO www.greatdecisions.org

and click on the topic under Resources, on the right-hand side of the page

The UN's post-2015 development agenda and leadership

by Stephen Browne and Thomas G. Weiss

The flag-lined approach to the entrance to the United Nations office in Geneva, Switzerland, November 2015. (GODONG/ROBERT HARDING/NEWSCOM)

There is a dramatic fork in the road for the United Nations and the United States in 2016. But unlike the late Yogi Berra, the next U.S. administration cannot merely "take it" but rather is required to act. While most American media and pundits are focused on international peace and security and the travails of the Security Council, much of the rest of the planet is instead often riveted on the challenges of poverty eradication and sustainable development. A new global push begins in 2016, when everyone will also be eyeing the "election" of the United Nations' next secretary-general.

Why new development objectives?

At the outset of the 21st century, 150 or so heads of state endorsed a set of eight measurable Millennium Development Goals (MDGs) with 18 concrete targets. While pundits dismiss the impact of goal setting, it is one of the few ways to aim at improvements and shame governments by holding their feet to the fire for poor results or even lackadaisical efforts.

While many judged the pursuit utopian, the record since 2000 is better than the generally slower progress in the 1990s

STEPHEN BROWNE *is a Senior Fellow at the CUNY Graduate Center's Ralph Bunche Institute, where* **THOMAS G. WEISS** *is Presidential Professor of Political Science and Director Emeritus. The authors have written extensively about the problems and prospects of the United Nations and are co-directors of the Future UN Development System Project.*

UNDP Administrator Helen Clark and Mbaranga Gasarabwe visit a small-scale mango farm operated by women. Mali, May 2010. (UNDP /UN PHOTO)

among most of the poorest countries (see chart on the right). Indeed, the 2015 final MDGs report showed that the proportion of people in dire poverty worldwide will have been more than halved, even ahead of the target year; all developing regions will have achieved gender parity in primary education; the clean water access goal will have been reached along with impressive results in fighting malaria and tuberculosis. In other areas, global measurements indicate some substantial shortfalls. Primary school enrolment is still not universal; chronic child malnutrition remains far too high; child and maternal mortality rates have fallen, but inadequately; and sanitation standards are short of their targets. While skeptics often indicate that the MDGs themselves deserve less credit for the plunge in poverty than growth in China and India, nonetheless more than 700 million people emerged from poverty. Meanwhile, the prospect of bad pub-

licity for failing to meet international targets undoubtedly motivated at least some countries to adopt measures that they might otherwise have not.

A few countries will have achieved all goals, but the majority will have fallen short on several. Some, especially those prone to armed conflict, have not advanced in economic terms for more than a generation. For them, targets will have meant little. And even those countries that are better off in 2015 than in 2000 may find it harder from their improved positions to attain the new goals.

A small group of UN staff compiled the MDGs in a single, succinct package that was measureable and time-bound. Although several UN organizations were slow to sign up, they all eventually did. The goals were the closest that the world organization has ever come to a realistic and realizable development agenda.

Starting in 2012, states and secretariats have toiled to frame a new set of "sustainable development goals," again intended to focus UN operations, but this time until 2030. In 2013, a high-level panel chaired by three serving heads of government proposed a new set of 12 goals and 50 measurable indi-

cators, already a quantum leap in range and ambition from the earlier millennium versions. The panel also laid down two important parameters. First, any new set of goals should build on the MDGs but have more breadth, including concerns about economic growth and jobs, promotion of peace and security and inclusive governance. Second, they should be universal, including all 193 UN member states in a global partnership that does not distinguish developing from developed countries (or the "global South" from the "North," in UN parlance).

The panel's report was the starting point for exhaustive consultations within an Open Working Group (OWG) of member states, which began deliberations in 2013. Open consultations have the merit of seeking wide consensus—a process that was not followed for the formulation of the MDGs, which were produced by a handful of senior UN officials.

The path to consensus among representatives of member states is to ensure that all their respective interests are included, along with those of multiple lobbying groups and advocates, including every UN development organization. A year-and-a-half later, the OWG

Before you read, download the companion **Glossary** that includes definitions and a guide to acronyms and abbreviations used in the article, as well as additional background material. Go to **www.great decisions.org** and select the topic in the Resources section on the right-hand side of the page.

UNDP'S MILLENNIUM DEVELOPMENT GOALS, 1990 – 2015

MILLENNIUM DEVELOPMENT GOAL	MADE PROGRESS	MET GOALS
1. The proportion of extremely poor people decreased by more than half since 1990.		✓
2. Five out of ten children in developing countries are now in school.	✓	
3. There are generally as many girls as boys enrolled in primary school today.		✓
4. The global under-five mortality rate declined by more than half.	✓	
5. The maternal mortality rate decreased by 45%.	✓	
6. The HIV/AIDS, malaria and TB epidemics have been halted and still fewer people are infected each year.		✓
7. Five out of ten people have access to clean drinking water today.		✓
8. Develop a global partnership for development	no clear deadline	

SOURCE AND TEXT: UNITED NATIONS DEVELOPMENT PROGRAMME

arrived at a list of no fewer than 17 development goals (see Table 1) and 169 explanatory paragraphs (with at least as many targets). The largest gathering ever of presidents and prime ministers at the UN summit of September 2015 adopted "Transforming Our World by 2030: A New Agenda for Global Action." Optimists called it "aspirational," whereas skeptics like Bjørn Lomborg noted that "having 169 priorities is the same as having none." William Easterly suggested a different "SDG" acronym: "senseless, dreamy, garbled." All too often the problem with UN deliberations is that process is more important than product; getting to an agreed text is a sufficient criterion for success, however lacklustre the result.

The Economist aptly characterized an earlier version as "something for everyone has produced too much for anyone." Indeed, the number of targets is so numerous that no country will be able to adopt them all. Among the first seven goals, there is a restatement and a further elaboration of most of the unrealized MDGs. And because "sustainability" implies environmental management, the majority of the 17 goals are wholly or partially concerned with managing resources, energy or climate change.

An exception is Goal 16 that, in acknowledgement of what is considered the main engine of development progress, deals with aspects of national governance that include building strong and inclusive institutions, promulgating the rule of law, respecting rights, and reducing corruption and "all forms of violence." Another exception is the final Goal 17 that concerns the "means of implementation," which contains some general statements acknowledging that the goals will necessitate substantial new resources for their realization. A central problem, which is especially pertinent for Goal 16, is that the last two umbrella goals are vague but shelter a large number of issues dear to the West and contested by many other countries.

The SDGs do not lack ambition, but if they are to have any practical importance, critical choices will have to be retrofitted onto this indigestible menu

Table 1: The 17 Sustainable Development Goals	
Goal 1	End poverty in all its forms everywhere.
Goal 2	End hunger, achieve food security and improved nutrition and promote sustainable agriculture.
Goal 3	Ensure healthy lives and promote well-being for all at all ages.
Goal 4	Ensure inclusive and equitable quality education and promote lifelong learning opportunities for all.
Goal 5	Achieve gender equality and empower all women and girls.
Goal 6	Ensure availability and sustainable management of water and sanitation for all.
Goal 7	Ensure access to affordable, reliable, sustainable and modern energy for all.
Goal 8	Promote sustained, inclusive and sustainable economic growth, full and productive employment and decent work for all.
Goal 9	Build resilient infrastructure, promote inclusive and sustainable industrialization and foster innovation.
Goal 10	Reduce inequality within and among countries.
Goal 11	Make cities and human settlements inclusive, safe, resilient and sustainable.
Goal 12	Ensure sustainable consumption and production patterns.
Goal 13	Take urgent action to combat climate change and its impacts.
Goal 14	Conserve and sustainably use the oceans, seas and marine resources for sustainable development.
Goal 15	Protect, restore and promote sustainable use of terrestrial ecosystems, sustainably manage forests, combat desertification, and halt and reverse land degradation and halt biodiversity loss.
Goal 16	Promote peaceful and inclusive societies for sustainable development, provide access to justice for all and build effective, accountable and inclusive institutions at all levels.
Goal 17	Strengthen the means of implementation and revitalize the global partnership for sustainable development.

of development aspirations. In some ways, the can has been kicked down the proverbial road as the actual contents of the agenda have been postponed until March 2016 when the Inter-Agency and Expert Group—a sub-group of 28 of the 193 national statistics offices that compose the UN's Statistical Commission—is to quantify targets where possible. Their indicators will, in effect, define the meaning of the SDGs and how they are monitored. Choices are necessary because not all countries can meet the (measurable) targets. And perhaps more importantly, their sheer number means that the earlier MDG advantage of being able to name and shame governments will largely have been removed.

Will all goals and targets be measured for every country? Or will a different set of goals be tailored to each? Or a mixture? How will their detailed application be measured? While the SDGs refer to least developed, landlocked and small island states, there is no mention of those prone to conflict, which will face the greatest development challenges. Readily available metrics existed for virtually every country for every MDG; how will new SDG concepts, such as security or governance, be determined?

Even once the shaping and honing has been done, better capacities for statistical compilation will be required. How will they be provided? And if the data can be trusted, who will monitor,

Speakers at the opening ceremony celebrate the adoption of the new Sustainable Development Goals during the Sixth Annual Social Good Summit on September 27, 2015, in New York. An initiative of the United Nations Foundation, Mashable, United Nations Development Program and the 92nd Street Y, the Social Good Summit explores how technology and new media can be leveraged to address global issues. (STUART RAMSON/AP IMAGES FOR UN FOUNDATION)

and how? How can observers, as Nate Silver's best seller asked, distinguish "the signal from the noise"?

Governments simply must be held to account if this exercise is to be even modestly meaningful. Yet governments—as the main obstacles to development—are the sole drivers of the review process. To ensure objectivity, civil society organizations, international nongovernmental organizations and the UN itself should track the SDGs. Indeed, the world body could well emulate its own practice in the human rights domain and institute "universal periodic reviews" of each country's development performance.

Apart from Goal 17 on means of implementation, the OWG did not go in depth on the resource implications of the SDGs; but it is clear that huge investments will be required to support the implementation of the post-2015 development agenda. Rather clumsily, the UN contrived to hold a conference on the financing of the agenda two months before the agenda was agreed. The Third International Conference on Financing for Development (FfD) was held in Addis Ababa in mid-July 2015.

Alliteratively, but not accurately, the outcome document of the July meeting was called the Addis Ababa Action Agenda (AAAA). In the age-old relationship between cart and horse, it might have been more logical to agree what needed to be done prior to determining the resources and actions required for implementation.

On a bright note, the Addis meeting did not—like virtually every UN development meeting before it—get bogged down in a sterile North-South debate about aid, prompting the UK development minister to declare that it was "a historic international deal that takes us beyond aid." The conference ended on time and was without fireworks or passion, which could also signify that the stakes were low. In fact, the outcome document outlines the requirement to blend domestic public and private finance before the section on "international development cooperation." The juxtaposition is important because of aid's diminishing role in relationship to other potential international resources. The discussion about Official Development Assistance (ODA) stopped short of making progress conditional on more aid and "welcomed

the increase in all forms of international finance" since the first FfD conference in 2002. The role of South-South cooperation was also recognized.

But for an "action" program, the language is infused more with exhortations than decisions. It reads in part like an alternative post-2015 agenda. A rare mention of the word "decide" occurs in the establishment of a "technology facilitation mechanism" based on an inter-agency task team of eight UN entities. In typically convoluted UN jargon, this mechanism is "for facilitating interaction, matchmaking and the establishment of networks between relevant stakeholders and multi-stakeholder partnerships."

The AAAA is also more explicit in its treatment of illicit financial flows and corruption, which bleed the African continent of more resources than can be offset by incoming aid. The document also calls for strengthening the work of the UN committee of experts on international cooperation in tax matters, a sensitive issue for several major donor countries.

There is also some language dealing with international migration and human trafficking. Signatories also "commit to ensuring the effective implementation of the United Nations Convention against Transnational Organized Crime," although actions will speak louder than these words.

A challenge for the SDGs agenda is the inherent tension between its universal nature—what is called "a shared global responsibility"—and the principle of "common but differentiated responsibility," or the idea from environmental law that wealthier, industrialized countries have a greater responsibility because they have for some time contributed much more to environmental deterioration. At stake is how to square that circle, or how to include the concept of national differentiation or differential responsibilities. The AAAA moved toward a balance between external aid and domestic resource mobilization.

The AAAA was also a step in the right direction, moving the international conversation away from financing for purely national goals such as education and clean water and toward global public goods such as halting climate change and pandemics. The document recognizes many new sources of development finance, including the Global Fund to Fight AIDS, Tuberculosis and Malaria, GAVI, the global Vaccine Alliance, and the Green Climate Fund. These sources are mainly funded by the traditional Western donors and are designed to finance the provision of global public goods. The section on trade also recognizes its contribution "to the promotion of sustainable development."

If suitably adjusted to include realistic targets, if a proper monitoring system is put in place and if adequate resources are available—obviously, some very big "if's"—this complex agenda is supposed to capture what UN publicity trumpets as "the world we want." This agenda nevertheless constitutes a gigantic challenge to the UN development system on which successful implementation will at least partially depend. But what constitutes this system, and will it be up to the job? In short, what is the UN we want and require? ∎

How fit for post-2015 purpose is the UN?

Development is usually described as one of the main pillars of the UN, the others being international peace and security, human rights, and humanitarian action. As distinct from the other pillars, the various organizations that make up the UN development system share long-term objectives. Almost every part of that system is also a member of the High-level Committee on Programmes and the UN Development Group, which oversee operational activities at the field level. Therefore, there is a "system" behind the UN's development pillar and aspirations.

This system undertakes the "operational activities" that account for about 60% of total annual UN spending (some $17 billion in 2013), employing 80,000 people, a majority of the organization's full-time staff. It includes more than 30 organizations (variously called funds, programs, offices and agencies). There are also an equivalent number of supportive functional commissions and research and training organizations, which are not included in the total. For example, the UN University alone has 16 specialized centers that do not appear in the UN's main alphabet soup.

Although it comprises organizations covering the gamut of development domains, the UN system cannot provide institutional solutions to all the challenges encompassed by the SDGs. For example, the World Trade Organization will play a major role for commerce but is outside the UN. In infrastructure and finance, the World Bank Group and regional development banks as well as the new Asian Infrastructure Investment Bank will be

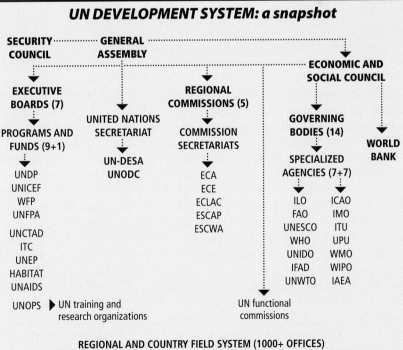

UN DEVELOPMENT SYSTEM: a snapshot

SECURITY COUNCIL

GENERAL ASSEMBLY

ECONOMIC AND SOCIAL COUNCIL

EXECUTIVE BOARDS (7)

REGIONAL COMMISSIONS (5)

UNITED NATIONS SECRETARIAT

GOVERNING BODIES (14)

PROGRAMS AND FUNDS (9+1)

COMMISSION SECRETARIATS

WORLD BANK

UN-DESA
UNODC

SPECIALIZED AGENCIES (7+7)

UNDP
UNICEF
WFP
UNFPA

ECA
ECE
ECLAC
ESCAP
ESCWA

ILO   ICAO
FAO   IMO
UNESCO   ITU
WHO   UPU
UNIDO   WMO
IFAD   WIPO
UNWTO   IAEA

UNCTAD
ITC
UNEP
HABITAT
UNAIDS

UNOPS ▶ UN training and research organizations

UN functional commissions

REGIONAL AND COUNTRY FIELD SYSTEM (1000+ OFFICES)
Many regional locations – between 5 and 20 separate UN offices per country

SOURCE: UNITED NATIONS

partners, but they are part of the UN system in name only or not at all. In health, a major role can be anticipated for the Global Fund and the GAVI Vaccine Alliance.

In addition to the role of such non-UN bodies, the landscape is changing for the UN in other ways. Competition comes from other global forums like the G20 and the World Economic Forum. Emerging powers like Brazil, China and India provide alternative forms of assistance to developing countries. More appropriate and specialized sources are available for the bread-and-butter technical assistance long provided by the UN system. Development inputs go far beyond aid, which is being supplanted

with alternative sources of funds and expertise—ranging from foundations like Gates to nongovernmental organizations of rival size, to foreign direct investment that is five times larger than ODA, and to remittances that are at least three times the size. And, of course, trade is booming, with many of the poorest countries in Africa enjoying substantial royalties from oil and mineral production.

Co-optation is the way to describe the increasing extent to which government and multilateral agency contributions to the UN development system are tied to donor conditions and earmarked for specific countries, priorities and groups rather than determined by the

Development System (UNDS) worldwide (and over 1,400 for the UN as a whole, including peace operations). The numbers, moreover, are growing not shrinking. Criticism is getting louder as impatience grows with proliferation, decentralization, rivalry, turf battles and redundancy.

Capacity is another variable. What exactly can the system do? How robust is the expertise within it? What are its comparative advantages, and how can they be maximized? Merely replicating the activities from the past is not viable, and limping along does not suffice, although it seems to be the default option.

Complacency characterizes the attitude of too many members of the international civil service who do not seem to recognize that there is a crisis, and that a transformative change must be made to prevent the UNDS from becoming a marginalized anachronism.

Another "C" is for "consolidation" or "centralization." The UN's structure would have puzzled even Rube Goldberg, the celebrated U.S. cartoonist whose elaborate contraptions a journalist described as a "symbol of man's capacity for exerting maximum effort to achieve minimal results." The structure and procedures, along with donor incentives, explain why individual UN organizations focus on their own substantive areas and eschew a coordinated UN path; they prefer to go it alone. Backed by separate budgets, governing boards, and organizational cultures as well as independent executive heads, an almost universal chorus sings the atonal tune praising decentralization and autonomy. The UN's principal organ charged with oversight, the Economic and Social Council, provides one of the main concert halls for this cacophony.

www.caglecartoons.com

UNITED NATIONS REFORM

Mike Keefe THE DENVER POST 2005

by foreign direct investment, private capital, worker remittances, export receipts, taxes and mining royalties.

Besides being hemmed in by an increasingly competitive environment, the UN has its own inherent weaknesses, giving urgency to considerations about its purpose in the post-2015 era. Five kinds of weaknesses characterize the current UN system: competition, coherence, co-optation, capacity and complacency.

Competition has squeezed the system out of the aid mainstream. The UN is now the source of less than 14% of total ODA. The UN's operations are essentially financed by ODA, which is less and less important in comparison

UN itself. Earmarking by donors threatens to undermine the capacity of the UN to address effectively a universal development agenda represented by the SDGs. Indeed, the single largest source of funding for the operational UN is the European Commission and its agencies, for which UN organizations act as implementing agencies.

Coherence, or actually lack thereof, is a long-standing lament. Few would deny that the system is atomized. Apart from the number of different entities, there is their physical dispersion. The headquarters of the main organizations are in 14 different countries (and 15 cities). There are also more than 1,000 representative offices of the UN

To be fair, there has been adaptation by the UN over time. Indeed, founders might well not recognize today what they created in 1945, when such problems as the environment and women's rights were not on the agenda—problems that have subsequently spawned a variety of institutional adaptations and changes. At the same time, our perspective reflects how empty the current glass is after seven decades. Robert Jackson was one of the operational giants of multilateralism for the Allies in World War II and the UN afterwards. He began his 1969 *Capacity Study's* evaluation of the UN development system by writing: "The machine as a whole has become unmanageable in the strictest sense of the word. As a result, it is becoming slower and more unwieldy like some prehistoric monster." That sentence infuriated heads of UN organizations then, but the lumbering dinosaur is now older and certainly not better adapted to the climate of the 21st century.

There have been serious debates but only half-hearted efforts at reform, including the 2006 "Delivering as One" report (DaO). But astonishingly, the most serious scrutiny about the fundamental role of the system took place in 1969; and we could do far worse than revisit the Jackson report's recommendations. While the importance of the world's body in helping to confront a growing litany of global challenges has never been greater, the UN is disjointed and demoralized. Former UN Under Secretary-General Margaret Joan Anstee lamented that after 45 years, the *Capacity Study* remained "the 'Bible' of UN reform because its precepts are lauded by everyone but put into effect by no one."

The UN needs to be fitter for purpose if it is to be a useful institution in the post-2015 era. But unlike most public organizations, there are no incentives to pursue cost-effectiveness because member states are either the UN's interested patrons or its patronized partners. Such cozy relationships are impediments, but they are also opportunities for reformers: impediments because any proposal that purports to reduce the UN's footprint will meet opposition (from donor countries that are hosts of UN organizations, or developing countries with a large UN presence); but opportunities as well because one or a few influential member states can work to champion change. Fortunately, there are initiatives to pursue.

The most recent overall reform blueprint consists of the 2006 DaO report of the High-level Panel on UN System-

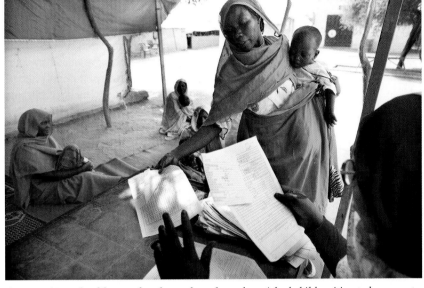

A nurse gives a health record to the mother of a malnourished child waiting to be seen at a clinic of the NGO Kuwait Patient Helping Fund in Abu Shouk camp for Internally Displaced Persons, North Darfur, Sudan. (ALBERT GONZÁLEZ FARRAN/UNAMID)

wide Coherence. The recommendations from this panel, convened by former Secretary-General Kofi Annan, are still pertinent but are only very slowly being implemented. Having more than 1,000 country representatives is wasteful, and while maintaining a universal presence, the UN's country operations should be scaled-back in a growing number of emerging and middle-income countries. The world body should concentrate more on those specific situations in which its operational role will remain indispensable, particularly in conflict-prone countries. In fragile environments, the UN should combine its operations with its other main roles of peacebuilding, including humanitarian relief, and the promotion of human rights and social justice.

The DaO report recommended that the UN system deliver as a unit instead of as a menagerie at the country level, but it never questioned why more than 20 different UN organizations still require separate offices in program countries, and overlooked the fact that transaction costs increased rather than decreased. While not achieving the hopes for one leader, one program, one fund and one office in more than a handful of cases, UN development organizations are collaborating more closely in some instances. An encour-

aging sign was the merger of four entities to form UN Women, the result of painstaking negotiation over four years—the first time in UN history that major institutional entities were closed down and consolidated. The panel also recommended a rapprochement of the UN with the World Bank, which appears to be taking place informally, through growing contacts between the Korean-born heads of the two institutions, hopefully leading to joint programs in some troubled states.

Most recommendations from 2006, however, remain moribund. The proposal to vest the UN Environment Programme with "real authority as the environmental policy pillar of the UN" was widely mooted at the Rio+20 conference in 2012, but it has barely advanced. The Commission for Sustainable Development was re-vamped but falls short of the authoritative Sustainable Development Board envisaged to oversee and drive the DaO initiative. Two of the recommendations that would have done more than any others to bring greater coherence to the system have not materialized: the appointment of a respected development thinker to oversee the entire system, and the establishment of single consolidated funds for the UN development system in each country.

The United Nations Stabilization Mission in Haiti's (MINUSTAH) Civil Affairs and the Brazilian UN Peacekeepers held a Civilian/Military Community event at a school in the volatile neighborhood of Cité Soleil.
(LOGAN ABASSI/MINUSTAH/UN PHOTO)

There have been fledgling efforts to promote coherence under Ban Ki-moon, the current UN Secretary-General. Some business practices are being harmonized. More system-wide evaluations are envisaged. A cautious plan has been proposed to align seven research and training entities. That such seemingly obvious steps are still merely under consideration and viewed as stretches is a reflection of the magnitude of the task.

Some new initiatives could have a beneficial impact. In an attempt to bring the different parts of the system together and more partners into the UN's work, the secretary-general has launched several programs: Every Woman, Every Child; Sustainable Energy for All; the Global Education First Initiative; Zero Hunger Challenge; the Scaling-Up Nutrition Movement; and the Call to Action on Sanitation. These initiatives demonstrate the continued proclivity for accretion—adding but never retiring redundant relics. However, if they encourage existing UN organizations to take charge and extend partnerships, perhaps they will have helped to move the UN toward the kind of transformation required.

The requisite overhaul is not only urgent but also unprecedented. Radical reform has been elusive and change incremental. As former UN Deputy Secretary-General Mark Malloch-Brown puts it: "a long period of tinkering with the UN machinery may actually allow the growing gap between performance and need to increase….[T]he call for reform is likely to grow steadily" and "the question remains when, not if." The authors' own research and interpretation of the last seven decades of development efforts show more and more moving parts but with less and less synergy, as well as higher transaction costs related to coordination for both host governments and for UN staff, but with too few results. ■

Future reform

The UN's operations, particularly in developing and transition countries, are its most visible feature, and most conversations about reform concern the operational delivery capabilities of the UN development system through its technical cooperation activities. But such assistance has diverged too far from the other primary function of the UN system—its contribution to the ways that states, organizations and individuals think about problems and formulate meaningful policies. The UN's development goals are the products of this ideational role, although in the case of the SDGs, the UN Secretariat's intellectual contribution has been minimal. This absence of original UN thinking belies the findings of a decade of research from the United Nations Intellectual History Project, which demonstrated the world organization's exceptional role in the generation of ideas, norms, principles, data and standards. In many ways, these efforts have been a singular contribution, one that can thrive even amid the system's institutional silos.

Human development

However, translating ideas into practice is where the UN falters. There are two parts to the problem. The first consists of attempting to define a unifying development paradigm by bringing together the many solid ideas that have emerged from the system. In the 1990s, for instance, the UN Development Programme (UNDP) came up with "human development," which was a value-driven riposte to the Washington Consensus that emphasized liberal economic reform without considering the human costs. Defined over the course of many global, regional and country reports, human development is a paradigm that places individual well-being, not only economic growth, as the central target of human progress. Inherent in the concept are the rights, capacities and opportunities of the individual and the creation of an enabling environment. Unfortunately, human development never caught on across the entire UN development system—not because of any inconsistency with UN values, but rather because the atomized system could never find and occupy common ground.

So, human development was "copyrighted" as a UNDP idea. The rest of the system was still defining development in narrower dimensions by organizational sectors and mandates: economic, social and environmental. These are the three facets of "sustainable development" that anchor the SDGs. However it is unlikely that sustainable development will "broaden the frame of reference and community in which development issues are understood, decisions are taken, and implementation is executed and evaluated," as outlined by Ban Ki-moon. In fact, it is likely to permit an array of isolated efforts to be displayed side-by-side, with different UN organizations championing favored angles. A coherent paradigm would require the kind of collaboration across agencies and perspectives that cannot easily come from the UN development system as currently configured.

The second part of the problem arises in putting the UN's ideas into practice—"operationalizing" development, however defined, by every part of the system. UN organizations are a source of original research and ideas, on which global norms and standards are based. They embody the universal values for which the UN is rightly cherished. In areas such as human rights, gender equality, health, employment and environmental standards, the UN is the critical source of value-based global norms that aspire to universal application. But the expansion in the numbers and scope of these standards is not matched by the efforts of the UN development system to help ensure compliance.

The MDGs' agenda at least focused the system on the goals that it had helped to establish. But too much of the UN's technical cooperation—the backbone of its operations—is spent on free-standing project initiatives, many only tenuously connected to the system's own norms. The World Health Organization cannot itself deliver better health to the world, including halting the spread of Ebola, but it can actively promote its own healthcare norms and raise funds for its own niche activities. The International Labor Organization mobilizes resources to help build labor-intensive rural roads and also sets up cooperatives, but its principal vocation is ensuring greater compliance with the conditions and safety standards it established for the world's workforce. The Office for Drugs and Crime has sought for many years to stamp out narcotics cultivation, without success; much more important are its efforts to promote and monitor compliance with the UN Convention against Corruption (of which it is the custodian) but here too headway is hard to verify. The UN Industrial Development Organization has played a role in helping industrial enterprises to phase out the use of ozone-destroying substances,

but it is also involved in many other industry-related activities that have no normative footings but are attractive to donors. The UN development system could be more effective if it were to expend more resources on issues in which it has been instrumental in setting standards, and less in areas where there are growing numbers of alternative sources of assistance.

Getting the UN system and its staff to think and act more normatively will necessitate changes in organizational culture. In 2013, the secretary-general revived a proposal originally put forward by his predecessor that he called "Human Rights Up Front." The purpose of the new initiative has been described as an attempt to ensure that the UN system "takes early and effective action, as mandated by the Charter and UN resolutions, to prevent or respond to large-scale violations of human rights or international humanitarian law. It seeks to achieve this by realizing a cultural change within the UN system, so that human rights and the protection of civilians are seen as a system-wide core responsibility." Officials are encouraged to embrace moral courage and prevent serious and large-scale human rights violations. It remains to be seen whether cultural change results, and whether

staff can count on the support of the UN's leadership in taking a moral stand on rights issues.

At the global level, the importance of having a system is nowhere more in evidence than in the UN's attempts to face up to major, longer-term development challenges. If the UN is to have an impact in improving the planet's environmental management, climate change, food security, migration and many other issues, it requires marshaling "coalitions of the willing" of different organizations within its own development pillar (technical, normative and operational).

2016 marks the beginning of a renewed development agenda and coincides with the last year of current Secretary-General Ban Ki-moon's tenure. One of his legacies seemingly will have been to preside over the continuing decline of the UN's development system. Inertia will not be a viable organizational strategy for the next secretary-general.

The discouraged reader may very well be tempted to ask, is the system actually capable of fundamental change? We have been asking that question in a series of public opinion surveys over the last four years among people worldwide who support and are usually familiar with the UN's work.

United Nations Secretary-General Ban Ki-moon rides a bike made of bamboo during a meeting with the Ghana Bamboo Bike Initiative at the UN Climate Conference in Warsaw, Poland, November 20, 2013. (ALIK KEPLICZ/AP PHOTO)

Samples in the U.S. would undoubtedly be more indifferent and probably more hostile toward the very notion of international cooperation and the role for the UN system. However, it is worth noting that a large majority of informed respondents worldwide in the latest expert survey of December 2014 were "optimists" (77%) who maintained that the system could change, while only a quarter remained pessimistic. The proportion of pessimists was smaller among emerging powers (15%) and larger among developed countries (31%). Over the years, voices from some 10,000 citizens (two thirds from the global South) have also identified possible directions for UN reform, with more optimists than pessimists.

Rankings of individual organizations have shown very wide ranges of perception of both relevance and effectiveness. An informed global expert public has called for the merger of many overlapping UN organizations. For the system as a whole, the most urgent and feasible changes are to modernize business practices, which are too complex, expand partnerships with other development organizations and clarify the relationship with the Washington-based financial institutions. The views in the global South about the urgency of UN reform are often more strident than those of the North, although the support for a UN system with less state control and more norm-making and operational autonomy are feeble everywhere.

Whether the UN's development glass is half-full or half-empty, clearly there is very substantial room for improvement to get the United Nations that we want for the world that we want, or even for the world that we have. Does an opportunity arise with the forthcoming election of the next secretary-general? ■

Next SG must be a reformer

For only the second time—the first was in 1996—the electoral campaigns for the American president and the United Nations secretary-general are running in parallel. Both promise to be long and protracted. Each has a growing slate of presumptive candidates pounding flesh and employing lobbyists.

But the next year will witness very different selection processes. U.S. presidential aspirants will be watched, tested, and paraded in front of respectful and hostile audiences in a vetting that is far more prolonged than the electoral campaign for most heads of state. Americans undoubtedly will be fatigued by and fed-up with the seemingly never-ending process, but the citizens of the planet are at the opposite end of the spectrum: they have virtually no say in selecting the UN's top official.

Indeed, the UN Charter says precious little about how the secretary-general is to be selected. If past is prelude, however, the successful candidate for the planet's top job will, as spelled out in Charter Article 97, be rubber-stamped by the General Assembly after being selected by an extraordinarily compact electoral college of five: the veto-wielding members of the Security Council—the U.S., the United Kingdom, China, France and Russia. The main "tests" will be geographic origin, which this time favors Eastern Europe, and perhaps gender. "Why not a female secretary-general for the first time?" rhetorically asks Equality Now, a network of women's rights groups.

After seven decades of elections for individuals based as much on accident as on merit, the decibel level is growing for a shakeup in the traditional UN process of leadership selection. The 1 for 7 Billion campaign emerged in 2015 and uses social media and other means to call for a more transparent process, including a shortlist for all member states to evaluate. Importantly, it has called for geography to be secondary and for the more inclusive process to identify a secretary-general who is "highly skilled, competent, persuasive and visionary." If seven billion constituents along with 188 other member states cannot vote, could their views at least be better represented? Could some modest accountability not be introduced into the usual great power manipulation? How about a basic job description?

Only Pollyanna would hope for a comprehensive vetting in 2016, but calls for change may have more traction than in the past. In early September 2015, the General Assembly passed resolution 69/321 that asked the presidents of the assembly and of the Security Council to send a joint letter to states describing the entire process and to "conduct informal dialogues or meetings" with declared candidates. It also called for candidates' names and CVs to be circulated.

An absolutely essential element of any candidate's platform should be a candidate's "vision" for the future shape of a reformed UN system and how to make the most of its 80,000 international civil servants (and some 125,000 military and civilian peacekeepers). While geopolitical change is beyond the writ of the secretary-general, shaking up the system and its staff members is not.

Resigning in utter frustration, the first incumbent, Trygve Lie of

Box 2: UN secretaries-general 1945–2016		
SECRETARY-GENERAL	**NATIONALITY**	**DATES OF SERVICE**
Trygve Halvdan Lie	Norway	2/1946–9/1952
Dag Hammarskjöld	Sweden	4/1953–9/1961
U Thant	Burma	9/1961–12/1971
Kurt Waldheim	Austria	1/1972–12/1981
Javier Pérez de Cuéllar	Peru	1/1982–12/1991
Boutros Boutros-Ghali	Egypt	1/1992–12/1996
Kofi Annan	Ghana	1/1997–12/2006
Ban Ki-moon	S. Korea	1/2007–12/2016

Norway, described his seven years at the helm as "the most impossible job in the world." In addition to being battered by politics, he and his successors have unsuccessfully tried to make sense of a fragmented and decentralized system engaged in virtually every sphere of human activity: peace and security operations; humanitarian assistance; promotion of human rights and justice; establishment of norms and conventions; and the provision of technical assistance for peace-building and development.

The job is all the more complex because within the system, the "boss" is only *primus inter pares*. The UN's specialized agencies are independently funded and managed, answering only to their own governors and donors. Even the special funds and programs of the UN proper are largely autonomous.

The last two decades have witnessed a few promising innovations: the International Criminal Court; the Global Compact; the Peacebuilding Commission; and the Human Rights Council. However, these innovations have added new moving parts. UN member states and secretariats normally respond to emerging problems by creating new mechanisms, often putting existing UN organizations in unworkable configurations but virtually never getting rid of old institutions. More and more organizations are at the table but without a common menu.

As indicated earlier, the painful process of formulating new SDGs has been a predictable, if lamentable, reflection of the cumbersome system at work. The UN's progressive marginalization is one reason not to be complacent about their implementation.

A second reason is the evidence from past attempts at reform that a strong leader committed to change, and with the vision and communication skills to match, can make a difference. Key reform initiatives could and should be on the radar screen of the next secretary-general. The question is not what and whether, but when and how.

President Barack Obama (center) and world leaders pose for a photograph before a UN Peacekeeping Summit, September 28, 2015, at UN headquarters. (ANDREW HARNIK/AP PHOTO)

Thus, it is critical to identify and elect a secretary-general who understands the flaws in the structure and staffing of the component parts of the dysfunctional UN family and has the knowledge, determination and charisma to confront and hopefully correct at least some of them.

Indeed, the chances for significant institutional change are normally enhanced during the "honeymoon," the first months of a secretary-general's term. Both Boutros Boutros-Ghali and Kofi Annan instituted their most sweeping staffing and management changes in 1992, 1997 and 2002. Let's insist on similar initiatives from 2016's successful candidate.

The 1 for 7 Billion campaign has also recommended a single term of six or seven years for the next secretary-general (instead of a renewable one of five years), a proposal that has been raised repeatedly over the years but without success. Doing so would require overcoming tradition and regional claims for parity but not a Charter revision. And it could eliminate the caution that customarily accompanies concerns for re-election and jolt the eventual nominee with a greater sense of urgency to strengthen — and actually transform — the world organization.

Policy implications in DC

While the UN should, it undoubtedly will not figure in the presidential debates or American voting decisions for the November 8, 2016, presidential election. Nonetheless, a crucial input will come from the presidential transition team about the UN's next leader, and what he or she should do with the atomized UN system.

In spite of the obvious shortcomings resulting from the SDGs kitchen-sink, these goals nonetheless provide a framework of an ambitious development agenda for 2016–30. This framework contains the vocabulary for the next administration to exert leadership in pushing for sensible priorities and sequencing for concessional finance and investment by the U.S. and by the Washington-based international financial institutions.

The same kind of supportive multilateral rhetoric and initiatives that characterized the early Obama and Bush administrations could well have an impact in Washington. Let's hope that the muddled process of formulating the SDGs will not be implemented by an ineffectual new UN secretary-general. The selection of that person in late 2016 will provide a crucial opportunity for the next U.S. administration to weigh in and help save the UN system from itself. ∎

discussion questions

1. Should there be more incentives provided by the UN to countries that are able to meet certain Sustainable Development Goals?

2. If nominated to be the next Secretary-General, what reforms would you push? In addition, what initiatives would you undertake in order to make the SDGs more successful?

3. Of the 17 Sustainable Development Goals, which is the one that seems the most likely to be achieved? What about the least? Why?

4. Do you think that there is too much power vested in the Security Council veto? How would you change this system without encroaching on any of the permanent member's interests?

5. Is there a global issue left unaddressed by the SDGs? Do you share the authors' opinion that the SDGs are trying to take on too much at once?

6. Which of the "five weaknesses" of the UN mentioned by the authors has the most detrimental effect on the organization? Which one is the easiest to solve and how should we go about it?

Don't forget: Ballots start on page 99!

suggested readings

Browne, Stephen, **The United Nations Development Programme and System.** New York, Routledge, 2011. 192 pp. Browne offers a brief overview of the system of organizations that delivers technical assistance in developing countries.

Browne, Stephen and Weiss, Thomas G. , eds., **Post-2015 UN Development: Making Change Happen?** New York: Routledge, 2014. 276 pp. This set of essays examines the problems and prospects of the development challenges facing the UN system.

Chesterman, Simon, ed., **Secretary of General? The UN Secretary-General in World Politics**. Cambridge: Cambridge University Press, 2007. 280 pp. Gordenker, Leon. **The UN Secretary-General and Secretariat**. London: Routledge, 2010. 126 pp. These books provide insights into the leadership and administration of the world organization.

Jolly, Richard, Emmerij, Louis and Weiss, Thomas G., **UN Ideas That Changed the World**. Bloomington: Indiana University Press, 2009. 339 pp. This final volume in the United Nations Intellectual History Project Series examines the UN's exceptional role in the generation of ideas, norms, principles, data and standards.

Murphy, Craig N., **The UN Development Programme: A Better Way?** New York, Cambridge University Press, 2006. 392 pp. This authoritative history of UNDP argues for the enduring relevance of the network's founding principles.

United Nations, **Delivering as One.** New York, United Nations, 2006. Available free online at: <http://www.un.org/en/ga/deliveringasone/pdf/mainreport.pdf>. This report offers an evaluation of the Development Program and System, and proposes solutions to UN structural fragmentation.

Weinlich, Silk, **Reforming Development Cooperation at the United Nations: An Analysis of Policy Positions and Actions of Key States on Reform Options**. Bonn: German Development Institute, 2011. 152 pp. Weinlich puts forward key issues from the point of view of key actors about the reform of the development system.

Weiss, Thomas G., **What's Wrong with the United Nations and How to Fix It**. Cambridge: Polity Press, 2016. This book contains a concise list of the UN's ailments and suggests possible prescriptions.

To access web links to these readings, as well as links to additional, shorter readings and suggested web sites,

GO TO www.greatdecisions.org

and click on the topic under Resources, on the right-hand side of the page

Climate geopolitics:
The road to Paris and beyond

by William Sweet

President Barack Obama looks at Bear Glacier, which has receded 1.8 miles in approximately 100 years, while on a boat tour to see the effects of climate change in Resurrection Cove in Seward, Alaska. (ANDREW HARNIK/AP PHOTO)

In what amounted to a full-court press, President Obama, Secretary of State Kerry, and White House chief science adviser John Holdren travelled to Alaska at the end of August 2015 to focus public attention on dangerous climate change. Noting that during the last 60 years warming has been twice as great in Alaska as in the contiguous U.S., the President said that the state now has one of the highest coastal erosion rates in the world and that its wildfire season is a month longer than it was in 1950. The point, he said, is that "climate change is no longer some far-off problem. It is happening here. It is happening now." Everything will be affected, he continued, as changes get more dramatic with each passing year. As for those who continue to deny or ignore the science, "they are increasingly alone. They are on their own shrinking island."

Amplifying the President's message, Holdren said that with the increase in average global temperature by 1.6° Fahrenheit since the end of the 19th century, more precipitation is falling as rain rather than snow, and more water is lost to evaporation, flood runoff and earlier snowmelt. In the Arctic, sea ice covers 40% less water than when satellite monitoring began in 1970, and the melting of permafrost is causing human communities to sink and methane—a greenhouse gas much more potent than carbon dioxide—to be released. Because of what Holdren called a greater "waviness" in the jet stream, the so-called polar vortex has moved south,

WILLIAM SWEET *is an adjunct professor of history and environmental policy in New York City who often writes about science and politics. He is completing a book about global climate diplomacy that will appear in 2016.*

(Left) Residents clear debris near the shoreline on November 23, 2013, in Tacloban, Leyte, Philippines, nearly two weeks after the devastating Typhoon Haiyan hit. The typhoon has been described as one of the most powerful ever to hit land, leaving thousands dead and hundreds of thousands homeless. (DONDI TAWATAO/GETTY IMAGES) *(Right) Pakistanis attend a funeral for unclaimed people who died from extreme weather—in this case, a devastating heat wave—in Karachi, Pakistan, June 26, 2015.* (SHAKIL ADIL/AP PHOTO)

producing stubbornly frigid winters throughout the upper plains states and Midwest.

The point of it all, self-evidently, was to rally U.S. support for policies to address climate change, in particular for a strong outcome at the Paris climate conference that will take place during the first two weeks of December 2015. Kerry compared the gravity of climate change to the crisis that faced the advanced industrial democracies in the 1930s. Leaders rose to the occasion then, he said, and can again now. But what Kerry did not say was this: climate change has come to be a highly partisan issue in U.S. politics, and as a result, U.S. leadership in global climate diplomacy is still widely seen as erratic, uncertain and unreliable.

As the U.S. heads into a presidential election year, the Republican candidates have unanimously cast doubt on whether costly action to address climate change is warranted, though there is some variation in their positions about whether the Earth is warming and whether human activity is largely to blame. Democrats are betting that a large majority of the public, even in the so-called "red states," wants to see

action. A steady drumbeat of alarming events and disconcerting scientific reports has clearly had an impact on public opinion and leaders. But as concern has climbed, there is also a growing awareness that even a country as rich and powerful as the U.S. cannot solve the whole problem all by itself. And so, even among those who are concerned about climate, people worry that the U.S. may not be getting other countries to do enough.

In California, where an ambitious bill to cut petroleum use by 50% by 2030 was under consideration in the summer of 2015, the Republican Assembly leader said her party was eager to help find solutions to the climate problem. "My son has asthma—of course I want clean air," she told *The New York Times*. "We want to be leaders," she said, "but not when there are no followers." As it happened, the California bill had to be withdrawn for lack of adequate support.

Visibility of warming

Scholars on climate policy used to routinely describe the problem as especially challenging because it is so abstract: a matter of gradually increasing long-term risks, none of them apparent to people in their daily lives. A favorite metaphor was the frog put in a pan of water that is very gradually heated. The frog notices nothing, swims happily around in circles…and then suddenly dies.

That metaphor is obsolete. In the last

years there has been a steady stream of unusual and violent weather events that were consistent with global warming, and in some cases almost certainly were directly caused by it. Easily the most dramatic was Typhoon Haiyan, which tore through Philippine villages at speeds up to 196 miles-per-hour on November 8, 2014, leaving more than 6,300 people dead. The year before, exceptionally severe flooding in India claimed the lives of several thousand people, a tragic event that, experts said, would become increasingly common as Himalayan glaciers melted and storm tracks moved. Last year, an equally unusual heat wave in Pakistan suffocated many hundreds in the country's urban slums. The same month, North Korea's official national news agency said the country was suffering its worst drought in a century.

Among such events, probably the most catastrophic was the severe drought that ravaged Syria beginning in 2006, setting the stage for that country's civil war and mass emigration. Experts attribute the misfortunes that followed more to the Assad government's inept and discriminatory reactions to the drought than to the drought itself. But climate and security specialists generally blame the drought in large part on global warming, referring to climate change in such situations as a "threat multiplier," as Obama noted in a speech to the Coast Guard Academy of May 20, 2015.

Before you read, download the companion **Glossary** that includes definitions and a guide to acronyms and abbreviations used in the article. Go to **www.great decisions.org** and select a topic in the Resources section on the right-hand side of the page.

Yale historian Timothy Snyder, best known for *Bloodlands*, his account of World War II's devastation of Eastern Europe and western Russia, worries we may be entering a new era of environmental panic and genocide. "So far, poor people in Africa and the Middle East have borne the brunt of the suffering. The mass murder of at least 500,000 Rwandans in 1994 followed a decline in agricultural production for several years before.... In Sudan, drought drove Arabs into the lands of African pastoralists in 2003. The Sudanese government sided with the Arabs and pursued a policy of eliminating the Zaghawa, Masalit and Fur peoples in Darfur and surrounding regions."

But Americans do not need to look across oceans to be concerned. Hurricane Katrina, Superstorm Sandy, the great Midwestern drought of 2012, the current California drought, the brutal winters of 2013 and 2014—both associated with the southward shift of the polar vortex—all of these events have been consistent with, or aggravated by, climate change. The Texas heat wave of 2011, as well as the Russian heat and fires of 2010—which killed tens of thousands and helped send global food prices soaring—were so far outside the range of normal probability, some experts say they were quite simply caused by global warming.

The scientific jury is still out on whether climate change was an important cause of the ongoing California drought. But there is no doubt among experts that higher rates of evaporation associated with higher average temperatures have been a major element in magnifying the drought's effects. Among the most dire were last year's unusually ferocious forest fires, some of which were the most terrifying ever experienced.

Looking ahead, a January 2015 report focused on the anticipated impacts of global warming in the U.S. heartland. The research project, chaired by former New York mayor Michael Bloomberg, former Treasury secretary Henry Paulson and the venture capitalist Thomas Steyer, painted a grim picture of what the Midwest will look like by century's end on "business as usual" projections.

The average Chicago resident will experience more summer days over 95°F than the average Texan does today, and the average Missourian as many as the average Arizonan, the "Risky Business" report concluded. Nevertheless, in the shorter run, higher winter temperatures might translate into lower heating bills and longer growing seasons.

Slouching toward Bethlehem?

Locally and regionally, not all the near-term effects of climate change are necessarily bad, which is a legitimate reason why many Americans are uncertain about whether there should be action to address climate change, how aggressive it should be and how much it should cost. However, anybody paying attention in recent years to scientific reports will have been treated to a steady stream of worse-than-expected findings.

On July 2015, according to the the National Snow and Ice Data Center, about half of Greenland's massive ice sheet had turned liquid since late spring, a highly abnormal event for the time of year; temperatures higher than 100° F in many part of western Europe were partly to blame. Four months earlier, there was news of the highest temperature ever recorded in Antarctica, 63.5°F.

In May, a NASA study was released indicating that the remaining portion of the Larsen Ice Shelf—a sheet covering an area about half the size of Rhode Island—would disintegrate completely within a few years; two thirds of the shelf had broken loose in 2002. If the entire world's fossil energy supplies were burned, the Antarctic ice sheet would melt in its entirety, causing sea levels to rise 50 meters, another study found.

In August, the *Journal of Glaciology* published a study indicating that the world's glaciers were retreating faster than ever before. A study in the April issue of *Nature Geoscience* had concluded that glaciers in western Canada would lose 70% of their mass by the end of the century.

NOAA, the National Oceanic and Atmospheric Administration, reported in July that the Northern Atmosphere during the first half of 2015 was not merely the hottest it had ever been, but a third of a degree warmer than any previous half-year in 135 years. With that kind of heating trend, melting glaciers and collapsing polar ice sheets, it is hardly surprising that seas are rising at accelerating rates. According to NASA, it is almost inevitable that ocean levels will climb by about three feet (or a

meter) in the coming decades, no matter what we do to curtail greenhouse emissions. Taking the combined risks from snowmelt and rising oceans into account, major deltaic river systems facing higher flood risks include the Chao Phraya (Thailand), Han (South Korea), Irrawaddy (Myanmar), Limpopo (southern Africa), Tone (Japan) and Yangtze (China). Surprisingly, the two systems in which risks may rise most sharply of all in the next decades are the Mississippi and Rhine.

With oceans absorbing most of the heat from global warming, questions are being raised about whether a saturation point is being reached and what will happen then. The oceans are also absorbing about half the carbon dioxide emitted into the atmosphere. Their acidification is one of the major factors in apocalyptic predictions of mass oceanic extinctions.

Climate activism

Because of the obvious effects of climate change, those most concerned increasingly see it as a moral issue, requiring direct action going beyond normal electoral politics. On college campuses, a campaign to induce universities to divest fossil fuel stocks has steadily gained ground, arousing intense controversy at some institutions such as Harvard. An analogous campaign has sought to get science museums to cut their ties with the Koch brothers because of the immense funds David H. and Charles G. Koch spend to support candidates who oppose aggressive action on climate, and to publicize work casting doubt on climate science. Greenpeace and the Sierra Club are among the organizations behind the anti-Koch petition drive.

Environmentalists have so far largely eschewed resort to civil disobedience, except in the case of the Key-stone pipeline project, which inspired many hundreds to turn out for protests in front of the White House and some to chain themselves to its fence. Several hundred were arrested. If global climate action is seen as grossly inadequate in the coming years, it can be safely assumed that much more civil disobedience will occur, and not just in the U.S.

Ironically, the U.S. public at large, though generally concerned about climate change, has been rather relaxed about the issue. In recent years, in fact, Americans seem to have become somewhat less sharply concerned, even as evidence of global warming piles up all around. Those who study the very complex and ambiguous attitudes of Americans have concluded that there really is no one public when it comes to climate change—there actually are a handful of publics with distinct mindsets. ∎

America's climate publics

Perhaps the most fundamental and abiding fact about U.S. public opinion on climate change is that it quite different from Europe's. Since the beginning of the 1990s, when the UN Framework Convention on Climate Change (UNFCCC) was negotiated and concluded in Rio de Janeiro, Europeans have been consistently worried about global warming and rank it high on their lists of issues deserving priority treatment. In most European countries, in contrast to the U.S., there has been hardly any partisan divide on the issue. Conservative and liberal governments alternate in power, without there being much discernible impact on a country's climate policy.

Students of the subject really are not sure why there is such a gulf between U.S. and European opinion, but a variety of factors clearly are at work besides just varying perceptions of the basic science. The top-down decision making apparatus of the European Union (EU) has helped steady policy, for example. So too have the European traditions of economic planning, where the costs and benefits of policies are customarily negotiated and allocated among major stakeholders, be they business, labor, regions or even demographic groups. It may just be that Europeans generally are aware almost from infancy that the benign climate in which their civilization has flourished is an anomaly; thus, any major change to it would almost certainly be for the worse. (Whether this is their attitude nobody seems to know, evidently because nobody has thought to ask.)

In any event, the difference is stark. In one survey taken in 2010—and there are many others yielding similar results—65% of Americans said they were "worried" about climate change, as compared to 84% of Europeans. "Only 43% of Americans [were] willing to sacrifice economically to slow global warming, compared to 69% of Europeans," Nigel Purvis and Andrew Stevenson observed in a German Marshall Fund paper. "While Europeans ranked climate change as one of the world's most serious problems (above international terrorism and a major global economic downturn), even among Democrats in the U.S. it ranked below health care, education, social security, the budget deficit and illegal immigration."

"According to one prominent conservative pollster," Purvis and Stevenson continued, "in the U.S. stopping 'climate change' is the least popular aspect of the climate agenda, paling in comparison to support for reducing dependence on foreign oil or creating clean energy jobs."

Climate communication findings

Yale's Anthony Leiserowitz and George Mason's Edward Maibach have done by far the most authoritative studies of U.S. opinion about global warming. Looking in detail at American attitudes over time, they concluded that there are really six U.S. climate publics: the alarmed, the concerned, the cautious, the disengaged, the doubtful and the dismissive. Those alarmed or concerned, as of 2012–13, represented well over a third of Americans, while those doubtful or dismissive were barely more than a fifth. About a quarter of the population was cautiously unde-cided, and only 8% outright dismissive of the whole problem. Plainly, quite a few more Americans are worried about climate change than not, and very few think it is a problem not worth worrying about at all.

By rather distinct majorities, Ameri-cans do want to see their elected offi-cials, as well as corporations and their fellow citizens, take action on climate. In a spring 2014 Leiserowitz-Maibach survey, Americans said by a 4–1 margin that they would reward political candi-dates who promised action on climate or punish those who resisted action. Yet at the same time Americans seem to be profoundly skeptical about how much the federal government can actually do. In a November 2013 poll, just 14% said they were very confident government policy could reduce global warming, while 46% had little to no confidence.

Separately, polling by Stanford psy-chologist Jon Krosnick has indicated that even in "red states" like Texas and Oklahoma, most people acknowledge the reality of global warming. These kinds of findings naturally have at-tracted the attention of Democratic strategists and leaders. The chief U.S. climate negotiator, Todd D. Stern, has expressed confidence that climate change action will be a winning posi-tion for Democrats in upcoming elec-tions. John Podesta, until recently Obama's top-level adviser with special responsibility for climate policy, now is serving as chairman of Hillary Clinton's presidential campaign. Podesta was the principal negotiator of a U.S.-China cli-mate agreement in fall 2014 that was widely hailed as a breakthrough in cli-mate diplomacy.

However the 2016 presidential pri-maries shake out, it is generally taken for granted that the Democratic candidate will favor continued strong action on cli-mate and, most likely, defend whatever agreement Obama co-negotiated in Paris in December 2015, if there is one. The Republican candidate will express skep-ticism about taking expensive actions on climate change and find reasons to be critical of the way Democrats have been conducting climate diplomacy. ∎

The China problem

A woman wearing a mask rides in the heavy smog on October 21, 2015, in Binzhou, Shan-dong Province, China. (CHINAFOTOPRESS/GETTY IMAGES)

The 1997 Kyoto Protocol, proceed-ing from the basic principle of "common but differentiated responsi-bility" as stated in the 1992 Framework Convention, required emissions cuts of the advanced industrial countries but not the developing countries, including fast-growing ones like China and India. Kyoto required Europe to cut its emis-sions 8% by 2008–12 by comparison with 1990, and the U.S., by 7%. Europe kept and exceeded that requirement, but the U.S. ended up rejecting the proto-col. Its emissions, instead of decreas-ing 7% in the commitment period, rose about 15%.

If in opting out of Kyoto the U.S. hoped to maneuver China in the direc-tion of accepting emissions limits, that strategy in the short and medium term was a complete failure. In the 15 years following Kyoto, China installed new coal generating capacity equivalent to England's entire electric power system every few years. Between 2005 and 2009 it added the equivalent of the en-tire U.S. coal fleet, which at that time was still producing about half of Ameri-ca's electricity. Between 2010 and 2013 it added half that amount again, burn-ing by the end about four times as much

coal as the U.S. and almost seven times as much as the EU. As a result, China surpassed the U.S. as the world's top carbon emitter around 2006 and, a de-cade later, was generating about twice the U.S. emissions—roughly 10 billion tons of CO_2 versus 5 billion.

And so, although the official U.S. attitude toward China had initially aroused considerable suspicion and hostility among all the countries that had ratified and implemented the proto-col, by the end of the first decade of this century foreign leaders were grudging-ly admitting that the U.S. had a point.

Projected PRC emissions

The Framework Convention, among other significant things, required indus-trialized countries to report their emis-sions on a regular basis. The treaty's secretariat compiles and edits those reports, posting them regularly on its website. Thus, one can say with au-thority, for example, that the EU kept and indeed surpassed its Kyoto com-mitment to cut its emissions by 8% by 2012—and that the U.S. did not.

Since China was not required to provide greenhouse gas reports, one must rely on a variety of independent

7

sources for estimates of its current and projected emissions, and those estimates vary widely. Among the major organizations assessing the situation are the Netherlands Environmental Assessment Agency, the International Energy Agency (IEA) and the Lawrence Berkeley Laboratory. The Dutch estimates, which usually are at the higher end, put China's 2013 emissions at 10.3 billion tons of CO_2, while the IEA and Lawrence Berkeley have them at about 8.5, a difference of more than 1.5 billion tons and an amount greater than Japan's 2013 total emissions.

Crude back-of-the-envelope projections based on any of those estimates would put China's 2030 emissions as much as three times higher than their 2000 levels, an outcome bordering on the catastrophic from a global point of view. At the 2009 Copenhagen climate conference, world leaders agreed that warming should be limited to 2° Celsius to ward off "dangerous climate change," another basic phrase in the UNFCCC. It is more than a little hard to see, on any reasonable forecasts, how China's projected emissions can be compatible with that goal.

U.S.-China 'breakthrough'

In October 2014, a month after a UN Climate Summit in New York and a large public demonstration in the city's streets, China and the U.S. announced a surprise bilateral agreement, committing China to have its emissions peak no later than 2030, and the U.S. to cut its emissions by 26%–28% by 2025 relative to 2005 levels. Previously the Chinese, with the support of virtually all developing countries, had flatly refused to make any kind of pledge at all about their future emissions. China's adoption of a peaking commitment represented a fundamental shift in its diplomatic position and reflected the government's sharper focus on climate policy.

The bilateral agreement, negotiated in great secrecy, owed a great deal to aggressive personal diplomacy on the part of the Americans. Secretary of State Kerry entertained a top-level Chinese counterpart at a famous seafood restaurant in Boston, taking the opportunity to tell him about how only decades earlier it would have been unthinkable to eat fish from the city's highly polluted harbor. Podesta travelled to China to negotiate details. Obama himself met with China's first-ranked vice premier Zhang Gaoli during the UN Climate Summit to seal the deal.

Podesta hailed the agreement as a breakthrough; he said China's clean energy commitment—the amount of non-carbon energy it would deploy by 2030—was like adding a whole new China on top of what they already are. But critics of the agreement could just as well say that the total increase in Chinese emissions by 2030 also will be just like adding another China—or even two. ∎

The road to Paris

The foundation stones for the ongoing conduct of climate diplomacy were laid in the 1980s and early 1990s, at a time when the adoption of the Montreal Protocol calling for the elimination of CFCs (chlorofluorocarbons) was setting an example of how new scientific knowledge could translate directly into global action. A G7 meeting in Toronto in June 1988 requested the UN Environment Program and the World Meteorological Organization to establish the Intergovernmental Panel on Climate Change. A week later, an experts' meeting on the changing atmosphere

Former U.S. Vice President Al Gore introduces a report on the melting of the Greenland ice sheet, on December 14, 2009, on the the 8th day of the UN Climate Change Conference in Copenhagen. (ATTILA KISBENEDEK/AFP/GETTY IMAGES)

in Toronto suggested the negotiation of a Framework Convention on Climate Change, on the model of the convention that had led to the Montreal Protocol. In December 1990, at the initiative of the tiny island state Malta, the UN authorized a formal negotiating process that would produce the 1992 UNFCCC.

The Framework Convention, finalized during a flashy Earth Summit in which many heads of state participated, enunciated the fundamental principles from which all subsequent climate diplomacy would proceed. Scientific uncertainty should not be an excuse for political inaction. The nations of the world should act to prevent dangerous climate change. Action should be based on the principle of common but differentiated responsibilities and capabilities. In each of the following years, there would be a Conference of the Parties (COP), at which the nations of the world would agree upon measures to advance the Convention's general objectives. Those principles are sometimes referred to as "constitutional," and, like the principles of the U.S. Constitution, they are destined to be endlessly discussed and reinterpreted, but rarely to be rejected or modified.

In keeping with the principle of common but differentiated responsibility, the Convention distinguished between developed countries, which would be required to make specific cuts in emissions, and all other countries, which would not. At the first Conference of Parties (COP-1) in Berlin, it was agreed that those cuts would be negotiated at Kyoto in 1997. German Chancellor

Angela Merkel, who at that time was environment minister in the government of Chancellor Helmut Kohl, played an important role.

The road to Copenhagen

The U.S. had a considerable influence in the shaping of the Kyoto Protocol, insisting for example on the inclusion of emissions trading devices—the Clean Development Mechanism, and Joint Implementation—allowing those subject to emissions cuts to purchase emissions permits from entities in countries more able to make the cuts. Nevertheless, the U.S. Senate voted almost unanimously on the eve of Kyoto not to ratify any agreement that required cuts by the U.S. but not by the biggest and fastest growing developing countries, like China. Largely at the best of Vice President Al Gore, the U.S. delegation agreed to a 7% cut at Kyoto, and President Bill Clinton vowed to keep the pledge even if the Senate did not ratify. As far as the U.S. was concerned, however, Kyoto was dead on arrival.

Soon after President George W. Bush took office, his administration repudiated Kyoto and let it be known that the U.S. would not be in a position to start cutting its greenhouse gas emissions until at least 2025. During the next eight years of negotiations, Bush's position made the U.S. almost irrelevant. The Europeans resisted the temptation to eject the U.S. from the COP process, while at the same time ensuring that the Kyoto Protocol would take effect without American participation. To meet entry-of-force requirements, the EU made a deal with President Vladimir Putin, in which Russia obtained membership in the World Trade Organization in exchange for its Kyoto ratification.

The EU proceeded to implement Kyoto successfully, explicitly hoping to set an example to the rest of the world, but without inducing the U.S. to budge. Increasingly its policies were looking well-intentioned but ineffectual and perhaps even sanctimonious. As German researcher Simon Schunz would put it, the EU simply failed to attain its most important policy objectives, and there was "a striking discrepancy

Some of around 1,000 people walk through the streets of Copenhagen on the last day of the UN Climate Summit in Copenhagen, Denmark, December 18, 2009. The demonstration was to protest against the Danish Police arrests of three spokespersons from the group Climate Justice Action. (JENS DIGE/POLFOTO/AP PHOTO)

between its undeniable long-term engagement in global climate politics, and its track record of attempted, but failed leadership by example."

At COP-13 in Bali, the EU and its diplomatic allies among the developing countries (including the most threatened island states), secured a commitment. The Bali Mandate called for a new comprehensive agreement to be reached at the end of 2009 on a "long-term global goal for emission reductions" and on "enhanced action" regarding mitigation (cuts in actual or projected emissions), climate change adaptation, technology, cooperation and international financing.

When most of the major world leaders convened at Copenhagen in December 2009 for COP-15—the first such meeting since Rio in 1992—optimism was running high. The two-part agenda for COP-15 called for agreement on a second round of Kyoto commitments, to cover the period 2012–20, and on a more comprehensive long-term program of climate action. Implicitly it was assumed that the U.S., now led by President Obama, who was striking a very different tone from his predecessor, would get on board.

Debacle or new start?

Those expectations turned out to be naïve. Well before the Copenhagen

conference started, the chief U.S. negotiator let it be known that America would not "do Kyoto"—it would not participate in the second commitment period (2012–20), implicitly or explicitly. The Europeans, in the throes of the worst economic crisis since the Great Depression, caved without a fight. With the conference hurtling toward collapse at the end of the first week, representatives of the developing countries rebelled when a draft treaty circulated that seemed to call into question the principle of common but differentiated responsibility. Representatives of nongovernmental organizations, many of them shut out of the over-booked conference center, seethed.

Meanwhile, the Intergovernmental Panel on Climate Change (IPCC), the main expert body providing the scientific basis for climate negotiations, had taken a hit. A huge volunteer effort involving many thousands of scientists, the IPCC produces comprehensive assessment reports roughly every five years covering the latest scientific findings, expected impacts and alternative policy scenarios. On the eve of the Copenhagen climate conference, there were revelations that it had been careless in its most recent report in handling some key issues (notably the speed with which Himalayan glaciers would

UN Secretary General Ban Ki-moon, left, and Chairman of the IPCC Rajendra K. Pachauri present a comprehensive report by the UN Climate Panel, summarizing the three interim reports previously released on climate changes, November 2, 2014, in Copenhagen, Denmark. (JENS DRESLING/POL-FOTO/AP PHOTO)

melt). Leaked e-mails suggested that some scientists perhaps were tailoring their statements to advance the alarmist cause.

In Copenhagen's eleventh hour, in a dramatic and widely reported development, President Obama and Secretary of State Hillary Clinton crashed a meeting that the leaders of Brazil, China and South Africa were having. They proceeded to hammer out an agreement on the outline of what came to be the Copenhagen Accord. It called upon the nations of the world to limit warming to 2°C, a major objective of the Europeans and especially of Germany. It also promised developing countries financial assistance from developed countries, eventually rising to $100 billion per year by 2020. But it did not require any specific emissions reductions of the industrialized countries, and instead called upon all major emitting countries to make voluntary pledges on emissions reduction, looking ahead to the year 2030.

The Copenhagen Accord could not win unanimous support of the conference, because of opposition from the governments of Cuba, Bolivia and Venezuela. Instead it was merely "noted" by the conference. Many of the major emitting countries did in fact make pledges in Copenhagen, including the U.S., which promised to cut its emissions 17% by 2025 relative to 2005 levels—not 1990, in contrast to the required Kyoto cuts. The effect, intended or not, was to make the U.S. Copenhagen cuts look bigger relative to other countries' Kyoto cuts than they actually were. Indeed, contrary to a widespread impression in the U.S. after Copenhagen, the pledged U.S. cuts were not greater than what Kyoto would have required.

Treaty prospects

Having achieved its diplomatic objectives at Copenhagen only by the skin of its teeth, the U.S. now faced an uphill battle in making its preferred global strategy work. From just about every other nation's point of view, first the U.S. had refused to play ball unless everybody else agreed to play with its ball—the notion of voluntary rather than mandatory cuts; then, having bullied everybody else into playing with its ball, it proceeded to deflate the ball, making 2005 the reference year for pledges rather than 1990.

During the following years, despite the long odds, the U.S. did largely rally the world to its approach based on voluntary pledges, which came to be formalized in the COP process as Independent Nationally Determined Contributions (INDCs). The U.S. success can be attributed in some part to tactful, persistent and methodical diplomacy. But the main factor, no doubt, was simply that Obama put his money where his mouth was.

He had signaled immediately upon being elected President in 2008 that anybody promoting clean, lower-carbon energy would now have a friend in the White House. The 2009 stimulus bill contained more than $30 billion in funding for such projects and the White House sharply boosted fuel efficiency standards for automobiles. But Obama did not talk about climate change in either of his presidential campaigns, and

he never went out of the way to talk about the issue in his first term.

Upon his reelection, however, Obama came out of the closet. On June 25, 2013, he delivered a major address at Georgetown University outlining a comprehensive program, the U.S. Climate Action Plan (CAP). It imposed even more demanding fuel standards for cars and trucks, a wide variety of measures to encourage energy conservation and innovation and support for every kind of low-carbon and zero-carbon technology, including nuclear power. Most importantly, greenhouse gas standards for electricity-generating plants were established—effectively shutting down a large fraction of the country's oldest and dirtiest coal-fired plants. The Georgetown speech delivered everything that Obama's environmentalist supporters had hoped to see from day one.

Obama's CAP made a convincing impression not only on America's European allies but also on China's leadership. It was generally considered the major precondition for the diplomatic breakthrough with China. Not only was the White House promising to make greenhouse gas emissions cuts, it was formulating and implementing specific policies that would achieve those cuts—and doing so in the face of enormous domestic political opposition.

Of course this opposition cuts both ways. All concerned foreign parties understood all too well that a climate treaty with demanding mandatory provisions would never win the approval of a Republican-controlled Senate, or a Senate in which the Republicans had a strong minority. In effect the U.S. Senate was holding hostage the whole world's climate diplomacy. Remarkably, most of the world's other diplomatic players seemed to accept that fact and were willing to agree on a process that would accommodate it.

The way the U.S. negotiating team and its expert advisers hoped to finesse the problem of the U.S. Senate was to win world agreement on a relatively short text that in some sense would be "legally binding," as called for in the Durban agenda for COP-21 in Paris.

(The Durban Mandate for the December 2015 meeting, analogous to the Berlin Mandate for Kyoto, was adopted at COP-17 in South Africa.) A much longer text, which would be somehow attached to the binding agreement, would include all the specific promises that countries had made in their INDCs, plus a variety of other measures. In others words, parties to the Paris treaty would make a legally binding commitment to take a long series of measures that would not be, as such, legally binding. In that fashion was the circle to be squared.

In assessing whatever would come out of Paris, the major criteria would be whether parties' combined INDCs would be large enough collectively to get the world onto a path that might stand some reasonable chance of keeping its warming below 2°C. Provisions to allow for continued strengthening of INDCs in the coming years could compensate for the fact that even if the combined commitments were not adequate initially, they might in time become satisfactory.

A month before the 196 member nations of the Framework Convention were to assemble in Paris to negotiate a new strategic agreement, the UN Climate Secretariat in Bonn issued an assessment of the aggregate pledges that had been submitted so far. It cited findings that the combined pledges might limit warming to 2.7°C in this century, which came closer to the two-degree target than most expert observers would have predicted. But not all such observers bought the claim. Some, like Joseph Romm of Climate Progress, said the correct number was closer to 3.5°C warming in this century.

Assessing Paris

Everybody agrees that a key part of the Paris agreement will concern the mechanisms put in place to get countries to do more to cut emissions over time. "Treaty mechanisms that allow a party to revise its commitment upward allow parties to lock in stronger measures internationally," wrote Daniel Bodansky and Elliot Diringer, two leading experts on climate diplomacy.

A woman working in the toxic smoke that comes out of the ground in Jharia, Jharkhand, India, in October 2014. Methane and other toxic gases constantly spew out from the open wounds in the Earth's crust near a coal mine in Jharia. (JONAS GRATZER/LIGHTROCKET/GETTY IMAGES)

(Bodansky was senior climate negotiator for the U.S., straddling the administrations of Bill Clinton and George W. Bush.) "For example, the Ramsar Wetlands Convention allows parties to list additional wetlands unilaterally. Over time, this has led to a huge increase in the number of wetlands listed as internationally important under the Ramsar Convention." Conversely, fail-safe provisions, for which there is precedent in the GATT (General Agreement on Tariffs and Trade) agreements, could allow for downward revision in certain well specified circumstances.

Going into Paris, the Europeans remained committed on paper to the principle of absolutely binding greenhouse gas emissions cuts. But just about everybody thought that was merely a pro forma negotiating position—or an item that would be traded perhaps for other desired goals. The Europeans were expected to yield in the end, and in fact, during the final months leading up to Paris, negotiators had started to formulate a two-part agreement and to decide what specifics would go into each part.

A much more explosive issue was the matter of financial assistance to developing countries. This is an issue of huge importance to the G-77 and the AOSIS bloc (Alliance of Small Island States)—and legitimately so, as those states worry increasingly about damage limitation, adaptation and emissions reduction. Bodansky and other leading experts agree that dangerous climate change will not be containable in the medium and long run unless the poor countries of the world get much more help than they are getting. But developed countries have been extremely slippery about their Copenhagen commitment to give at least $100 billion per year to help developing countries cope with climate change. The U.S. Congress has flatly refused to authorize any funds in fulfillment of the promise. If the Paris agreement contains binding language requiring rich countries to deliver concretely on the promise, that alone could kill the agreement in the U.S.

In the final months approaching Paris, it was evident to all that if there were an agreement, it would not be an agreement with relatively simple and easily summarized provisions, like the basic principles found in the UNFCCC or the rich country cuts specified in the Kyoto Protocol. Rather, it would be a complex document with several orders of statements and a great many details, many of them quite important. Assessment of the treaty—above all whether it might get the world heading in the direction of a two-degree path—will be a challenging task. ∎

discussion questions

1. Climate change is a long-term problem affecting all countries. To what extent are international political solutions to climate change feasible? Is change more likely to come from private actors and NGOs, rather than governments?

2. The benefits of tackling climate change are huge but spread across the entire world population. Meanwhile, the costs associated with reducing greenhouse gas emissions fall onto a small number of highly polluting industries, with disproportional political leverage in the U.S. and elsewhere. Given this situation, what could be done to frame the issue so that it highlights the positive aspects of tackling climate change?

3. What are the biggest points of contention between U.S. Democrats and Republicans on the climate change debate? Why do you think that is and how will it evolve in the future?

4. How much do you think climate change will factor into the next presidential election? Do you think, as the article suggests, that the Democratic candidate will use the support for climate change legislation against its Republican opponent?

5. What possible incentives could developed countries give the developing countries to curb their emissions? Is it unfair for them to curb emissions to levels wealthy nations long surpassed—i.e. do developing countries have the "right to development?"

6. Do you think that the denial of climate change, or refusing to acknowledge it as an issue, will continue to hinder U.S. presidential candidates? Is there a chance that this stance could become popular enough that it benefits candidates?

7. Is there any chance that the climate change debate will become the main concern of the American people, or will it constantly be overshadowed by other issues such as global terrorism, the economy or public welfare?

Don't forget: Ballots start on page 99!

suggested readings

Benedick, Richard Elliott, **Ozone Diplomacy: New Directions in Safeguarding the Planet.** Cambridge, MA, Harvard University Press, 1991 and 1998. 449 pp. Though not a new book, this is an absorbing account of the diplomacy that ultimately inspired the climate negotiations, by the American diplomat who led the U.S. team during the most crucial years. Particularly startling is Benedick's account of U.S. world ozone leadership under President Ronald Reagan.

Carlarne, Cinnamon P., **Climate Change Law and Policy: EU and U.S. Perspectives.** New York, Oxford University Press, 2010. 350 pp. This detail-rich book offers an authoritative compare-and-contrast account of American and European policies and attitudes toward climate policy. It also provides incisive analysis of recent climate negotiations.

Klein, Naomi, **This Changes Everything: Capitalism vs. the Climate.** New York, Simon & Shuster, 2014. 576 pp. This bestseller makes the case that radical ideological change, both economic and political, is a prerequisite for meeting the challenge of climate change.

Nordhaus, William D., **The Climate Casino: Risk, Uncertainty and Economics for a Warming World.** New Haven, CT, Yale University Press, 2015. 392 pp. (paper). A noted Yale University economist, Norhaus offers a comprehensive analysis of the costs and benefits associated with global warming. He makes a convincing case for universal participation in carbon cutting regimes.

Oreskes, Naomi and Conway, Erik M., **The Collapse of Western Civilization: A View from the Future.** New York, Columbia University Press, 2014. 104 pp. This sobering work imagines the world of 2093, in which the globe has been devastated by the effects of climate change.

Pope Francis, **Laudato Si' (Praise Be to Him): On Care for our Common Home.** Vatican: The Holy See, 2015. 184 pp. (encyclical letter). Available free online at: <http://w2.vatican.va/content/francesco/en/encyclicals/documents/papa-francesco_20150524_enciclica-laudato-si.html>. The scope of this much-anticipated papal encyclical, issued in summer 2015, extends far beyond climate change. But the letter includes a comprehensive list of the causes and effects of global warming according to the Church. It takes the position that indifference in the face of alarming scientific knowledge is sinful.

Sachs, Jeffrey D., **The Age of Sustainable Development.** New York, Columbia University Press, 2015. 544 pp. This book provides comprehensive coverage of the relationships between economy, society and the environment. It is currently the go-to point of departure for anyone looking to study sustainable development.

To access web links to these readings, as well as links to additional, shorter readings and suggested web sites,

GO TO www.greatdecisions.org

and click on the topic under Resources, on the right-hand side of the page

Cuba and the U.S.

by Michael Shifter and Ben Raderstorf

A man wears a T-shirt printed with the American flag as he passes a tourist in a Che Guevara T-shirt in Havana, December 22, 2014. As diplomatic relations between the U.S. and Cuba thaw, an unexpected outburst of American flag waving in Cuba has followed. (THE NEW YORK TIMES/REDUX)

On the morning of December 17, 2014, an unremarkable sunny day quickly transformed into a whirlwind of excitement as the news spread. Something big was happening. Church bells rang out in Old Havana and crowds gathered around whatever television sets they could find to watch Cuban President Raúl Castro announce the biggest diplomatic shift in U.S.-Cuban relations in several generations. At the same moment, 1,100 miles north in Washington, DC, U.S. President Barack Obama delivered a similar message to the American people.

A change—in Cuba and in the U.S.-Cuban relationship—had long seemed overdue. Shifting political winds and economic realities, time and again, prevented change in Cuba's relationship with the U.S. and the world economy. Over the last quarter century, almost everything relating to the island had been entrenched—stuck in a cold war reality as intransigent as it was outdated.

The last GREAT DECISIONS article on Cuba, in 2009, aptly described a country "on the verge" of political, diplomatic, and economic changes. Six years later, the same could still be said. To many observers, Cuba and its relationship with the U.S. have been perpetually on the brink of change,

MICHAEL SHIFTER *is president of the Inter-American Dialogue and an adjunct professor of Latin American Studies at Georgetown University's School of Foreign Service.*

BEN RADERSTORF *is a program assistant in the Peter D. Bell Rule of Law Program at the Inter-American Dialogue.*

but with fundamental change never coming to pass. This stubborn durability of the status quo is what made so many wonder why the current rapprochement had not come sooner. Even now, when a shift has finally arrived, the process is sure to still be slow and difficult. The road to reconciliation, reform and opening is a long and winding one, and will almost inevitably have unexpected turns. For Cuba especially, this is a chance at a restart of sorts—but one burdened by a complicated history.

Earlier thaw

By many accounts, the current changes should have occurred a quarter-century ago. In 1989 and 1990, the Cuban economy collapsed after the fall of the Berlin Wall and the dismantling of the Soviet Union. It entered a severe depression understatedly referred to as the *período especial,* the special period. By the summer of 1991, many were speculating that Fidel Castro's government would collapse under economic and political strain. Communism around the world was disintegrating and old conflicts were subsiding as the cold war faded into memory. During the 1990s, the Cuban government liberalized narrow but key industries out of desperation. This coincided with a relative tourism boom, largely from Canada and Europe. At the same time, President Bill Clinton lifted some restrictions on remittances and family travel and moved toward a more conciliatory approach. As he once told an Oval Office confidant, "anybody with half a brain could see the embargo was counterproductive."

But the incipient thaw was to be short-lived. A number of factors upended Clinton's intentions and cemented U.S.-Cuban hostility for almost two decades. The budding 1990s rapprochement ground to a halt when Cuba shot down two American civilian planes that had been dropping propa-

---

Before you read, download the companion **Glossary** that includes definitions and a guide to acronyms and abbreviations used in the article. Go to **www.great decisions.org** and select a topic in the Resources section on the right-hand side of the page.

ganda leaflets over the island in 1996. This incident turned politics in Washington against reconciliation, leading Clinton to sign the Helms-Burton act, tightening sanctions and transferring final authority over the embargo from the presidency to Congress. Then, the divisive Elián González affair potentially cost Al Gore precious Cuban American votes in Florida and, theoretically, the 2000 presidential election. The controversy that the case stirred—in particular, a striking photo of a crying boy taken from his relatives at gunpoint after the U.S. Supreme Court ordered Elián back to Cuba—further discouraged U.S. politicians from considering anything other than a hardline approach. Around the same time, Hugo Chávez's rise to power in oil-rich Venezuela in 1999 provided a new lifeline, with generous energy deals and other forms of financial support subsidizing the Cuban economy, making reforms less necessary and pushing reconciliation with the U.S. further off the table.

Cuban Five

After George W. Bush was elected, the possibility of a change became even more remote. In 2001, five Cubans allegedly sent to Florida to monitor the activities of anti-Castro exile groups were convicted on espionage charges. Portrayed at home as unjustly imprisoned heroes, the "Cuban Five" became a rallying cry for Havana as the diplomatic relationship between the two countries spiraled downward. In 2003, Bush announced the creation of a Commission for Assistance to a Free Cuba and in 2004, under the commission's recommendations, sanctions were tightened significantly, in an effort to finally topple communism in Cuba. By 2006, an overt propaganda war broke out between the U.S. interests section in Havana and the Castro government, including billboards and lighted signs, along with attempts to obscure them.

But then Barack Obama was elected president. His critical statements on the embargo during the campaign and the offer in his 2009 inauguration

speech to "extend a hand" to those willing to "unclench their fist" seemed to mark a new opportunity for progress. Indeed, after entering office, he again lifted restrictions on remittances and family travel, and a larger opening seemed imminent. However, even Obama seemed unable to overcome the recurring pattern of frustrated opportunities. In 2009, Alan Gross, a USAID contractor, was imprisoned in Cuba for delivering communications equipment to religious groups—or dissidents, according to the Cuban government. The arrest became the latest obstacle to improved relations. The Cuban government sentenced him to 15 years in prison for allegedly aiming to "destroy the revolution," and, in turn, the U.S. government insisted he be freed. At the same time, Havana redoubled its calls for the release of the Cuban Five, and the possibility of change faded back to deadlock.

This was largely the state of affairs for the first six years of Obama's presidency—at least on the surface. Below, two key developments were slowly taking shape. First, starting in 2011, Raúl Castro's government began a set of limited economic reforms attempting to "update" the Cuban economic model to the 21st century. The changes included greater freedoms for small businesses, deregulation of state industries, and opening up the agricultural sector to a number of small producers and cooperatives. These reforms recognized that total state control of the economy was unsustainable, and that attracting investment would require more economic flexibility. The need for reform also became more pressing as the Venezuelan economy began to lose steam after 2011, casting doubt on Cuba's economic future.

Second, in early 2013, fresh from his reelection victory, Obama instructed his foreign policy team to take a new look at the relationship with Cuba. Given the green light from the White House for "exploratory talks," American and Cuban negotiators began a series of secret meetings, first in Toronto and then at the Vatican, where Pope Francis emerged as a crucial mediating figure, directly encouraging both sides to make concessions. Through nine different meetings, those talks eventually secured the release of Alan Gross, the remaining imprisoned members of the Cuban Five, and an unnamed American intelligence asset who had been apprehended in Cuba. To the surprise of many observers, the negotiations also paved the way for the historic joint announcement by Obama and Castro that their countries were seeking to fully normalize relations.

Since December 2014, the reconciliation has proceeded consistently and without, to date, any major setbacks. Through numerous obstacles, the efforts have already been enormously fruitful, bringing U.S.-Cuban relations to their best point since before the revolution. Immediately after the announcement, Obama used executive authority to loosen many of the restrictions under the embargo—including raising remittance caps further, expanding travel permissions, marginally increasing export and import allowances, and re-

U.S. President Barack Obama and Cuban President Raúl Castro shake hands at the Summit of the Americas in Panama City, Panama, April 11, 2015. (PABLO MARTINEZ MONSIVAIS/AP PHOTO)

moving some banking and communications prohibitions. On April 10 and 11, both the U.S. and Cuban leaders attended the Summit of the Americas in Panama City, sitting down for an hour-long discussion that Obama described as "frank" and a "historic meeting," and that Castro called an opportunity for serious discussion where "everything can

be on the table." This was the first time that presidents from the two countries had met face-to-face since 1958, when Dwight Eisenhower and Gen. Fulgencio Batista (the military strongman overthrown a year later by the Cuban revolution) sat down together, coincidentally also in Panama.

In diplomatic terms too, the progress has been impressive. On May 29, the U.S. Department of State announced that Cuba had officially been rescinded from its list of State Sponsors of Terrorism, a longtime demand of the Cuban government, allowing the country expanded access to international banking and commerce. While opponents in Congress decried the removal, they made no efforts to stop it—a telling sign of how much the politics of Cuba had changed in Washington. Finally, at 12:01am on July 20, the U.S. and Cuban governments officially established embassies in Havana and Washington, respectively. While the embassy buildings were the same—previously they had been unofficial diplomatic out-

posts, or "interests sections," under the protection of the Swiss embassy—the symbolism was immense. The stately Cuban mansion in the Meridian Hill neighborhood of Washington, DC, and the imposing American concrete building on the seaside Malecón esplanade in Havana are visible symbols of the new relationship between the two

countries. Their openings marked, albeit with little pomp, the reestablishment of diplomatic relations for the first time since they were abruptly severed in 1961, the same year Barack Obama was born. John Kerry's visit to Havana in August to formally inaugurate the embassy was the first time a U.S. Secretary of State had set foot on the island

since 1945, two years after he was born.

For Cuba, the ongoing normalization with the U.S. will be an inflection point—in one direction or another. December 17, 2014, will almost surely mark a critical date not only for U.S.-Cuban relations, but also for the Cuban political, economic and diplomatic reality as a whole. ∎

Adjusting political institutions for long-term stability

A large part of the challenges Cuba faces in the years to come—and by far the most uncertain—is wrestling with its own political system. While they may not be publicly visible or widely known, internal tensions and debates within the government and Communist Party of Cuba will have an enormous influence on all other changes the island will see in the coming years and decades.

Raúl Castro, aged 84, has stated that he will step down as President and First Secretary of the Communist Party when his current term ends in 2018. It will be the first time in 57 years that Cuba is not led by a Castro. For practical and symbolic reasons alike, such a transition would be monumental. His retirement will presumably usher in a new genera-

tion of younger leaders, many of whom were born after Fidel Castro took power and none of whom fought in the revolution. While it is hard to know how open the new generation will be to reforms, their decisions will likely be less ideologically rigid than those of the Castro governments. They also represent a generational transition in Cuba as a whole—young Cubans are overwhelmingly more interested in openness, trade and engagement and far less attached to the politics of communism than their parents. The transition of power will open the door to a new world of policies and possibilities less rooted in the ideological battles of Cuba's past.

Symbolically, the change could be even more important. When Castro steps down, state institutions will lose

the charismatic authority and revolutionary legitimacy that has anchored the government for over half a century. The few revolutionary leaders still alive and in power, of whom Raúl Castro is the most important, are some of the last links between the Cuba of today and the Cuba of 1959. While a rare opinion poll conducted in March showed tepid support for the Castro brothers—Raúl and Fidel at 47% and 44% approval, respectively—their firm control over the affairs of state has been almost unquestioned. The next generation of leaders will not be guaranteed the same legitimacy.

As power in the Cuban government becomes less monolithic, politics are likely to become more complex. The new governing class will be forced to reflect on the nature and purpose of communism in Cuba. They will have to balance the growing generational divide, both demographically and ideologically. This will be even truer after Raúl, Fidel and the rest of the original leaders eventually pass away.

Role of Miguel Díaz-Canel

The internal workings of the Cuban government and Communist Party are opaque; without democratic accountability, the dynamics of power lie mostly in the shadows. That said, in the past years one figure has emerged as a possible defining leader in post-Castro Cuba. Miguel Díaz-Canel, an electrical engineer and longtime party loyalist, was tapped as First Vice-President of the Council of State in 2013, making him second in command to Raúl Castro.

Cuban First Vice-President Miguel Díaz-Canel prepares to cast his vote at a polling station in Nautico neighborhood in Havana on April 19, 2015, during municipal elections. (ADALBERTO ROQUE/AFP/GETTY IMAGES)

At 55, he is youthful by Cuban political standards—his predecessor in the position, José Ramón Machado Ventura, is now 85 years old. Until recently, Díaz-Canel has kept a relatively low profile. His path to the Vice-Presidency has been a traditional one, diligently working his way up through the Communist Party structure first in provincial governance, and then in Havana. He was appointed to the Politburo, the executive committee of the Communist Party, in 2003, and served as minister of higher education from 2009 to 2012. All the while he kept his head down, earning a reputation for hard work and technocratic commitment to the party line. In the past year, however, he has increasingly become a public and diplomatic face for the government.

Relatively little is known about Díaz-Canel's ideology and how he would navigate the manifold debates and questions that are bound to accompany Castro's retirement. On one hand, Raúl Castro himself praised his "solid ideological firmness" and some inside and outside Cuba described him as a "hardliner." On the other hand, many observers suspect him to be more sympathetic to the perspectives of Cuba's younger generations who overwhelmingly favor greater openness. He was even, until recently, supposedly quite active on Facebook. However, it is crucial to note that his ascension is far from guaranteed. In the past, political fights and other internal dynamics have sidelined rising stars in the Cuban government with little warning; Díaz-Canel may be no exception.

Political struggles behind the scenes

Whoever next leads Cuba will have to navigate and mediate a growing internal debate that likely already exists—in the party, the government, and the country—about the path forward. While the government is widely considered to be politically stable, the unified ideological front it projects does not necessarily reflect the truth. Furthermore, the differences between political hardliners committed to a closed system and the presumably more reformist moderates who urge incremental political change

Cuban soldiers bearing their national flag march in the May Day parade at Revolution Square in Havana, Cuba, May 1, 2011. (JAVIER GALEANO/AP PHOTO)

and greater openness is only expected to grow in coming years.

These political questions reveal a large and complex web of power networks behind the Castro government. The core institutions, from the Communist Party to the Cuban Revolutionary Armed Forces, are multifaceted. Not unlike the Chinese and Vietnamese governments, formal political power in the Cuban state is distributed relatively widely. Power is held by majority vote of the 31-member Council of State, which in turn is officially elected by and reports to the more than 600 members of the National Assembly of People's Power. In addition, the sprawling bureaucracy and public sector—which altogether accounts for a stunning 75% of Cuba's gross domestic product (GDP)—is overseen by the 34 members of the Council of Ministers, with portfolios as specific as the steel industry or the construction sector, over which each minister has extensive control. The same complexity is true for the various political bodies of the Communist Party of Cuba—which is nominally separate from the state—and the regional and municipal Assemblies of People's Power and the local People's Councils. The political networks extend as far as the infamous neighborhood-level Committees for the Defense of the Revolution, designed to keep tabs on suspicious and subversive activity community by com-

munity. Under the Castro governments, all of these political institutions have been closely controlled from the top—but that cohesion may not last.

Above all, the most important political institution in coming years is likely to be the military—the Cuban Revolutionary Armed Forces (FAR). According to many analysts, it has long been the most influential institution in Cuba. It not only controls affairs of defense, but also has wide economic interests, ranging from the Cuban Import-Export Corporation to Gaviota, the state tourism firm. Additionally, the FAR has an unparalleled claim to competency in Cuba, especially compared to the other state institutions which have a long history of dysfunction and inefficiency. In the 1970s and 1980s, the Cuban armed forces were among the world's most professional and capable—evidenced by their multiple successful overseas victories, helping repel invading forces twice in Angola and once in Ethiopia. Historically, the military's role in Cuba's foreign policy is second only to that of its doctors—including the 246 health workers sent to fight Ebola in West Africa, the most of any country. And while the relative militarization of Cuba declined after the end of the cold war, the FAR's political and, increasingly, economic clout has remained strong. Naturally, the Castro brothers rarely had trouble controlling the generals—after all, most of them fought behind Fidel in the revolution and Raúl was the head of the FAR for almost 50 years. The same may not be true for prospective future leaders, many of whom, like Díaz-Canel, are civilians. With this broad network of institutions to manage and oversee, the leadership will have to balance a wide variety of voices and interests as they navigate a complex political landscape.

Political reforms on the horizon?

Most opponents of the ongoing claim that ending the embargo will only strengthen the Communist Party and the Castro regime. They argue that democracy—defined by free and fair elections—should be a prerequisite to ending the embargo. Sen. Marco Rubio, a prominent critic of Obama's Cuba policy, argued that it "will tighten this regime's grip on power for decades to come." And opponents are not alone in focusing on democracy. Proponents of

lifting the embargo, too, have used it as an argument, claiming that engagement can help bring about a democratic transition. The President himself has repeatedly claimed that more openness can help "empower the Cuban people."

In either case, most Cubans see a turn to democracy as unlikely under any circumstances. Only 37% believe an opening with the U.S. will help change the political system and just 19% think that it could lead the government to allow other political parties. Indeed, democracy on the island remains a long way off. That said, the pressure for more accountability and representation has grown substantially in the past 20 years, a trend that should only continue. In particular, according to the few reliable polls available, younger Cubans are substantially more interested in democracy, elections, and political pluralism than their parents.

Of course, a change is far from guaranteed. After Castro, the single-party government could prove to be resilient

and stable in the long term—making few to no changes. Alternatively, future leaders could also find themselves threatened by democratic pressure and crack down even harder on opposition groups, leading to rampant corruption and increased authoritarianism. In a third scenario, the government could even collapse outright, leading to chaos and instability. Most likely though, Cuba will pursue modest but consistent measures that attempt to increase political inclusion and accountability without a full transition to a democratic system. In doing so, the government has to thread the needle between appearing flexible to public demands while also holding on to power. In a telling sign, the Communist Party in April approved a new General Election Law. While few details about the law have been announced (and will likely not be known until 2016) the reforms may, at least according to some analysts, include dramatic changes to how Cuba's leaders are selected.   ■

Rethinking the economic model

The more immediate task for Cuba is its economy. The island's flagging state-run system remains badly in need of revitalization, reform and renewal, even with the ongoing changes.

In recent years, economic growth has fallen to 1.3% annually, down from as high as 12% in 2005. Some of that decline has been fueled by the economic collapse in Venezuela over the last four years—a portion of the mid-2000s growth was financed by oil subsidies, credit, investment and trade, facilitated under the presidency of Hugo Chávez. As the Venezuelan economy has gone south, Cuba has again found itself at risk of losing an external patron that kept it afloat. At the same time, state-owned agricultural, industrial and service sectors are notoriously inefficient and unproductive. The economy also struggles with an unusual dual-currency regime with two different pesos: one

that is convertible and pegged to the U.S. dollar, one that is not. The system—which originated in a post-cold war attempt to attract hard currency from abroad—nominally values convertible and nonconvertible pesos at a one-to-one rate. In reality, the two pesos trade at approximately 26 to 1. The peculiar arrangement is a constant source of confusion and inefficiency. It also enables questionable accounting practices on the part of state-run industries; the two dissonant exchange rates hide the price of imports and make exports seem unprofitable. At a certain point, the two will have to be reconciled, but doing so will come with costs. As *The Economist* noted, raising the value of the non-convertible peso could "stoke inflation and lead to widespread shortages," while devaluing the convertible one "would be fiercely resisted by those with savings in the harder currency."

All of these are problems that Raúl Castro's government has recognized for years, and has—with extreme caution and slowness—sought to correct. In 2010, Raúl made the stakes clear: he declared in a nationally televised address, "we reform, or we sink." In the same year, his brother Fidel surprised many around the world when he admitted to an American journalist that "the Cuban model doesn't even work for us anymore."

While the reforms have been halting and so far yielded fairly disappointing results, the trend toward greater market activity is clear. The number of independent, self-employed Cubans, or *cuentapropistas,* has spiked since 2010 as everyday Cubans begin operating home-cooking restaurants, hawking produce and electronics from street side stores and stalls, running tailoring and laundry businesses from their houses and performing other small-scale services. At present, the officially licensed cuentapropistas number nearly half a million. When informal industries, private and cooperative agriculture and other activities are factored in, the overall private sector is far larger. According to official government figures, up to 1.6 million Cubans (34% of total employment) could be characterized as private sector employees in 2012. The goal is supposedly to employ 40% of the workforce in nonstate industries by next year. A 2014 estimate held that 25.3% of Cuba's GDP is generated by the private and cooperative sector—up from 5% in 1989, surpassing state-run industries (but not the state itself) for the first time. That said, it is worth remembering that the government could very well be inflating these figures. And even if not, "private sector" is a slippery term that risks exaggerating the scale of market activity. Experts claim that up to 10% of Cuban workers are likely simultaneously employed in state and nonstate activities—for example, working for a state owned industry but also operating a small enterprise—inflating the nonstate statistics. Even more importantly, almost all nonstate economic activity is at the peripheries of society. The state still dominates three quarters of the economy, the entirety of the island's industry and almost all large-scale economic activity.

Abandon or preserve the socialist state?

As a result, the economic reform efforts to date amount to low-hanging fruit. Liberalizing cuentapropistas, agricultural cooperatives and other forms of individual and small-scale private enterprise has required almost no adjustment of the economic model. Giving licenses to roadside restaurants and allowing individual farmers to till fallow government land involves few concessions by the public sector economy. Moreover, business restrictions, investment regulations and taxes remain very harsh for the newly licensed enterprises. Pressures for this to change in the years ahead are, however, expected to mount. Díaz-Canel has publicly admitted that most of the "progress [has been] on the issues that are easiest to solve. What is left are the more important choices that will be decisive in the development of [the] country." Castro, for his part, has insisted that the underlying Marxist model is not on the table, that the reforms are simply "updating [the] economic model in order to build a prosperous and sustainable socialism." But taking steps toward more market activity without abandoning the "ongoing revolution" is more difficult than it sounds.

On the one hand, the historical trend does not seem to favor the Cuban socialist model. Open markets are a difficult beast to contain, however much the government tries. Greater migration, remittances, internet freedom, tourism, imports, Western media and—of course—American dollars will increase pressure for market reforms, especially around foreign investment. Yet on the other hand, seemingly solid and cred-ible predictions that the Communist system would come crumbling down have been repeatedly and consistently wrong. The regime has been remarkably resilient. After more than five decades, a Castro is still in power and, despite important changes on the margins, the revolutionary fundamentals of the economy remain intact.

But if Cuba does continue this process of reform, two historical comparisons provide interesting reference points: China and Vietnam. Among the four other remaining Communist states outside Cuba, they have both undergone relatively successful, nearly comprehensive, although not identical, transitions to thriving and globalized market economies (the same cannot be said for the other two, Laos and North Korea). If Cuba were to follow the Chinese and Vietnamese path, it could attempt a similar economic and diplomatic transformation without a change in political leadership—surely a tempting possibility. However, several key differences would make such a path far more difficult. The first is demographics. According to Julia Sweig and Michael Bustamante, "Cuba is an underdeveloped country with developed-world problems." Unlike China and Vietnam, which both began their transitions with large, young, poor and largely non-service sector workforces—a powerful resource for an aspiring manufacturing export economy—Cuba's population is aging and mostly already employed

(Left) Private vendors in Havana sell handmade clothing to tourists. (CYNTHIA CARRIS/REDUX) *(Right) Yunior Parra, a real estate agent, conducts business on a bench along the Prado in Havana, June 10, 2015. Cubans are now allowed to buy and sell their homes.* (PHOTO BY SUZANNE KREITER/THE BOSTON GLOBE/GETTY IMAGES)

Pictured: the Convertible Peso and the regular peso, or Moneda Nacional. Most state-run businesses serving average Cubans still use Moneda Nacional, which is often found to be counterfeit. Moneda Nacional is valued at 1/26th of the Convertible Peso, which is used principally by foreigners and Cuba's small but growing economic elite. (CHRISTIAN FRANZ TRAGNI/ REDUX)

in the service sector. In part because of relatively successful education and healthcare systems, along with other social policies, the Cuban population is skewed much older than its neighbors. The island has a median age of 40 years old, compared to 28 years for the rest of Latin America and the Caribbean. As a result, Cubans would be unlikely to flock to low-wage export-sector jobs even if they existed. The aging population could also discourage investment, especially as large numbers of young Cubans presumably will continue to migrate out of the country. Cuba is also, of course, a relatively small island—which limits its economic options—and close geographically to the U.S. Its Caribbean culture, social structure and history markedly differentiate it from China and Vietnam.

Finally, and perhaps most importantly, a rapid and full-scale transition to a market economy would require an ideological shift that the Castro governments have categorically rejected for decades. In a speech to the National Assembly, just days after the announcement of the diplomatic thaw, Raúl Castro declared that "we must not expect that in order for relations with the U.S. to improve, Cuba will abandon the ideas that it has struggled for." For the country as a whole to forsake them so dramatically, even under dif-

ferent leadership, would be surprising indeed. Even beyond the Castro brothers, Cuba is defined by an animated sense of nationalism—strong even for Latin America—for which a radical reversal would be, for many Cubans, tantamount to surrender.

Investment and financing

As a result, Cuba's likely path forward seems to be marginal economic reforms and a slow, measured transition to a hybrid state-market economy—although other possibilities exist, including a more troubling path of semi-capitalist oligarchy and kleptocracy akin to many post-Soviet countries. But if a slow market transition is to prevail, the primary challenge will be investment and financing. Underlying many of its economic problems—beyond inefficiency and barriers to commerce—are disastrously low investment rates, something that "updating" the economic model has done little to change. On average, Cuba invests only about 10% of GDP, compared to a regional average of almost 25% across Latin America. For Cuba to bridge this gap, since neither saving nor borrowing is an option, it needs billions of dollars of new capital. According to Marino Murillo, the Minister of Planning and Economy, "Cuba needs from $2 billion to $2.5 billion a year in direct foreign investment to advance its socialist socio-economic model, prosperous and sustainable."

As part of the ongoing reforms, the Castro government has begun to open the doors wider to foreigners looking to get a piece of the Cuban economy, particularly in agriculture and tourism. In 2014, the government released a list of 246 projects as part of a Portfolio of Opportunities for Foreign Investment, and has cut taxes on profits, streamlined approval mechanisms and otherwise made investing simpler, although even further changes in investment laws are supposedly forthcoming. Because the Cuban government's reporting on capital inflows is almost nonexistent, estimating how effective these measures have been is difficult. However, anecdotal evidence suggests that European, Latin American and Asian firms

have begun to explore investment opportunities. American individuals and firms, of course, are still almost entirely barred from investing in the country by the embargo.

Cuba has also attempted to woo foreign governments directly. China, for example, has increased loans to the island in recent years, particularly for infrastructure projects. The biggest investment by far, though, has been a nearly $1 billion partnership with Brazil to establish a massive, deep-water port in Mariel Bay on the country's north shore. The cornerstone of a new 180-square mile "special economic development zone" in which commerce, investment and trade will supposedly be liberalized, Mariel is an audacious project. The same harbor that launched a mass exodus in 1980—as tens of thousands fled a country stuck in the past—could potentially become a symbol of Cuba's future. Both Brazil and Cuba hope the port will become a crucial transit point for the larger "New Panamax" container ships that will begin flowing through the Panama Canal when an ongoing expansion is complete in 2016. As Brazilian President Dilma Rousseff said at the project's inauguration, Mariel is "the first container-terminal port in the Caribbean with the capacity to integrate into the inter-oceanic logistical chain."

For many Cubans, the hopes for Mariel are even higher than increased trade. The project—along with Cuba's highly educated population—has even fed talk among some Cubans that their country could one day become the "Singapore of the Caribbean." That scenario, though, seems almost impossible. Concerns about the Mariel project abound, both inside and outside the country. In public and in private, Brazilian officials and firms have expressed growing concerns that the slow pace of economic, investment and trade reforms will hamstring the project before it is even complete. What is increasingly clear is that while Mariel could well be important, it will not likely be a silver bullet for Cuba's economic woes. ∎

Reintegration into a transformed world

The final challenge for Cuba in the years ahead is one that it doesn't entirely control—rebuilding relationships with the rest of the world.

First and foremost, the path to reconciliation with the U.S. has only just begun. Over half a century of diplomatic isolation, economic separation and outright hostility has sown deep mutual distrust and misgivings. Metaphorically speaking, the Straits of Florida may be the widest 93 miles on earth—a powerful symbol of both the closeness and distance between the two worlds. Richard Blanco, in his poem "Cosas del Mar" (Matters of the Sea) read at the opening of the U.S. Embassy in Havana, described how "the sea doesn't matter. What matters is this—that we all belong to the sea between us."

As one of the last and most visible vestiges of the cold war, the U.S.-Cuba relationship has inherited some of that conflict's passion and acrimony. American and Cuban politicians still generally view the other as a dangerous enemy—Cubans see the U.S. as the imperialist hegemon bent on quashing its much smaller neighbor, while Americans see the Castro government as a brutal dictatorship using force to repress 11 million people. Neither image is entirely fair, and both countries have begun to relax their misgivings, but these assumptions will still be hard to shake.

Considering this legacy, the diplomatic thaw over the past year has been impressive. First, the release of Alan Gross and the remaining three members of the Cuban Five was a symbolic step forward for both countries. Then, the face-to-face meeting between Obama and Castro at the Summit of the Americas exceeded many expectations, particularly in tone. That Raúl Castro opened his remarks with "I agree with everything that [President Obama] has just said," was noteworthy in itself, a phrase that would have been unthinkable at any other time since 1961. Both leaders were notably conciliatory and quick to praise the other, Obama noting Castro's

"openness and courtesy" and Castro thanking Obama for his bravery. Castro also offered his apologies to President Obama, "because none of this is his fault"—referring to the long history of animosity between the two countries. Finally, the opening of embassies and restoring diplomatic relations on July 20 marked the biggest practical step. More than anything, the reestablishment of diplomatic relationships will facilitate faster, easier and more direct communication in the future.

The most important obstacle still to overcome is the embargo itself—or, as the Cubans call it, *el bloqueo,* the blockade. Both Barack Obama and Raúl Castro have called for its immediate removal. Yet ending the 54-year-old trade ban is largely out of both of their hands. It is also unlikely to happen in the coming year. While Obama's push to normalize relations with the island has restarted debate in Washington, the embargo remains politically tricky, especially under a Republican-controlled Congress. Shortly after the push to normalize was announced, John Boehner, then the Speaker of the House and a main gatekeeper to any changes, firmly discounted the possibility. "Relations with the Castro regime should not be

revisited, let alone normalized," he said, "until the Cuban people enjoy freedom—and not one second sooner." There is little indication that current Speaker Paul Ryan will approach the issue differently. Senate majority leader Mitch McConnell similarly opposed the President's plan, and opposition from other Republican members of Congress has at times been even blunter. As a result, even if a majority of both houses supported lifting the embargo, the leadership would be unlikely to bring a vote to the floor. The strongest possibility is that aspects of the sanctions, such as the travel ban for U.S. citizens, will be eroded by specific legislative measures, slowly reducing economic restrictions on the island. This is especially true if Cuba shows some willingness to open up on political questions.

Things will not necessarily change outright after the 2016 election either. Of the Republican candidates for President who have expressed a position, all, with the exception of businessman Donald Trump and Sen. Rand Paul, oppose the rapprochement with Cuba, with Gov. Jeb Bush, Sen. Marco Rubio, and Sen. Ted Cruz most vocally critical (all three of whom have close ties to the

A classic American car passes in front of some signs that read in English "Long Live Free Cuba" in Havana, Cuba, June 16, 2015. (DESMOND BOYLAN/AP PHOTO)

Cuban American community, historically a staunch supporter of the embargo, even if current polls are changing). For some, it has become a prominent line of attack on the Obama administration. According to Senator Rubio, the Cuba deal makes the President "the single worst negotiator we have had in the White House in my lifetime," adding that if elected he will be "committed to doing everything [he] can to unravel as many of these changes as possible." Especially if a Republican wins in 2016, the chances of the status quo changing soon are small.

In the longer term, though, the trend is clearly toward repeal. Ending the embargo is overwhelmingly popular among American voters—and support is rising. A Pew Research Center poll in July found that an astounding 72% of voters supported lifting the embargo, up from 66% in January. Importantly, this included large majorities across all demographics, age groups and political parties—including 59% of registered Republicans and 55% of those identifying as "conservative Republicans." A November 2015 poll by the Atlantic Council similarly showed broad support for repeal in the "heartland" states of the country. Even the Cuban American community in south Florida, historically a powerful advocate for the embargo, has lost its conviction. According to the 2014 FIU Cuba Poll, "a slight majority (52%) of the Cuban American community in Miami-Dade County opposes continuing the U.S. embargo." In comparison, 85% of respondents in the same survey in 1993 favored tightening trade sanctions. While this trend is true across age groups, it is largely driven by changes in attitudes among young Cuban Americans.

Beyond the embargo, for the Cubans, full normalization of relations is also contingent on the U.S. naval base Guantánamo Bay. Under a 1903 treaty, the U.S. government officially leases the land from Cuba in perpetuity—for $4,085 annually. Since the revolution, though, Cuba considers the lease to be invalid and has refused to cash the checks (with the exception of one in

1959, which they maintain was a clerical mistake). While not a strict precondition, the Cubans have insisted that the base's return be a part of the negotiations. As Raúl Castro said in January, "normalizing bilateral relations" will not be possible until the U.S. returns "the territory illegally occupied by the Guantánamo naval base." At present, reports indicate that the Obama administration has been working for some time on a plan to close the detention center. This would only be the first step, but if such an effort were successful it could open the door to a conversation about the base as a whole. Both countries also believe that the other owes financial restitution—some U.S. politicians and businesspeople believe Cuba should pay compensation for the American-owned properties expropriated after the revolution, and the Cuban government maintains that the U.S. owes reparations to the Cuban people for "the human and economic damage that they're suffered" under the embargo. Although a working group is in place, neither is likely to happen, or at least not beyond symbolic gestures—but the issue will still play a role in future negotiations.

Political tensions

Last of all, a full rapprochement will have to address political tensions between the two countries. Although Obama has been less vocal than his predecessors and Republican opponents on the question of democracy, the U.S. government remains committed to political change in Cuba, as well as greater individual freedoms and respect for human rights. Cuba, on the other hand, continues to see any attempt to spur political change—even through engagement—as an undue incursion and a threat to its sovereignty.

The main conflict is the millions of dollars annually that Congress appropriates for program work in Cuba, including democracy promotion, civil society training and communications support—all of which Cuba sees as clandestine attempts to undermine their sovereignty. While the U.S. has indicated it is willing to change the programs, it will almost

certainly not give up its relationships with civil society and dissident groups in Cuba, creating one of the more sensitive issues to be dealt with in coming negotiations. At the same time, the Castro government may have to make some concessions when it comes to human rights, political prisoners and civic freedoms if it wants to see the embargo removed soon. These decisions will almost certainly extend long beyond the presidency of Barack Obama and, perhaps, that of Raúl Castro.

Re-engaging with Latin America and the world

Meanwhile, Cuba—should it choose to do so—also has far to go in reintegrating into a world that has changed dramatically since 1959. Even though Washington has stood alone, at least since the end of the cold war, in seeking to isolate the island, Cuba still lives relatively apart from its neighbors and the world. This is partly due to aspects of the Helms-Burton Act that restrict international finance. Recent connections and attempts at engagement between Cuba and other Latin American countries, while substantial, have only been a first step.

The disconnect between Cuba and the rest of Latin America comes, above all, from a lack of shared experiences. Amidst claims of "Latin American solidarity" stemming from the rise of new left-wing governments around the region after 2000, the trials, struggles and debates that Cuba has lived through are fundamentally different. Because Cuba has mostly lived apart from Latin America for five decades, it has not seen the changes brought to the region by modern economic and political trends, including the rise of a new middle class, the expansion of trade, the Internet revolution, the widespread emergence of independent civil society and modern, technologically sophisticated industry. Nor has it faced many of the problems with which most Latin American countries have struggled. These include criminal violence, deteriorating rule of law, expanding drug abuse and political dysfunction. Above all, even though it has benefited from the economic support of its neighbors—particularly Venezuela, in the form of generous energy deals—its commercial relationships are extremely limited. In part, this is a self-imposed isolation. The government's tight control of imports, exports and foreign investment (a regime some Cubans call the *autobloqueo*, the self-blockade) have in the past made it difficult for foreign firms even in friendly countries to do business with the island. These are issues with which the Cuban government is already grappling—in particular through Mariel, investment reforms and bilateral trade and finance projects—and will almost certainly continue to do so in the future.

In coming years, Cuba will also have to reexamine its general isolation from international institutions. While the Organization of American States conditionally lifted Cuba's 47-year suspension in 2009, the Castro government has not shown interest in meeting the conditions required to regain full membership. And even though Raúl Castro attended the Summit of the Americas in 2015, Cuba has still focused its diplomatic energy on the Community of Latin American and Caribbean States (CELAC), a younger hemispheric body that excludes the U.S. and Canada. Yet CELAC remains mostly in its infancy, and has so far failed to promote the degree of Latin American diplomatic integration that many had hoped for.

At the same time, CELAC is decidedly Latin American, and Cuba will have to address whether or not its regional relationships should also include the U.S. and Canada at the table. Lastly, through the decades of the embargo, Cuba has also been excluded from the international financial community—a divide that should be bridged if it wants to reenergize its economy. While membership in the Bretton Woods institutions (chiefly the IMF and the World Bank) seems still to be a remote possibility while the U.S. embargo stands and the economy remains opaque, the CAF-Development Bank of Latin America, a regional development bank headquartered in Venezuela, has expressed interest in Cuba possibly joining.

Edwardo Clark, a Cuban-American, holds an American flag and a Cuban flag as he celebrates outside the new Cuban Embassy in Washington, DC, July 20, 2015. (ANDREW HARNIK/AP PHOTO)

What kind of country does Cuba want to be?

From the perspective of the White House, the best option in Cuba may simply be to get out of the way. As Obama stated in Panama City, when the U.S. inserts itself "in ways that go beyond persuasion, it's counterproductive. It backfires. That's been part of our history—which is why countries keep on trying to use us as an excuse for their own governance failures. Let's take away the excuse." In historical terms, the ongoing rapprochement is significant. In a single stroke, the Obama administration's change in policy has broken through over half a century of mistrust, antagonism and political intransigence. Above all, this moment has created an enormous opportunity for the island and its 11 million people. It opens the door for Cuba to leave its past behind and to choose a new future.

The changes that Cuba faces in the years ahead will be complicated, difficult and will take time. Washington may have to learn to be patient with the island—rarely its first instinct. As Secretary of State Kerry said at the opening of the U.S. Embassy in Havana, "U.S. policy is not the anvil on which Cuba's future will be forged. Decades of good intentions aside, the policies of the past have not led to a democratic transition in Cuba. It would be equally unrealistic to expect normalizing relations to have, in a short term, a transformational impact. After all, Cuba's future is for Cubans to shape." In other words, the fundamental question now is what does Cuba want to become?

To be clear, this does not mean Cuba will choose the future that Washington would prefer, that its choices will be prudent, or even that the opportunities for growth and renewal will be seized at all. Cuba could just as well try to protect the status quo as it could gamble on greater reforms. Its economy could smoothly transition from state to free market, or it could break down into oligarchy and kleptocracy. This is most likely the brink of a new era of political opening in Cuba, but the temptation to repress may still win out.

In any case, the island's journey as it rejoins the modern world has only just begun. The U.S. has taken an important step in attempting to engage rather than isolate—and it will continue to do so. But Americans must also recognize that they are only a supporting actor in the debates and struggles ahead. The fate of Cuba is, perhaps more than any time since the revolution, firmly in Cuban hands. ∎

discussion questions

1. Who benefits the most from ending the embargo—the U.S. or Cuba? Is there a clear winner and loser or is it mutually beneficial? Besides the economic benefits, how will the abolition of the embargo affect U.S-Cuba relations?

2. Do Cuban Americans support or oppose the U.S. embargo against Cuba? How has the community's opinion evolved since the embargo was first imposed in 1960?

3. Will Raúl Castro be more like a Deng Xiaoping or Mikhail Gorbachev? In other words, will the economic opening of Cuba strengthen Castro's grip over the country or will it bring about the downfall of the regime?

4. What impact has the U.S. embargo had on Cuba's relations with other nations? Is Cuba able to trade freely and attract foreign investment? Conversely, will restoring ties with Cuba increase the U.S.' ability to influence other governments in Latin America?

5. Is returning Guantánamo a necessary condition for the normalization of U.S.-Cuba relations? Could you envision a deal where the U.S. would be able to maintain its military presence on the island?

6. With Obama leaving office in 2017, and Castro the following year, what kind of leader will both sides require to continue the groundwork already laid for improved relations?

7. Human rights violations and absence of freedom continue to this day in Cuba. For the U.S., the respect of human rights is an essential condition for normalization and a requirement of U.S. law. For Cuba, it is a direct threat to its mode of control, to be resisted at all costs. What is an acceptable *modus vivendi* for both sides?

suggested readings

Domínguez, Jorge I., Hernández, Rafael, and Barberia, Lorena G. , eds., **Debating U.S.-Cuban Relations: Shall We Play Ball?** New York, Routledge, 2012. 288 pp. A comprehensive volume covering the complexities and nuances of economic, political, security, people-to-people and global issues in U.S.-Cuba relations, with chapters by many of the most prominent Cuba scholars and analysts.

Erikson, Daniel P., **The Cuba Wars: Fidel Castro, the United States, and the Next Revolution.** New York, Bloomsbury Press, 2008. 368 pp. This critical look at long-running political narratives about Cuba is written by one of the leading policy experts on the country, currently a State Department official deeply involved in the ongoing opening.

Feinberg, Richard E., "The New Cuban Economy: What Roles for Foreign Investment?" **The Brookings Institution**, 2012. Available free online at: <http://www.brookings.edu/~/media/Research/Files/Papers/2012/12/cuba-economy-feinberg/cuba-economy-feinberg-9.pdf?_lang=en>. This paper offers a clear-headed analysis of possibilities and obstacles facing foreign investment in the Cuban economy.

——— and Piccone, Ted, eds., **Cuba's Economic Change in Comparative Perspective**. Brookings Institution, 2014. 119 pp. Available free online at <http://www.brookings.edu/~/media/research/files/papers/2014/11/cuba-economic-change-comparative-perspective/cubas-economic-change--english--web.pdf>. This collection of papers from many of the leading international and Cuban economists considers the challenges and obstacles to economic reform on the island.

Frank, Marc, **Cuban Revelations: Behind the Scenes in Havana**. Gainsville, FL, University Press of Florida, 2013. 344 pp. In this book, a freelance journalist with two decades of experience in Cuba explores an inside perspective on the Cuban economy, government and society from 1994 to 2013.

LeoGrande, William M. and Kornbluh, Peter, **Back Channel to Cuba: The Hidden History of Negotiations between Washington and Havana**. Chapel Hill, NC, The University of North Carolina Press, 2014. 544 pp. LeoGrande and Kornbluh chronicle the long history of unofficial communication and coordination between the U.S. and Cuban governments.

Mesa-Lago, Carmelo and Pérez-López, Jorge, **Cuba Under Raúl Castro: Assessing the Reforms**. Boulder, CO, Lynne Rienner Publishers, Inc., 2013. 293 pp. This book is the authoritative account of the economic reforms attempted by the government of Raúl Castro and their limitations.

Sullivan, Mark P., "Cuba: U.S. Policy and Issues for the 113th Congress." **Congressional Research Service**, July 31, 2014. 74 pp. Available free online at: <https://www.fas.org/sgp/crs/row/R43024.pdf>. This report summarizes the political issues that faced U.S. foreign policy towards Cuba shortly preceding the announcement of the diplomatic opening.

Suchlicki, Jaime, **Cuba: From Columbus to Castro and Beyond**. Washington, D.C., Brassey's, Inc., 2002. 278 pp. Suchlicki writes a thorough, approachable history of the island of Cuba, placing the Castro government in a complex historical context.

Sweig, Julia E. and Bustamante, Michael J. , "Cuba After Communism: The Economic Reforms That Are Transforming the Island." **Foreign Affairs**, 2013. Available free online at: <https://www.foreignaffairs.com/articles/cuba/2013-06-11/cuba-after-communism>. This article provides an in-depth look at the possibilities for economic reforms in Cuba and considers their likely consequences.

To access web links to these readings, as well as links to additional, shorter readings and suggested web sites,
GO TO www.greatdecisions.org
and click on the topic under Resources, on the right-hand side of the page

Global Discussion Questions

No decision in foreign policy is made in a vacuum, and the repercussions of any single decision have far-reaching effects across the range of strategic interests on the U.S. policy agenda. This GREAT DECISIONS feature is intended to facilitate the discussion of this year's topics in a global context, to discuss the linkages between the topics and to encourage consideration of the broader impact of decisionmaking.

1. Consider "The future of Kurdistan" in the context of "The rise of ISIS." Is the Peshmerga fight against ISIS strengthening or weakening Kurdish aspirations for an independent state? Will the West align itself with the Kurds, to the detriment of its more traditional allies such as Turkey?

2. Consider "The rise of ISIS" in the context of "Shifting alliances in the Middle East." Where does ISIS fit in the political dynamics of the region? If regime security is paramount to Arab states, why have they not gathered a coalition to defeat the jihadist group? Moreover, with features of a proto-state, does ISIS value regime security as much as neighboring countries? Or is it trumped by other political objectives?

3. Consider "Climate geopolitics" in the context of "The rise of ISIS." How much has climate change contributed to the unrest in Syria and Iraq? Will extreme events attributable to climate change such as droughts lead to further destabilization of the Middle East? What is the process by which disaffected populations, with diminishing agricultural capacity, might radicalize and join the ranks of jihadist groups?

4. Consider "The UN's post-2015 development agenda and leadership" in the context of "Climate geopolitics." Do the UN SDGs focus enough on this issue of climate change? What is the role of the UN in this issue? Should it take the lead, or leave it to individual nations? Can UN structural reform enhance the organization's ability to tackle climate change? What other areas of the UN mandate such as the protection of human rights, peacekeeping, conflict prevention and poverty alleviation could be affected by climate change? How?

5. Consider "Climate geopolitics" in the context of "International migration." How much has climate change contributed to the migration crisis, with people fleeing the Middle East at unprecedented rates? In the future, will we see mass migration from the countries most at risk from climate change? Does the risk of a climate or environmental refugee crisis make the issue of tackling climate change more immediate?

6. Consider "Cuba and the U.S." in the context of "Korean choices." Could the normalization of relations and the lifting of the U.S. embargo on Cuba serve as a template for South Korean reengagement with the North? What are the similarities between the two issues and where do they diverge? Cuba is the latest communist regime to enter the globalized economy: does this put further pressure on Kim Jong Un to end his country's autarkic system?

7. Consider "The rise of ISIS" in the context of "International migration." Is the mass flight of civilians helping ISIS consolidate its hold over parts of Syria? After one of the perpetrators of the Paris attacks was found to have allegedly entered the EU through Greece, is it reasonable to fear that ISIS could take advantage of the migrant crisis, by infiltrating jihadists among the refugees arriving in Europe?

8. Consider "The future of Kurdistan" in the context of "Korean choices." South Korea has been the third largest supporter of Iraqi Kurdistan in terms of personnel and resources sent, behind the U.S and the UK. Why does South Korea have such an interest in the struggle of the Kurds? Can any parallels be drawn between the Korean peninsula's colonial history and the Kurdish struggle for independence? Is South Korea's interest in the KRG purely economic?

9. Consider "Cuba and the U.S." in the context of "International migration." Many Cubans have risked their lives crossing the Straits of Florida in order to come to the U.S. Should one expect a surge or decrease in migration from Cuba to the U.S. once the embargo is lifted? Why are Cuban Americans, who immigrated to the U.S. in the aftermath of the Cuban revolution, so vocally against lifting the embargo? How have subsequent migration waves from Cuba changed the Cuban American opinion on the matter?

10. Consider "Korean choices" in the context of "Shifting alliances in the Middle East." Can the concepts used to explain regional political dynamics in the Middle East—regime security, as well as internal and external security dilemmas—shed some light on international relations in northeast Asia?

About the balloting process...

Dear Great Decisions Participants,

My name is Dr. Lauren Prather and I have been working with the Foreign Policy Association (FPA) for the last two years on the National Opinion Ballot (NOB). You have likely received emails from me about the NOB. We thought this year I might write to you to explain a bit my interest in assisting the FPA with fielding the NOB.

My research is primarily focused in international relations. I received my PhD in political science from Stanford University, where I worked with some of the top public opinion and international relations researchers in the field. I am now a faculty member at the School of Global Policy and Strategy at the University of California, San Diego (UCSD). My research interests are broadly revealed in the title of my dissertation: *Self-Interest, Group Interest, and Values: The Determinants of Mass Attitudes towards Foreign Aid in Donor Countries.*

As anyone who studies public opinion about foreign policy knows, one of the key difficulties is that the public is often uniformed or misinformed about the topics. This is where you come in! The Great Decisions participants are some of the most informed Americans about foreign policy issues, and the NOB is the perfect opportunity to voice those opinions.

The NOB is also one of the only public opinion surveys in the United States that attempts to gather the opinions of the educated public. Thus, it has great value to researchers and policymakers alike. Some of the questions in which researchers are interested in include the following:

- Are the opinions of the educated public significantly different from those of the average American?
- How does public opinion about foreign policy change over time?
- How does public opinion on one foreign policy issue relate to public opinion on other foreign policy issues? For example, are people who support U.S. government policies to mitigate climate change more or less willing to support drilling in the Arctic?
- How do different segments of the population, men or women, liberals or conservatives, view foreign policy choices?

In order to answer this type of questions, the NOB needed to have certain attributes. We needed to have a way to organize the ballots by participant across all topics. That way, we know, for example, how participant #47 responded to the question about climate change mitigation and how he or she responded to the question about drilling, even if those were in different topics in the NOB.

Furthermore, in order to understand how public opinion has changed over time, we needed a way to measure #47's opinion on, for example, drilling in 2014 and a way to measure #47's opinion on drilling in 2015. When you signed on with your email address to enter the ballot the past couple of years, you were assigned a random number (like #47). **Only** this number is connected to your responses and **never** your email address.

In fact, as a researcher, I must receive the approval of my Institutional Review Board by demonstrating that your data would be protected at all times, and that your responses would be both confidential and anonymous. I do this by using only secure computing networks and by storing your identifying information separately from your responses to the NOB. My work with the FPA has received approval from Stanford and now also from UCSD.

While I hope this provides some assurances about the security of your personal data, I understand that there have been some difficulties with simply going online to take the survey. Each year we continue to improve on these practices, but it is a learning process.

You will find the paper ballot in every briefing book in addition to directions for each topic on how to record your opinion online. You will be asked to use the unique hyperlink for each topic to record your response. Because we would still very much like to match your responses across topics, and to previous years if you have completed the ballot online, we will ask you to use your email address. Again, you will be given a random number or the number assigned to you in previous years; this, rather than your email address will be matched to your responses.

If you have any questions or comments, I am always happy to respond via email at LPrather@ucsd.edu. To learn more about my research and teaching, you can visit my website www.laurenprather.org.

I'll end where I should have begun by thanking everyone who has participated in the NOB over the years. I have learned a tremendous amount about your foreign policy views and it has greatly informed my own research. In the future, I hope to communicate to the scholarly and policy communities how the educated American public thinks about foreign policy.

Sincerely,

Lauren Prather

2016 National Opinion Ballot

First, we'd like to ask you for some information about your participation in the Great Decisions program. If you are not currently a Great Decisions program member, please skip to the "background" section in the next column.

How long have you participated in the Great Decisions program (i.e., attended one or more discussion sessions)?

- ❏ This is the first year I have participated.
- ❏ I participated in one previous year.
- ❏ I participated in more than one previous year.

How did you learn about the Great Decisions program?

- ❏ Word of mouth
- ❏ Local library
- ❏ Foreign Policy Association website
- ❏ Promotional brochure
- ❏ Other organization _____

Where does your Great Decisions group meet?

- ❏ Private home
- ❏ Library
- ❏ Community center
- ❏ Learning in retirement
- ❏ Other _____

How many hours, on average, do you spend reading one *Great Decisions* chapter?

- ❏ Less than 1 hour
- ❏ 1–2 hours
- ❏ 3–4 hours
- ❏ More than 4 hours

Would you say you have or have not changed your opinion in a fairly significant way as a result of taking part in the Great Decisions program?

- ❏ Have
- ❏ Have not
- ❏ Not sure

Background Section: Next, we'd like to ask you some information about your background.

How strongly do you agree or disagree with the following statement? Although the media often reports about national and international events and developments, this news is seldom as interesting as the things that happen directly in our own community and neighborhood.

- ❏ Agree strongly
- ❏ Agree somewhat
- ❏ Neither agree nor disagree
- ❏ Disagree somewhat
- ❏ Disagree strongly

Generally speaking, how interested are you in politics?

- ❏ Very much interested
- ❏ Somewhat interested
- ❏ Not too interested
- ❏ Not interested at all

Do you think it is best for the future of the U.S. if it takes an active role in world affairs or stays out of world affairs?

- ❏ Takes an active role in world affairs
- ❏ Stays out of world affairs

How often are you asked for your opinion on foreign policy?

- ❏ Often
- ❏ Sometimes
- ❏ Never

Have you been abroad during the last two years?

- ❏ Yes   ❏ No

Do you know, or are you learning, a foreign language?

- ❏ Yes   ❏ No

Do you have any close friends or family who live in other countries?

- ❏ Yes   ❏ No

Do you donate to any charities that help the poor in other countries?

❑ Yes   ❑ No

Generally speaking, do you usually think of yourself as a Republican, a Democrat, an Independent, or something else?

❑ Republican

❑ Democrat

❑ Independent

❑ Other _____

What is your gender?

❑ Male

❑ Female

What race do you consider yourself?

❑ White/Caucasian

❑ Black/African-American

❑ Asian-American

❑ Native American

❑ Hispanic/Latino

❑ Other (please specify) _____

How important is religion in your life?

❑ Very important

❑ Somewhat important

❑ Not too important

❑ Not at all important

What is your age?   _____

Are you currently employed?

❑ Full-time employee

❑ Part time employee

❑ Self-employed

❑ Unemployed

❑ Retired

❑ Student

❑ Homemaker

What are the first three digits of your zip code? (This will allow us to do a state-by-state breakdown of results.)

_____   _____   _____

Can you give us an estimate of your household income in 2015 before taxes?

❑ Below $30,000

❑ $30,000-$50,000

❑ $50,000-$75,000

❑ $75,000-$100,000

❑ $100,000-$150,000

❑ Over $150,000

❑ Not sure

❑ Prefer not to say

What is the highest level of education you have completed?

❑ Did not graduate from high school

❑ High school graduate

❑ Some college, but no degree (yet)

❑ 2-year college degree

❑ 4-year college degree

❑ Some postgraduate work, but no degree (yet)

❑ Postgraduate degree (MA, MBA, MD, JD, PhD, etc.)

Now we would like to ask you some ballot questions from previous years:

1. From 2004's "Middle Eastern Political Reform": Do you believe that "some cultures are incompatible with democracy"?

❑ Yes

❑ No

2. From 2015's "Sectarianism in the Middle East": In terms of the political situation in the Middle East, which is more important?

❑ Democratic governments, even if there is less stability in the region

❑ Stable governments, even if there is less democracy in the region

3. From 1997's "Terrorism and Crime": For each of the following statements, indicate whether you agree or disagree?

	AGREE	DISAGREE
Homegrown terrorism is a greater menace than terrorism fostered overseas	❑	❑
The inconvenience of tightened security at airports and other public places is a price worth paying for safety from terrorist attacks	❑	❑
The U.S. should mount retaliatory strikes against governments that sponsor terrorist attacks on Americans	❑	❑
The CIA should work with anyone who can help catch terrorists, even "unsavory characters"	❑	❑
There are circumstances under which the use of terrorism may be justified	❑	❑

4. From 2015's "Sectarianism in the Middle East": To what extent do you agree or disagree that the U.S. should consider recognizing a free nation for Kurdish people called Kurdistan?

- ❑ Agree strongly
- ❑ Agree somewhat
- ❑ Disagree somewhat
- ❑ Disagree strongly
- ❑ Not sure

5. From 2007's "International Migration": Do you agree or disagree with the following statements?

	Agree	Agree with reservations	Disagree	Disagree with reservations
Building a fence on the U.S.-Mexico border is an effective way to slow illegal immigration				
Illegal immigration to the U.S. hurts the economy				
Illegal immigrants already in the U.S. should be allowed to stay				

6. From 1992's "Refugee Crisis": Do you agree or disagree with the following statements regarding U.S. policy on admitting refugees?

	Agree	Agree with reservations	Disagree	Disagree with reservations
The U.S. should distinguish between refugees from political persecution and those fleeing economic hardship				
The U.S. should not broaden the definition of refugees to allow more into the U.S.				
The U.S. should be less strict about requirements that refugees prove "fear of persecution"				

7. From 2007's "International Migration": Do you think it is a contradiction to support the free movement of goods and services that characterizes globalization, on the one hand, and to limit the free flow of workers, on the other hand?

- ❑ Yes
- ❑ No

8. From 1997's "Northeast Asia": In its security strategy in Northeast Asia, the U.S. should (pick one):

- ❑ Continue to play the role of regional policeman
- ❑ Renegotiate security alliances and establish a traditional balance of power in the region
- ❑ Withdraw U.S. military forces from Northeast Asia to U.S. territory
- ❑ Other

9. From 1999's "U.S. Role in the UN": For each of the following activities, check whether the UN, private/nongovernmental organizations or unilateral/regional actors perform them best:

	UN	Private/ NGO	Unilateral/ Regional
Disaster relief			
Health/medical assistance			
Developmental assistance			
International trade arrangements			
Human rights watch			
Arms limitations			
Conflict resolution			

10. From 2006's "The UN: post-summit outlook": Do you agree or disagree with the following statements?

	AGREE	DISAGREE
UN staff should be hired on the basis of skills and experience, not because they come from a certain region or country	❏	❏
A reformed, more effective UN central administration will take power away from developing countries in the General Assembly	❏	❏
The UN member states focus too strongly on their individual interests to reach agreements on UN reform	❏	❏
Reforming the UN is a continuous process rather than a series of discrete decisions	❏	❏

11. From 1988's "The Global Environment": What is the most effective way for the U.S. to respond to environmental problems?

❏ Legislate strict domestic laws setting restrictions on pollution

❏ Seek bilateral and multilateral agreements on environmental issues

❏ Let free market forces deal with environmental problems

❏ Give tax incentives to companies combatting pollution

12. From 2007's "Global Warming": Which statement most closely expresses your concern about the impact of climate change?

❏ Climate change is "the greatest hoax ever perpetrated on the American people"

❏ Climate change is a "planetary emergency"

❏ There is not enough information at this time to determine the long-term impact of climate change

13. From 2009's "Cuba": Do you think it would be in the best interests of the U.S. to: (select one)

❏ Drop the current U.S. embargo against trade with Cuba

❏ Develop trade relations with Cuba that go beyond the current "cash only" agricultural sales, but short of lifting the embargo

❏ Maintain the trade embargo with Cuba until there is a real change in its government's philosophy

14. From 2009's "Cuba": With Raúl Castro at the helm as president, pursuing a path of limited economic opening, Cuba is on the verge of a huge political transition. Do you think Raúl's leadership will:

❏ Breathe new life into the Cuban Revolution

❏ Sow the seeds for Cuba to evolve into a different kind of society altogether

Topic 1. Shifting alliances in the Middle East

1. Have you engaged in any of the following activities related to the "Shifting alliances in the Middle East" topic? Mark all that you have done or mark none of the above.

- ❏ Read the article on the Middle East in the 2016 *Great Decisions* briefing book
- ❏ Discussed the article on the Middle East with a Great Decisions discussion group
- ❏ Discussed the article on the Middle East with friends and family
- ❏ Followed news related to the Middle East
- ❏ Taken a class in which you learned about issues related to the Middle East
- ❏ Have or had a job related to the Middle East
- ❏ Traveled to the Middle East
- ❏ None of the above

2. How interested would you say you are in issues related to the Middle East?

- ❏ Very interested
- ❏ Somewhat interested
- ❏ Not too interested
- ❏ Not at all interested

3. How closely have you been following news about the Middle East?

- ❏ Very closely
- ❏ Somewhat closely
- ❏ Not too closely
- ❏ Not at all closely

4. Which event do you think had the biggest impact on the political dynamics of the Middle East?

- ❏ The 2003 U.S. invasion of Iraq and its subsequent withdrawal in 2011
- ❏ The Arab spring and the ensuing civil wars
- ❏ The rise of ISIS
- ❏ The Iran nuclear deal

5. Do you think that the Iran nuclear deal will bring about:

- ❏ More stability in the region
- ❏ Less stability in the region

Would you like to share any other thoughts with us about Middle East Alliances? If so, please use the space below.

Topic 2. The Rise of ISIS

1. Have you engaged in any of the following activities related to "The rise of ISIS" topic? Mark all that you have done or mark none of the above.

- ❏ Read the article on ISIS in the 2016 *Great Decisions* briefing book
- ❏ Discussed the article on ISIS with a Great Decisions discussion group
- ❏ Discussed the article on ISIS with friends and family
- ❏ Followed news related to ISIS
- ❏ Taken a class in which you learned about issues related to ISIS
- ❏ Have or had a job related to ISIS
- ❏ Traveled to Iraq and/or Syria
- ❏ None of the above

2. How interested would you say you are in issues related to ISIS?

- ❏ Very interested
- ❏ Somewhat interested
- ❏ Not too interested
- ❏ Not at all interested

3. How closely have you been following news about ISIS?

- ❏ Very closely
- ❏ Somewhat closely
- ❏ Not too closely
- ❏ Not at all closely

4. To what extent do you agree or disagree with the following statement? "The U.S. government's strategy of 'degrading and ultimately defeating' is working against ISIS."

- ❏ Agree strongly
- ❏ Agree somewhat
- ❏ Neither agree nor disagree
- ❏ Disagree somewhat
- ❏ Disagree strongly

5. Do you support or oppose of U.S. airstrikes against ISIS?

- ❏ Strongly support
- ❏ Somewhat support
- ❏ Neither support or oppose
- ❏ Somewhat oppose
- ❏ Strongly oppose

6. Do you support or oppose sending weapons to moderate groups to fight ISIS?

- ❏ Strongly support
- ❏ Somewhat support
- ❏ Neither support or oppose
- ❏ Somewhat oppose
- ❏ Strongly oppose

7. Would you support or oppose the U.S. sending ground troops to fight ISIS?

- ❏ Strongly support
- ❏ Somewhat support
- ❏ Neither support or oppose
- ❏ Somewhat oppose
- ❏ Strongly oppose

8. When it comes to the U.S. committing military forces to fight against ISIS, which of the following best describes your point of view?

- ❏ Favor sending troops in for as long as it takes to get the job done
- ❏ Favor sending in troops for a short period to allow the Iraqi Army to take over
- ❏ Do not favor sending any troops at all

9. If Iraq were to fall into the hands of Islamic militants, do you think this would be a serious setback for U.S. prestige in the world, only a minor setback or not a setback at all?

- ❏ Serious setback for U.S. prestige in the world
- ❏ Minor setback for U.S. prestige in the world
- ❏ Not a setback at all for U.S. prestige in the world

10. Do you think the U.S. should have removed all troops from Iraq in 2011, or should the U.S. have left some troops there?

- ❏ The U.S. should have removed all troops from Iraq in 2011.
- ❏ The U.S. should have left some troops.

11. How confident are you that the U.S. and its allies will defeat ISIS?

- ❏ Very confident
- ❏ Somewhat confident
- ❏ Not too confident
- ❏ Not confident at all

12. Do you think that ISIS is more or less powerful than they were 6 months ago or are they equally as powerful?

- ❏ ISIS is more powerful than they were 6 months ago
- ❏ ISIS is less powerful than they were 6 months ago
- ❏ ISIS is equally as powerful as they were 6 months ago.

13. Do you think that ISIS is a major threat, a minor threat, or not a threat at all to U.S. national security?

- ❏ Major threat to U.S. national security
- ❏ Minor threat to U.S. national security
- ❏ Not a threat at all to U.S. national security

14. Do you think that ISIS is a major threat, a minor threat, or not a threat at all to America's allies in the Middle East?

- ❏ Major threat to America's allies in the Middle East
- ❏ Minor threat to America's allies in the Middle East
- ❏ Not a threat at all to America's allies in the Middle East

15. Which of the following statements about Islamic extremist groups like ISIS do you agree with more:

- ❏ We should use military strength to destroy Islamic extremists groups once and for all.
- ❏ We should accept that we cannot destroy Islamic extremists groups by using military force.

16. Would you like to share any other thoughts with us about the rise of ISIS? If so, please use the space below.

. . . .

. . . .

. . . .

. . . .

. . . .

Topic 3. The Future of Kurdistan

1. Have you engaged in any of the following activities related to "The Future of Kurdistan" topic? Mark all that you have done or mark none of the above.

❑ Read the article on the Kurds in the 2016 *Great Decisions* briefing book

❑ Discussed the article on the Kurds with a Great Decisions discussion group

❑ Discussed the article on the Kurds with friends and family

❑ Followed news related to the Kurds

❑ Taken a class in which you learned about issues related to the Kurds

❑ Have or had a job related to the Kurds

❑ Travelled to a Kurdish region of the world

❑ None of the above

2. How interested would you say you are in issues related to the Kurds?

❑ Very interested

❑ Somewhat interested

❑ Not too interested

❑ Not at all interested

3. How closely have you been following news about the Kurds?

❑ Very closely

❑ Somewhat closely

❑ Not too closely

❑ Not at all closely

4. Overall, to what extent do you support or oppose the direct shipping of U.S. military equipment to the Kurdish Peshmerga opposing ISIS in Iraq?

❑ Support strongly

❑ Support somewhat

❑ Neither support nor oppose

❑ Oppose somewhat

❑ Oppose strongly

5. What do you think is more likely in Iraq's future—reconciliation and co-operation between Arab and Kurdish factions, or separation and division between these two groups?

❑ Reconciliation and co-operation between Arab and Kurdish factions is more likely.

❑ Separation and division between Arab and Kurdish factions is more likely.

6. To what extent do you support or oppose the Kurdish region of Iraq breaking away completely from the country and declaring independence?

❑ Support strongly

❑ Support somewhat

❑ Neither support nor oppose

❑ Oppose somewhat

❑ Oppose strongly

7. If the Kurds were to declare independence from Iraq and establish a new country, to what extent would you support or oppose the U.S. government recognizing the new country?

❑ Support strongly

❑ Support somewhat

❑ Neither support nor oppose

❑ Oppose somewhat

❑ Oppose strongly

8. There are also a significant number of Kurds living in Turkey. If the Kurds were to declare independence from Turkey and establish a new country, to what extent would you support or oppose the US government recognizing the new country?

❑ Support strongly

❑ Support somewhat

❑ Neither support nor oppose

❑ Oppose somewhat

❑ Oppose strongly

9. To what extent do you support or oppose the Turkish government's bombing of Kurdish regions in Turkey against militants fighting for independence?

❑ Support strongly

❑ Support somewhat

❑ Neither support nor oppose

❑ Oppose somewhat

❑ Oppose strongly

10. Would you like to share any other thoughts with us about the future of Kurdistan? If so, please use the space below

. . . .

. . . .

. . . .

Topic 4. International Migration

1. Have you engaged in any of the following activities related to the "International Migration" topic? Mark all that you have done or mark none of the above.

❑ Read the article on migration in the 2016 *Great Decisions* briefing book

❑ Discussed the article on migration with a Great Decisions discussion group

❑ Discussed the article on migration with friends and family

❑ Followed news related to migration

❑ Taken a class in which you learned about issues related to migration

❑ Have or had a job related to migration

❑ None of the above

2. How interested would you say you are in issues related to migration?

❑ Very interested

❑ Somewhat interested

❑ Not too interested

❑ Not at all interested

3. How closely have you been following news about migration?

❑ Very closely

❑ Somewhat closely

❑ Not too closely

❑ Not at all closely

4. How likely is it that Congress will pass immigration reform legislation?

❑ Very likely

❑ Somewhat likely

❑ Not too likely

❑ Not likely at all

5. To what extent do you approve of Congress passing immigration reform legislation?

❑ Approve strongly

❑ Approve somewhat

❑ Neither approve nor disapprove

❑ Disapprove somewhat

❑ Disapprove strongly

6. To what extent do you approve or disapprove of the way President Obama is dealing with immigration?

❑ Approve strongly

❑ Approve somewhat

❑ Neither approve nor disapprove

❑ Disapprove somewhat

❑ Disapprove strongly

7. Would you say that immigration helps the U.S. more than it hurts it, or immigration hurts the U.S. more than it helps it?

❑ Immigration helps the U.S. more than it hurts it.

❑ Immigration hurts the U.S. more than it helps it.

8. What effect do you feel that the influx of migrant workers has made in your country?

❑ Increased wages substantially

❑ Increased wages moderately

❑ Increased wages minimally

❑ Neither increased nor decreased wages

❑ Decreased wages minimally

❑ Decreased wages moderately

❑ Decreased wages substantially

9. Here is a list of possible concerns some people have expressed over illegal immigration. For each one, please tell me if you are very concerned, somewhat concerned, not very concerned or not at all concerned about it.

9.1. Changing the culture of the country.

❑ Very concerned

❑ Somewhat concerned

❑ Not too concerned

❑ Not concerned at all

9.2. Leading to an increase in crime.

❑ Very concerned

❑ Somewhat concerned

❑ Not too concerned

❑ Not concerned at all

9.3. Leading to an increase in terrorism.

- ❏ Very concerned
- ❏ Somewhat concerned
- ❏ Not too concerned
- ❏ Not concerned at all

9.4. Taking jobs away from U.S. citizens.

- ❏ Very concerned
- ❏ Somewhat concerned
- ❏ Not too concerned
- ❏ Not concerned at all

9.5. Overburdening government programs and services.

- ❏ Very concerned
- ❏ Somewhat concerned
- ❏ Not too concerned
- ❏ Not concerned at all

10. Here is a list of positive things some people have expressed that come from legal immigration. For each one, tell me if you think it is a major benefit of immigration into the country, a minor benefit, or not a benefit at all.

10.1. Bringing in new cultures to the country.

- ❏ Major benefit
- ❏ Minor benefit
- ❏ Not a benefit at all

10.2. Performing jobs that U.S. citizens mostly do not want.

- ❏ Major benefit
- ❏ Minor benefit
- ❏ Not a benefit at all

10.3. Bringing needed expertise and skills to the country.

- ❏ Major benefit
- ❏ Minor benefit
- ❏ Not a benefit at all

10.4. Adding new ideas and entrepreneurial spirit.

- ❏ Major benefit
- ❏ Minor benefit
- ❏ Not a benefit at all

11. People come to the U.S. for different purposes. When you think about "immigrants," which of these types of people do you normally have in mind? Please select all that apply or select none of the above.

- ❏ People who come to apply for refugee status
- ❏ People who come to work paid jobs
- ❏ People who come to live with their spouse or civil partner
- ❏ People who come to study
- ❏ None of the above

12. Do you think the U.S. does or does not have a responsibility to take in refugees fleeing from other countries?

- ❏ The U.S. has a responsibility to take in refugees fleeing other countries
- ❏ The U.S. does not have a responsibility to take in refugees fleeing other countries

13. To what extent, would you support or oppose the U.S. government offering financial support to charities or the European Union in order to help refugees?

- ❏ Support strongly
- ❏ Support somewhat
- ❏ Neither support nor oppose
- ❏ Oppose somewhat
- ❏ Oppose strongly

14. Which comes closer to your opinion on dealing with the Syrian refugees?

- ❏ It's a European problem—the U.S. doesn't have a role to play
- ❏ It's a global problem—the U.S. needs to step up and do its part

15. Would you like to share any other thoughts with us about international migration? If so, please use the space below.

. . . .

. . . .

. . . .

. . . .

. . . .

. . . .

Topic 5. Korean Choices

1. Have you engaged in any of the following activities related to the "Korean Choices" topic? Mark all that you have done or mark none of the above.

- ❏ Read the article on the Koreas in the 2016 *Great Decisions* briefing book
- ❏ Discussed the article on the Koreas with a Great Decisions discussion group
- ❏ Discussed the article on the Koreas with friends and family
- ❏ Followed news related to the Koreas
- ❏ Taken a class in which you learned about issues related to the Koreas
- ❏ Have or had a job related to the Koreas
- ❏ Traveled to the Korean peninsula
- ❏ None of the above

2. How interested would you say you are in issues related to the Koreas?

- ❏ Very interested
- ❏ Somewhat interested
- ❏ Not too interested
- ❏ Not at all interested

3. How closely have you been following news about the Koreas?

- ❏ Very closely
- ❏ Somewhat closely
- ❏ Not too closely
- ❏ Not at all closely

4. For each of the following countries, do you feel that the country is a close ally of the U.S., is friendly but not a close ally, is unfriendly but is not an enemy, or is unfriendly and is an enemy of the U.S.?

4.1 North Korea
- ❏ Close ally of the U.S.
- ❏ Friendly, but not a close ally of the U.S.
- ❏ Unfriendly, but not an enemy of the U.S.
- ❏ Unfriendly, and is an enemy of the U.S.

4.2 South Korea
- ❏ Close ally of the U.S.
- ❏ Friendly, but not a close ally of the U.S.
- ❏ Unfriendly, but not an enemy of the U.S.
- ❏ Unfriendly, and is an enemy of the U.S.

4.3 China
- ❏ Close ally of the U.S.
- ❏ Friendly, but not a close ally of the U.S.
- ❏ Unfriendly, but not an enemy of the U.S.
- ❏ Unfriendly, and is an enemy of the U.S.

4.4 Japan
- ❏ Close ally of the U.S.
- ❏ Friendly, but not a close ally of the U.S.
- ❏ Unfriendly, but not an enemy of the U.S.
- ❏ Unfriendly, and is an enemy of the U.S.

5. How much influence you think each of the following countries have in the world? Please answer on a 0 to 10 scale; 0 meaning they are not at all influential and 10 meaning they are extremely influential.

5.1. South Korea

NOT AT ALL INFLUENTIAL   0   1   2   3   4   5   6   7   8   9   10   EXTREMELY INFLUENTIAL

5.2. North Korea

NOT AT ALL INFLUENTIAL   0   1   2   3   4   5   6   7   8   9   10   EXTREMELY INFLUENTIAL

5.3. China

NOT AT ALL INFLUENTIAL   0   1   2   3   4   5   6   7   8   9   10   EXTREMELY INFLUENTIAL

5.4. Japan

NOT AT ALL INFLUENTIAL   0   1   2   3   4   5   6   7   8   9   10   EXTREMELY INFLUENTIAL

6. The U.S. currently has about 30,000 troops in South Korea. In your view, is that too many, too few, or about right?

- ❏ Too many troops
- ❏ Too few troops
- ❏ About the right amount of troops

7. Do you think the U.S. should or should not maintain long-term military bases in South Korea?

- ❏ Should maintain long-term military bases in South Korea
- ❏ Should not maintain long-term military bases in South Korea

8. In America's relations with South Korea, the U.S. should place a high or low priority on each of the following.

8.1 Preventing North Korea from building up its nuclear capability.

- ❏ High priority
- ❏ Low priority

8.2 Trying to bring about regime change in North Korea.

- ❏ High priority
- ❏ Low priority

8.3 Protecting freedom of navigation on the sea-lanes in the region.

- ❏ High priority
- ❏ Low priority

8.4 Building a regional security alliance between the U.S. and East Asian countries.

- ❏ High priority
- ❏ Low priority

8.5 Building a regional free trade area with the U.S. and East Asian countries.

- ❏ High priority
- ❏ Low priority

8.6 Limiting the rise of China's power.

- ❏ High priority
- ❏ Low priority

9. What is South Korea's most significant socio-economic challenge?

- ❏ The demographic challenge
- ❏ The welfare challenge
- ❏ The equity challenge
- ❏ The happiness challenge

10. Do you think the U.S. should or should not have diplomatic relations with North Korea?

- ❏ The U.S. should have diplomatic relations with North Korea
- ❏ The U.S. should not have diplomatic relations with North Korea

11. The U.S. currently has economic sanctions in place against North Korea. Do you think it should increase sanctions, decrease sanctions, keep sanctions at their current level or eliminate sanctions entirely?

- ❏ Increase sanctions
- ❏ Decrease sanctions
- ❏ Keep sanctions at their current level
- ❏ Eliminate sanctions entirely

12. Do you think that persistent tension between South and North Korea is a major threat, a minor threat, or not a threat at all to U.S. national security?

- ❏ Major threat to U.S. national security
- ❏ Minor threat to U.S. national security
- ❏ Not a threat at all to U.S. national security

13. Do you think that the persistent tension between South and North Korea is a major threat, a minor threat, or not a threat at all to America's allies in Northeast Asia?

- ❏ Major threat to America's allies in Northeast Asia
- ❏ Minor threat to America's allies in Northeast Asia
- ❏ Not a threat at all to America's allies in Northeast Asia

14. How likely is that unification of the Korean peninsula will happen in the next decade?

- ❏ Very likely
- ❏ Somewhat likely
- ❏ Somewhat unlikely
- ❏ Very unlikely

15. Would you like to share any other thoughts with us about the Korean Choices? If so, please use the space below.

. . . .

. . . .

. . . .

. . . .

Topic 6. The United Nations post-2015

1. Have you engaged in any of the following activities related to "The United Nations post-2015" topic? Mark all that you have done or mark none of the above.

- ❏ Read the article on the UN in the 2016 *Great Decisions* briefing book
- ❏ Discussed the article on the UN with a Great Decisions discussion group
- ❏ Discussed the article on the UN with friends and family
- ❏ Followed news related to the UN
- ❏ Taken a class in which you learned about issues related to the UN
- ❏ Have or had a job related to the UN
- ❏ None of the above

2. How interested would you say you are in issues related to the United Nations?

- ❏ Very interested
- ❏ Somewhat interested
- ❏ Not too interested
- ❏ Not at all interested

3. How closely have you been following news about the UN?

- ❏ Very closely
- ❏ Somewhat closely
- ❏ Not too closely
- ❏ Not at all closely

4. What is your opinion of the UN?

- ❏ Very favorable
- ❏ Somewhat favorable
- ❏ Somewhat unfavorable
- ❏ Very unfavorable

5. How effective is the UN in trying to solve the problems it faces?

- ❏ Very effective
- ❏ Somewhat effective
- ❏ Not too effective
- ❏ Not at all effective

7. Should the United Nations be in charge of the worldwide effort to combat climate change and all countries, including the U.S., should report to the UN on this effort, or should it be up to individual countries to make decisions on their own?

- ❏ The United Nations should be in charge of the effort to combat climate change and all countries, including the U.S., should report to the UN on this effort
- ❏ Combating climate change should be up to individual countries to make decisions on their own

8. The UN contributes to raising the standards of living around the world. To what extent do you agree or disagree with this statement?

- ❏ Agree strongly
- ❏ Agree somewhat
- ❏ Neither agree nor disagree
- ❏ Disagree somewhat
- ❏ Disagree strongly

9. The U.S. should cooperate fully with the UN. To what extent do you agree or disagree with this statement?

- ❏ Agree strongly
- ❏ Agree somewhat
- ❏ Neither agree nor disagree
- ❏ Disagree somewhat
- ❏ Disagree strongly

10. The UN is central to solving conflicts in the world. To what extent do you agree or disagree with this statement?

- ❏ Agree strongly
- ❏ Agree somewhat
- ❏ Neither agree nor disagree
- ❏ Disagree somewhat
- ❏ Disagree strongly

11. The UN should remain headquartered in the U.S. To what extent do you agree or disagree with this statement?

- ❏ Agree strongly
- ❏ Agree somewhat
- ❏ Neither agree nor disagree
- ❏ Disagree somewhat
- ❏ Disagree strongly

12. It is important for the U.S. to be an active member of the UN. To what extent do you agree or disagree with this statement?

- ❏ Agree strongly
- ❏ Agree somewhat
- ❏ Neither agree nor disagree
- ❏ Disagree somewhat
- ❏ Disagree strongly

13. How important is it that the UN play a role in the following areas:

13.1. Providing humanitarian aid in times of crisis.

- ❏ Very important
- ❏ Somewhat important
- ❏ Not too important
- ❏ Not important at all

13.2. Advocating for and protecting human rights.

- ❏ Very important
- ❏ Somewhat important
- ❏ Not too important
- ❏ Not important at all

13.3. Peacekeeping

- ❏ Very important
- ❏ Somewhat important
- ❏ Not too important
- ❏ Not important at all

13.4. Conflict prevention

- ❏ Very important
- ❏ Somewhat important
- ❏ Not too important
- ❏ Not important at all

13.5. Conflict resolution

- ❏ Very important
- ❏ Somewhat important
- ❏ Not too important
- ❏ Not important at all

13.6. Poverty alleviation

- ❏ Very important
- ❏ Somewhat important
- ❏ Not too important
- ❏ Not important at all

13.7. Confronting climate change

- ❏ Very important
- ❏ Somewhat important
- ❏ Not too important
- ❏ Not important at all

14. Thinking of the same list of areas, which is the one area where the UN can make the most difference? Please select one or select none of the above.

- ❏ Providing humanitarian aid in times of crisis
- ❏ Advocating for and protecting human rights
- ❏ Peacekeeping
- ❏ Conflict prevention
- ❏ Conflict resolution
- ❏ Poverty alleviation
- ❏ Confronting climate change
- ❏ None of the above

15. Members of the UN General Assembly have agreed on a set of principles called the Universal Declaration of Human Rights. Some say the UN should actively promote such human rights principles in member states. Others say this is improper interference in a country's internal affairs and human rights should be left to each country. Do you think the UN should or should not actively promote human rights in member states?

- ❏ The UN should actively promote human rights in member states
- ❏ The UN should not actively promote human rights in member states

16. Would you like to share any other thoughts with us about the United Nations post-2015? If so, please use the space below.

. . . .

. . . .

. . . .

. . . .

. . . .

. . . .

Topic 7. Climate geopolitics

1. Have you engaged in any of the following activities related to the "Climate geopolitics" topic? Mark all that you have done or mark none of the above.

- ❏ Read the article on climate change in the 2016 *Great Decisions* briefing book
- ❏ Discussed the article on climate change with a Great Decisions discussion group
- ❏ Discussed the article on climate change with friends and family
- ❏ Followed news related to climate change
- ❏ Taken a class in which you learned about issues related to climate change
- ❏ Have or had a job related to climate change
- ❏ None of the above

2. How interested would you say you are in issues related to climate change?

- ❏ Very interested
- ❏ Somewhat interested
- ❏ Not too interested
- ❏ Not at all interested

3. How closely have you been following news about climate change?

- ❏ Very closely
- ❏ Somewhat closely
- ❏ Not too closely
- ❏ Not at all closely

4. Do you think that climate change is or is not caused by human activity?

- ❏ Climate change is caused by human activity
- ❏ Climate change is not caused by human activity

5. Do you think that tackling climate change is or is not a moral issue?

- ❏ Climate change is a moral issue
- ❏ Climate change is not a moral issue

6. How concerned you are, if at all, about global climate change?

- ❏ Very concerned
- ❏ Somewhat concerned
- ❏ Not too concerned
- ❏ Not at all concerned

7. To what extent do you approve or disapprove of the way President Obama is dealing with climate change?

- ❏ Strongly approve
- ❏ Somewhat approve
- ❏ Neither approve nor disapprove
- ❏ Somewhat disapprove
- ❏ Strongly disapprove

8. When it comes to the new limits on carbon dioxide emissions being set by the Obama administration and the EPA, which comes closer to your point of view?

- ❏ Action is needed because coal plants are a major source of carbon pollution. These reductions will mean cleaner air and reduce the health care costs associated with asthma and respiratory diseases by billions of dollars. Significantly lowering carbon pollution is the critical step in addressing climate change and the natural disasters and property damage it causes. These reductions will help create a new generation of clean energy and jobs.

- ❏ Coal plant carbon emissions have already dropped over the last decade and this action will mean fewer jobs. The compliance costs for electric companies will be three times more expensive than any current EPA regulation, which means higher prices. Consumers and businesses will both end up paying more for electricity. These regulations will mean only a small change to the global climate as carbon emissions in China, India and other developing countries will continue to rise.

9. All else equal, would you like the next president to be someone who favors government action to address climate change, or someone who opposes such action?

- ❏ The next president should be someone who favors government action to address climate change
- ❏ The next president should be someone who oppose government action to address climate change

10. A candidate who believes climate change is man-made and action should be taken to combat it is:

- ❏ Completely acceptable
- ❏ Somewhat acceptable
- ❏ Somewhat unacceptable
- ❏ Completely unacceptable

11. *"When people ask me if I believe global warming has been happening, I'm not qualified to debate the science over climate change, because I am not a scientist. […]. I am not qualified to make this decision. But I am astute enough to understand that every proposal to deal with climate change involves hurting our economy and killing American jobs."*

If a candidate says this, would this make you:

- ❏ More likely to vote for this candidate
- ❏ Less likely to vote for this candidate
- ❏ It would not affect how likely I would be to vote for this candidate

12. Now let me read you a few statements about the issue of climate change. Tell me to what extent you agree or disagree with that statement, or if you are unsure.

12.1. It is possible to combat climate change and have a strong economy with good jobs simultaneously; we don't have to choose one over the other.

- ❏ Agree strongly
- ❏ Agree somewhat
- ❏ Neither agree nor disagree
- ❏ Disagree somewhat
- ❏ Disagree strongly

12.2. Taking action to combat climate change will create more jobs because it will encourage us to innovate, invest in new technologies and move to clean energy like wind and solar.

- ❏ Agree strongly
- ❏ Agree somewhat
- ❏ Neither agree nor disagree
- ❏ Disagree somewhat
- ❏ Disagree strongly

12.3. By refusing to take action on climate change, the older generation is going to leave future generations to clean up the mess of their climate pollution.

- ❏ Agree strongly
- ❏ Agree somewhat
- ❏ Neither agree nor disagree
- ❏ Disagree somewhat
- ❏ Disagree strongly

12.4. Climate change is significantly increasing the number and severity of extreme weather events, such as hurricanes, flooding, wildfires, and droughts in the U.S.

- ❏ Agree strongly
- ❏ Agree somewhat
- ❏ Neither agree nor disagree
- ❏ Disagree somewhat
- ❏ Disagree strongly

13. When, if ever, do you think the consequences of climate change will personally affect people like you and your family?

- ❏ It is already affecting us; in your lifetime
- ❏ In the next generation or your kids' lifetime
- ❏ Not for several generations
- ❏ Never

14. To what extent do you agree or disagree that developed countries have a responsibility to help poorer nations with the effects of climate change?

- ❏ Agree strongly
- ❏ Agree somewhat
- ❏ Neither agree nor disagree
- ❏ Disagree somewhat
- ❏ Disagree strongly

15. Would you like to share any other thoughts with us about climate geopolitics? If so, please use the space below.

. . . .

. . . .

. . . .

. . . .

. . . .

Topic 8. Cuba and the U.S.

1. Have you engaged in any of the following activities related to the "Cuba and the U.S." topic? Mark all that you have done or mark none of the above.

- ❑ Read the article on Cuba in the 2016 *Great Decisions* briefing book
- ❑ Discussed the article on Cuba with a Great Decisions discussion group
- ❑ Discussed the article on Cuba with friends and family
- ❑ Followed news related to Cuba
- ❑ Taken a class in which you learned about issues related to Cuba
- ❑ Have or had a job related to Cuba
- ❑ Traveled to Cuba
- ❑ None of the above

2. How interested would you say you are in issues related to Cuba?

- ❑ Very interested
- ❑ Somewhat interested
- ❑ Not too interested
- ❑ Not at all interested

3. How closely have you been following news about Cuba?

- ❑ Very closely
- ❑ Somewhat closely
- ❑ Not too closely
- ❑ Not at all closely

4. What is your opinion of Cuba?

- ❑ Very favorable
- ❑ Somewhat favorable
- ❑ Somewhat unfavorable
- ❑ Very unfavorable

5. To what extent do you approve or disapprove of the way Barack Obama is handling the U.S. relationship with Cuba?

- ❑ Very much approve
- ❑ Somewhat approve
- ❑ Neither approve nor disapprove
- ❑ Somewhat disapprove
- ❑ Very much disapprove

6. On December 17, 2014, the Cuban government and the U.S. government announced that they would begin to normalize their relations. Do you think the announcement favors Cuba more, favors the U.S. more, or favors both equally?

- ❑ Favors Cuba more
- ❑ Favors the U.S. more
- ❑ Favors both equally

7. To what extent do you approve or disapprove of the U.S. re-establishing diplomatic relations with Cuba?

- ❑ Very much approve
- ❑ Somewhat approve
- ❑ Neither approve nor disapprove
- ❑ Somewhat disapprove
- ❑ Very much disapprove

8. Do you think re-establishing diplomatic relations with Cuba will lead to more democracy for Cuba, less democracy for Cuba, or it will not make much of a difference?

- ❑ More democracy for Cuba
- ❑ Less democracy for Cuba
- ❑ Will not make much difference

9. To what extent would you approve or disapprove the U.S. ending its trade embargo against Cuba, allowing U.S. companies to do business in Cuba and Cuban companies to do business in the U.S.?

- ❑ Very much approve
- ❑ Somewhat approve
- ❑ Neither approve nor disapprove
- ❑ Somewhat disapprove
- ❑ Very much disapprove

10. If travel restrictions were lifted, how likely would you be to visit Cuba?

- ❑ Very likely
- ❑ Somewhat likely
- ❑ Not too likely
- ❑ Not likely at all

11. Would you like to share any other thoughts with us about Cuba and the U.S.? If so, please use the space below.

. . . .

. . . .

1/RUSSIA

In your opinion, does the government of Russia respect the personal freedoms of its people?

Yes	1.9%
No	87.8%
Not sure	10.13%

Do you approve or disapprove of the way Barack Obama handled or is handling the situation involving Russia and Ukraine?

Approve strongly	18.2%
Approve somewhat	46.5%
Disapprove somewhat	18%
Disapprove strongly	12.2%
Not sure	5.1%

To what extent do you favor or oppose each of the following potential actions by the United States?

	FAVOR	OPPOSE	NOT SURE
The U.S. increasing economic and diplomatic sanctions on Russia	64.7%	18.9%	16.4%
The U.S. favoring Ukraine as a member of NATO	27.6%	46.8%	25.6%
The U.S. sending arms and military supplies to the Ukrainian government	40.1%	36.3%	23.6%
The U.S. working with Russia to peacefully resolve tensions in the region	92.6%	3%	4.4%
The U.S. staying out of Russian affairs	21.5%	45.3%	33.2%

Do you think that growing tension between Russia and its neighbors is a major threat, a minor threat, or not a threat to the well being of the United States?

A major threat	35.3%
A minor threat	49.2%
Not a threat	12.2%
Not sure	3.3%

Do you think that growing tension between Russia and its neighbors is a major threat, a minor threat, or not a threat to the well being of America's NATO allies?

A major threat	60.6%
A minor threat	33.6%
Not a threat	4.4%
Not sure	1.4%

2/PRIVACY

How concerned are you personally about the privacy of personal information you give out on the Internet, as well as privacy regarding what you do on the Internet?

Very concerned	45.8%
Somewhat concerned	36.7%
Not too concerned	14.2%
Not at all concerned	3.0%
Not sure	0.3%

How concerned are you personally about each of the following?

1. *Large online databases that publish telephone directories, property tax information, legal information, and other publicly available records that allow database subscribers to investigate the lives of ordinary Americans.*

Very concerned	38.5%
Somewhat concerned	32%
Not too concerned	23.5%
Not at all concerned	5.8%
Not sure	0.2%

2. *Corporate websites gathering marketing information about consumers by tracking their web browsing habits.*

Very concerned	41.4%
Somewhat concerned	38.2%
Not too concerned	16.3%
Not at all concerned	3.6%
Not sure	0.5%

3. *Internet advertisers gathering marketing information about people who click on their ads by tracking their web browsing habits.*

Very concerned	38.7%
Somewhat concerned	38%
Not too concerned	18.3%
Not at all concerned	4.5%
Not sure	0.5%

4. *The government's ability to "tap" into a suspect's computer and monitor their Internet usage.*

Very concerned	44.2%
Somewhat concerned	28.6%
Not too concerned	18.9%
Not at all concerned	7.5%
Not sure	0.8%

5. *The government's ability to "tap" into suspects' home computer files.*

Very concerned	48.3%
Somewhat concerned	25.5%
Not too concerned	16.1%
Not at all concerned	9.5%
Not sure	0.6%

6. *Software that allows the government to "tap" into email, searching for incriminating evidence of any kind.*

Very concerned	51.5%
Somewhat concerned	31%
Not too concerned	11.6%
Not at all concerned	5.6%
Not sure	0.3%

As you may know, as part of its efforts to investigate terrorism, a federal government agency obtained records from larger U.S. telephone and internet companies in order to compile telephone call logs and Internet service providers (ISPs). Based on what you have heard or read about the program, would you say you approve or disapprove of this government program?

Approve strongly	15.1%
Approve somewhat	41.6%
Disapprove somewhat	23.1%
Disapprove strongly	15.7%
Not sure	4.5%

As you may know, a former U.S. government contractor named Edward Snowden is the source of the information about the government program that created the database of telephone logs and Internet communications. Do you think it was right or wrong for him to collect and share that information?

Right	28%
Wrong	51%
Not sure	21%

Do you think it was right or wrong for the newspapers who reported on the program leaked by Edward Snowden to publish that information?

Right	50.4%
Wrong	35.3%
Not sure	14.3%

Is American monitoring of _____ acceptable or unacceptable?

	ACCEPT-ABLE	UN-ACCEPT-ABLE	NOT SURE
Other countries' citizens	36.8%	39.4%	23.8%
Other countries' leaders	33.7%	46.5%	19.8%
American citizens abroad	36.7%	42.5%	20.8%
American citizens living in the U.S.	19.5%	59.8%	20.7%
Suspected terrorists abroad	95.2%	1.5%	3.3%
Suspected terrorists living in the U.S.	95.5%	1.3%	3.2%

3/SECTARIANISM

How much emphasis should the U.S. place on the Middle East when creating American foreign policy?

A great deal	64%
Some	31.4%
A little	3.1%
None at all	0.5%
Not sure	1%

Do you agree or disagree that the United States should consider recognizing a free nation for Kurdish people called Kurdistan?

Agree strongly	31%
Agree somewhat	43.1%
Disagree somewhat	7.4%
Disagree strongly	2.3%
Not sure	16.2%

To what extent do you agree or disagree that President Obama made a mistake in returning forces to Iraq after the rise of ISIS in summer 2014?

Agree strongly	14.2%
Agree somewhat	24.4%
Disagree somewhat	35.7%
Disagree strongly	25.7%

If airstrikes are not enough to stop ISIS, do you favor or oppose the U.S. sending more ground troops to Iraq to fight the Islamic State?

Favor	16.4%
Oppose	62.7%
Not sure	20.9%

In terms of the political situation in the Middle East, which is more important?

Democratic governments, even if there is less stability in the region	15.3%
Stable governments, even if there is less democracy in the region	84.7%

Please select which of the following statements is closer to your own view:

Because Muslim religious, social and political traditions are incompatible with Western ways violent conflict is inevitable.	17.6%
Because most Muslims are like people everywhere, we can find common ground and violent conflict between the civilizations is not inevitable.	82.4%

4/INDIA

How much do you think India takes the interests of the U.S. into account when making foreign policy decisions?

A lot	8.1%
Somewhat	44.7%
Little	42.3%
None	2.1%
Not sure	2.8%

How much do you think the U.S. takes Indian interests into account when making foreign policy decisions?

A lot	5.2%
Somewhat	48.3%
Little	40.4%
None	3.3%
Not sure	2.8%

In your opinion, are relations between the U.S. and India improving, worsening or staying the same?

Improving	39.8%
Worsening	9.5%
Staying the same	39.4%
Not sure	11.3%

The five permanent members of the United Nations Security Council are China, France, Russia, Britain and the United States. Some people have proposed that the permanent membership should be expanded. Would you favor or oppose India becoming a permanent member?

Favor	54.2%
Oppose	22.1%
Not sure	23.7%

To what extent do you see tensions between India and Pakistan as a possible threat to the vital interests of the United States in the next 10 years?

Critical threat	16.4%
An important, but not critical threat	72.1%
Not an important threat at all	8.3%
Not sure	3.2%

India and the U.S. have agreed that the U.S. will sell nuclear technology to India and that India will allow the UN's nuclear agency to inspect some of its nuclear power plants. Which argument comes closer to your view?

Selling India civilian nuclear technology is a good idea because it strengthens U.S.-India relations and contributes to peace and stability in Asia.	59.7%
Selling India civilian nuclear technology is a bad idea because it suggests to other countries that they can develop nuclear weapons and get away with it.	20.1%
Not sure	20.2%

Do you think that India will play a greater role or a lesser role in international politics in the next 10 years than it does today?

Greater role	83.8%
Lesser role	1.3%
Same role	12.8%
Not sure	2.1%

How much do you trust India to act responsibly in world politics?

Very much	11.3%
Somewhat	67.1%
Not too much	17.3%
Not at all	0.9%
Not sure	3.4%

How much do you trust India to keep its international commitments?

Very much	15.2%
Somewhat	64.2%
Not too much	15.2%
Not at all	0.8%
Not sure	4.6%

In general do you think that India practices fair trade or unfair trade with the U.S.?

Fair trade	27.3%
Unfair trade	25.8%
Not sure	46.9%

Do you think the U.S. should have a free trade agreement that would lower barriers to trade with India?

Yes	60.9%
No	16.1%
Not sure	23%

Do you think U.S. economic aid to India should be increased, kept the same, decreased or stopped altogether?

Increased	11.4%
Kept the same	50.5%
Decreased	21.3%
Stopped altogether	4.3%
Not sure	12.5%

At present, are the U.S. and India mostly rivals or mostly partners?

Mostly rivals	5.8%
Mostly partners	77.8%
Not sure	16.4%

If India becomes significantly more powerful economically would you view this development as mainly positive or mainly negative?

Mainly positive	92.3%
Mainly negative	3.2%
Not sure	4.5%

If India becomes significantly more powerful militarily would you view this development as mainly positive or mainly negative?

Mainly positive	35.6%
Mainly negative	43.7%
Not sure	20.7%

5/AFRICA

Do you think the amount of foreign aid the U.S. gives to African countries in general should be increased, kept the same, decreased or stopped altogether?

Increased	38.5%
Kept the same	44%
Decreased	15.5%
Stopped altogether	2%

Thinking about the recent Ebola outbreak, what do you think should happen to foreign visitors coming to the United States from West Africa?

They should be allowed to enter the U.S. as long as they do not show symptoms of Ebola.	51.6%
They should be quarantined upon their arrival in the U.S. until it's certain they do not have Ebola.	38.1%
They should not be allowed to enter the U.S. until the Ebola epidemic in West Africa is over.	4.1%
Not sure	6.2%

To what extent do you see civil wars in

Do you think the U.S. government should increase, keep the same, decrease or stop altogether the following types of assistance to Egypt?

	INCREASE	KEEP SAME	DECREASE	STOP	NOT SURE
Economic aid	21%	55%	14.1%	5.2%	4.7%
Military aid	4.5%	28.4%	39.5%	19.9%	7.7%
Democracy aid	25%	31.8%	15.6%	14.1%	13.5%

Do you think the amount of foreign aid the U.S. gives to each of the following countries should be increased, kept the same, decreased or stopped altogether?

	INCREASED	KEPT THE SAME	DECREASED	STOPPED ALTOGETHER
Egypt	10%	46.8%	37.5%	5.7%
Libya	9.5%	34.5%	34.9%	21.1%
Tunisia	31.4%	50.4%	11.8%	6.4%
Kenya	26%	56.3%	13.7%	4.8%
Nigeria	20.4%	50%	21.9%	7.7%
Ghana	21.5%	61%	13.9%	3.6%
South Africa	13.6%	59.8%	19.1%	7.5%

Africa as a possible threat to the vital interests of the United States in the next 10 years?

Critical threat	13%
An important, but not critical threat	65.9%
Not an important threat at all	17.9%
Not sure	3.2%

As you may know, the United States participated in a NATO military campaign against forces loyal to Muammar Qaddafi in Libya, which was led by Britain and France, not the U.S. What level of participation should the U.S. have taken in Libya?

Taken the leading role in the campaign	4.5%
Taken a major role but not the leading role	40.9%
Taken a minor role	35.2%
Not participated at all	14.7%
Not sure	4.7%

Should the U.S. government have taken a more active role in helping Egypt during its transition to democracy?

Yes	25.5%
No	52.7%
Not sure	21.8%

6/SYRIA'S REFUGEE CRISIS

When it comes to U.S. policy in Syria which statement do you agree with most?

The U.S. should have provided Syrian rebels with more aid sooner	32.3%
The U.S. should not have gotten involved at all	12.7%
The U.S. did the best it could in a difficult situation	45.7%
Not sure	9.3%

Do you approve or disapprove of the way Barack Obama has reacted to the civil war in Syria?

Approve strongly	13.6%
Approve somewhat	41.5%
Disapprove somewhat	21.2%
Disapprove strongly	13.8%
Not sure	9.9%

Do you think the U.S. has a responsibility to do something about the fighting in Syria between government forces and anti-government rebels, or doesn't the U.S. have this responsibility?

The U.S. has a responsibility to do something	34.2%
The U.S. does not have a responsibility to do something	47.9%
Not sure	17.9%

In general, do you support or oppose Western countries sending arms and military supplies to anti-government groups in Syria?

Support strongly	11.6%
Support somewhat	43.7%
Oppose somewhat	22%
Oppose strongly	10.9%
Not sure	11.8%

In general, do you support or oppose Arab countries sending arms and military supplies to anti-government groups in Syria?

Support strongly	31.6%
Support somewhat	37.2%
Oppose somewhat	12.1%
Oppose strongly	8.2%
Not sure	10.9%

How should the international community respond to events in Syria? Check all options you support.

Enforce sanctions	73%
Send humanitarian aid	93.5%
Evacuate refugees	72.1%
Send in ground forces	7.9%
Impose a no-fly zone over Syria	43.5%
Conduct airstrikes against Syrian government targets	25.7%

Copies of the National Opinion Ballot Report are available upon request. The NOBR is also available at www. fpa.org as a downloadable PDF.

7/HUMAN TRAFFICKING

How much focus should the U.S. government place on ending human trafficking relative to other domestic and international problems?

A lot of focus	44.3%
Some focus	47.1%
Not too much focus	7.2%
No focus at all	1.1%
Not sure	0.3%

Do you think the U.S. government should increase, keep the same or decrease the amount of money it gives other countries to fight human trafficking?

Increase	41.7%
Keep the same	38.1%
Decrease	6.4%
Not sure	13.8%

Do you think the U.S. government should impose economic sanctions on countries with high rates of human trafficking?

Yes	58.9%
No	21.1%
Not sure	20%

Do you think that prostitution should be legalized in the United States?

Yes	32.2%
No	48.5%
Not sure	19.3%

Do you think that it is right or wrong for other countries like the Netherlands to legalize prostitution?

Right	49.3%
Wrong	18.9%
Not sure	31.8%

Do you think the United States should be allied with countries like the Netherlands that have legalized prostitution?

Yes	79%
No	6.2%
Not sure	14.8%

Ballots for this year's topics begin on page 99!

8/BRAZIL

How much do you think Brazil takes the interests of the U.S. into account when making foreign policy decisions?

A lot	7.6%
Somewhat	31.9%
Little	49.3%
None	6.5%
Not sure	4.7%

How much do you think the U.S. takes Brazil's interests into account when making foreign policy decisions?

A lot	1.4%
Somewhat	28.5%
Little	56.8%
None	10.3%
Not sure	3%

In your opinion, are relations between the U.S. and Brazil improving, worsening or staying about the same?

Improving	9.8%
Worsening	31.2%
Staying about the same	51.1%
Not sure	7.9%

The five permanent members of the United Nations Security Council are China, France, Russia, Britain and the United States. Some people have proposed that the permanent membership should be expanded. Would you favor or oppose Brazil becoming a permanent member?

Favor	38.2%
Oppose	33.6%
Not sure	28.2%

Do you think that Brazil will play a greater role or a lesser role in international politics in the next 10 years than it does today?

Greater role	73.8%
Lesser role	3.3%
Same role	18.8%
Not sure	4.1%

How much do you trust Brazil to act responsibly in world politics?

Very much	6.6%
Somewhat	63.7%
Not too much	22.5%
Not at all	1.7%
Not sure	5.5%

How much do you trust Brazil to keep its international commitments?

Very much	10.9%
Somewhat	67.4%
Not too much	13.4%
Not at all	0.6%
Not sure	7.7%

In general do you think that Brazil practices fair trade or unfair trade with the United States?

Fair trade	31.8%
Unfair trade	11.7%
Not sure	56.5%

Do you think the U.S. should have a free trade agreement that would lower barriers to trade with Brazil?

Yes	70.9%
No	10.7%
Not sure	18.4%

Would you approve or disapprove of the U.S. working with Brazil to preserve and protect the Amazon rain forest?

Approve strongly	78.3%
Approve somewhat	19.3%
Disapprove somewhat	1.2%
Disapprove strongly	0.6%
Not sure	0.6%

Which do you think are more important in U.S.-Brazil relations: economic interests or environmental interests?

Economic interests	36.5%
Environmental interests	51.7%
Not sure	11.8%

Do you think U.S. economic aid to Brazil should be increased, kept the same, decreased, or stopped altogether?

Increased	9.6%
Kept the same	52.5%
Decreased	11.7%
Stopped altogether	19.3%
Not sure	6.9%

At present, are the U.S. and Brazil mostly rivals or mostly partners?

Mostly rivals	19.4%
Mostly partners	47.6%
Not sure	33%

If Brazil becomes significantly more powerful economically would you view this development as mainly positive or mainly negative?

Mainly positive	90.3%
Mainly negative	2.8%
Not sure	6.9%

If Brazil becomes significantly more powerful militarily would you view this development as mainly positive or mainly negative?

Mainly positive	21.9%
Mainly negative	52.3%
Not sure	25.8%

In your opinion, did Brazil's hosting of the World Cup help its image around the world, hurt its image around the world, or did it have no impact on Brazil's image?

Help Brazil's image	46.9%
Hurt Brazil's image	18.3%
Had no impact on Brazil's image	23.5%
Not sure	11.3%

Become a Member

For nearly a century, members of the Association have played key roles in government, think tanks, academia and the private sector.

Make a Donation

Your support helps the FOREIGN POLICY ASSOCIATION's programs dedicated to global affairs education.

As an active participant in the FPA's Great Decisions program, we encourage you to join the community today's foreign policy thought leaders.

Member—$250

Benefits:
- Free admission to all Associate events (includes member's family)
- Discounted admission for all other guests to Associate events
- Complimentary GREAT DECISIONS briefing book
- Complimentary issue of FPA's annual *National Opinion Ballot Report*

Visit us online at

www.fpa.org/membership

Make a fully tax-deductible contribution to FPA's Annual Fund 2016.

To contribute to the Annual Fund 2016, visit us online at **www.fpa.org** or call the Membership Department at

(800) 628-5754 ext. 333

The generosity of donors who contribute $500 or more is acknowledged in FPA's *Annual Report.*

All financial contributions are tax-deductible to the fullest extent of the law under section 501 (c)(3) of the IRS code.

FPA also offers membership at the SPONSOR MEMBER and PATRON MEMBER levels. To learn more, visit us online at www.fpa.org/membership or call (800) 628-5754 ext. 333.

Return this form by mail to: Foreign Policy Association, 470 Park Avenue South, New York, N.Y. 10016. *Or fax to:* (212) 481-9275.

ORDER ONLINE: WWW.GREATDECISIONS.ORG

OR CALL (800) 477-5836

FOR MEMBERSHIP: WWW.FPA.ORG/MEMBERSHIP

❑ MR.   ❑ MRS.   ❑ MS.   ❑ DR.   ❑ PROF.

NAME _____

ADDRESS _____

_____**APT/FLOOR** _____

CITY _____ **STATE** _____ **ZIP** _____

TEL _____

E-MAIL _____

❑ AMEX   ❑ VISA   ❑ MC   ❑ DISCOVER
❑ CHECK (ENCLOSED)

CHECKS SHOULD BE PAYABLE TO FOREIGN POLICY ASSOCIATION.

CARD NO.

SIGNATURE OF CARDHOLDER

EXP. DATE (MM/YY)

PRODUCT	QTY	PRICE	COST
GREAT DECISIONS 2016 Briefing Book (FPA 31649)		$25	
SPECIAL OFFER TEN PACK SPECIAL GREAT DECISIONS 2016 (FPA31656) *Includes 10% discount		$225	
GREAT DECISIONS TELEVISION SERIES GD ON DVD 2016(FPA31650)		$40	
GREAT DECISIONS 2016 TEACHER'S PACKET (1 Briefing Book, 1 Teacher's Guide and 1 DVD (FPA31652) E-MAIL: (REQUIRED)		$70	
GREAT DECISIONS CLASSROOM-PACKET (1 Teacher's Packet & 30 Briefing Books (FPA31653) E-MAIL: (REQUIRED)		$570	
MEMBERSHIP		$250	
ANNUAL FUND 2016 (ANY AMOUNT)			

SUBTOTAL	$
plus S & H*	$
TOTAL	$

For details and shipping charges, call FPA's Sales Department at (800) 477-5836.
Orders mailed to FPA without the shipping charge will be held.